DARKROOM ART

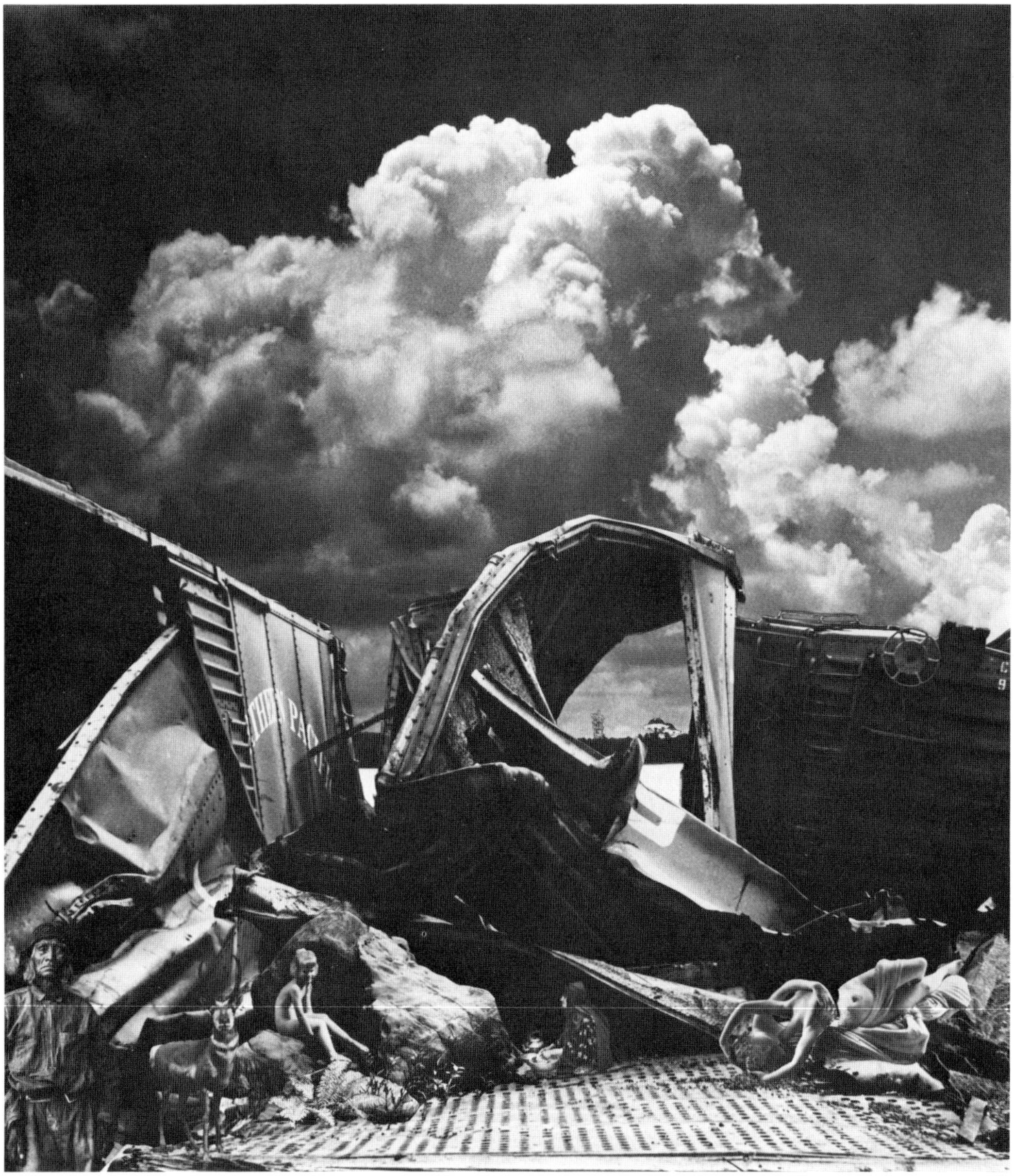

The techniques used by Jim Farber to create this image, entitled In the Ruins, *are described in chapter 10.*

DARKROOM ART

JERRY BURCHFIELD

AMPHOTO

American Photographic Book Publishing
An Imprint of Watson-Guptill Publications
New York, New York

First published in 1981 in New York, New York by American Photographic Book Publishing, an imprint of Watson-Guptill Publications, a division of Billboard Publications, Inc., 1515 Broadway, New York, NY 10036.

Library of Congress Cataloging in Publication Data

Burchfield, Jerry
Darkroom Art.

Includes index.
1. Photography—Special effects. I. Title.

TR148.B87   778.8   80-29426

ISBN 0-8174-3709-6 (hardbound)

ISBN 0-8174-3708-8 (paperbound)

Manufactured in the United States of America

Contents

Preface

Darkroom Art is for those with darkroom experience who want to go beyond the basics. With today's advanced technology, almost anyone can make a photograph. This gives photographers freedom to concentrate on the images instead of on the technical procedures. But many find straight images from the camera are not enough. They discover that the darkroom not only offers an opportunity to refine their photographs, but also to step into a realm beyond the limits of *camera reality*.

This book serves as a guide and reference. The techniques covered vary from methods to improve the straight camera image to procedures which alter and even make an abstraction of the photograph. Many of the topics covered may upset the purist. But photography is a medium, an image-making tool, and need not be limited in its application. The word *photography* means *writing with light*, and consequently any image made with light-sensitive materials can be considered a photograph.

This book will be of value to both advanced photographers and beginning enthusiasts. The range of subjects is extensive and includes contrast masking, making black-and-white and color internegatives, the Sabattier effect in color and in black and white, duo-tone solarization, multiple printing, high-contrast techniques, posterization, toning for performance, bleaching, and adding dyes to prints.

To take advantage of most photographic processes, it is necessary to have a basic understanding of how the medium works, good intuitive sense, and a lot of desire. Too many people place all their emphasis on technique and equipment, eventually becoming "technicrats." Some find it so overwhelming they lose interest in photography. I present a variety of image-making options in a straightforward way that is not overly technical. However, effective use of these methods depends on how you apply them and how much experimenting you are willing to do.

The photographs in the book are by a variety of photographers. Some are newcomers, but many are well known in the field. The photographers are credited in the captions; all other photographs not attributed by name are mine. I would like to give special thanks to the photographers who contributed to this book. Their creations serve as visual representations of the techniques discussed and illustrate some of the options open to you through special effects in the darkroom.

This book reflects years of work with the medium. In my case, it is a direct result of spending too much time in the dark. I owe a special thanks to Lou Jacobs, Jr., for his generous help and advice; Tom and Michele Grimm for their inspiration; Mark Chamberlain for his patience and support; and the rest of the crew at BC Space—G.J. Pelissero and Nan Schwarz—who helped keep the ball rolling. Finally, the person who deserves the most credit is my wife, Barbara, who not only helped with the book, but put up with me.

Jerry Burchfield
June, 1980

1

Film Processing Alternatives and Special Effects

Processing film is one of the most critical and uncreative procedures in the photographic process. It is critical because, if not handled properly, all your long, hard hours of shooting can be totally lost. Once you've processed film a few times, it may become repetitious and boring. However, there are ways to vary your film processing techniques that will improve the diversity and quality of your work while adding to your repertoire of visual effects. This chapter covers different approaches to film processing that can save the day if you've made an error in shooting, plus a variety of methods to achieve special effects.

Pushing and Pulling Film

Don't despair if shooting conditions don't permit normal exposures or if you accidentally forget to adjust your meter for the proper film speed and expose a whole roll of film incorrectly. There is a way out. Acceptable results can still be obtained with either black-and-white or color films by making adjustments in the film processing.

Photographers continually run into situations where they can't make normal hand-held exposures due to inadequate lighting. Rather than give up the shot, they may use a tripod, add supplementary lighting, or underexpose and push film development to compensate for the underexposure. Since supplementary lighting equipment and tripods are not always on hand, push processing has become a popular alternative.

If you're in a shooting situation where push processing is a necessity, adjust the ASA setting on your meter until you can get an exposure reading that allows you to shoot the picture. For example, with a 400 ASA film such as Kodak's Tri-X, double the ASA setting so that it reads 800. This adjustment makes it easier to get a reading in low light conditions. It also means your film will be underexposed one stop and need to be push processed in order to be printable. If doubling the ASA once is not enough, continue to increase the ASA until you get an acceptable meter reading.

Overexposed film can also be saved by altering the film-processing procedure. This is normally referred to as "pulling" film. The development time is reduced to compensate for the overexposure.

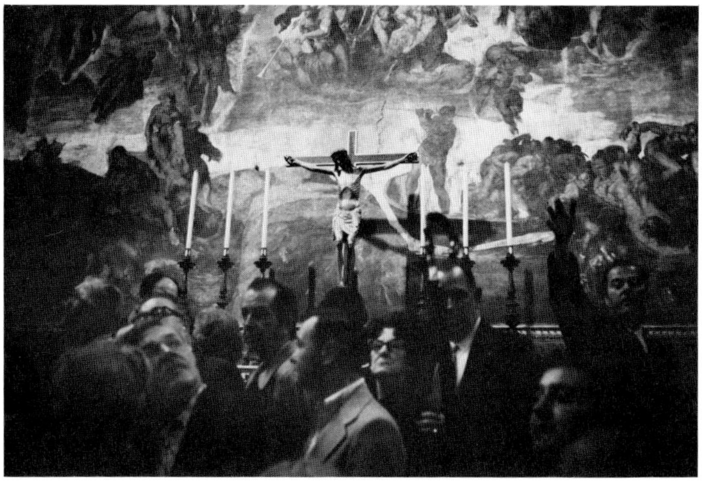

Low-light conditions, and a crowd of anxious tourists, made push process necessary for this photograph of the Sistine Chapel. Kodak Tri-X film was shot at ASA 1000, and the development was increased by 50 percent.

Processing Requirements. Both pushing and pulling are based on making adjustments in the film development time. It doesn't matter what size or type of film you use, the basic principle is the same with either black-and-white or color films. The following chart provides a guide to follow for pushing and pulling either black-and-white or color film with your normal developer.

Chemistry for Color Film. When pushing or pulling color films, use the normal processing chemistry recommended for that particular type of film. With color negative films, C-41 chemistry is normally used; but push processing should be avoided with these films because it has a minimal effect. With transparency films, E-6 chemistry is used to develop everything except Kodachrome and some foreign films. Only try to push or pull E-6 transparency films. Kodachrome and many foreign films cannot have the processing altered.

You can either have a custom lab push or pull your color film, or you can purchase C-41 and E-6 chemistry and do it yourself. If you need to have your film pushed or pulled more than one stop, you'll probably have to process it yourself, since most custom labs have automated film processors that are designed to make only one stop alterations.

Chemistry for Black-and-White Film. With black-and-white films you can either use your normal developer, or a special high-energy developer such as Acufine or Diafine. These special developers let you use a higher than normal ASA while reducing the problems of increased contrast and grain which occur when film is push processed.

PUSH & PULL PROCESSING ADJUSTMENTS

(Example based on 400 ASA film)

Film ASA	Film Exposure	Change in Developer Time
1600	2 stops underexposed	Increase by 75%
1000	1 1/3 stops underexposed	Increase by 50%
800	1 stop underexposed	Increase by 35%
400	Normal	Use Normal Time
200	1 stop overexposed	Decrease by 35%
100	2 stops overexposed	Decrease by 50%

The Effects of Pushing and Pulling

Contrast and grain structure are altered whenever film is pushed or pulled. When film is developed, it begins developing uniformly. The shadow areas of the image, which received the least amount of exposure, develop the fastest, and first; while the highlights and middle values continue developing long after the shadow areas have ceased to be affected by the developer. Consequently, when film is pushed, only the highlights and the middle values are affected by the increased processing time. This not only increases contrast, it also increases the size of the silver particles that make up the grain of the film. That's why prints made from pushed film tend to have a grainier appearance than prints made from normally processed negatives.

Many photographers capitalize on the characteristics of push processing and use the increased contrast and grain effectively in their images, while other photographers use special developers, like Acufine, to gain the advantage of the increased film speed without sacrificing grain and contrast. Whichever approach you choose, remember that push processing does *not* increase shadow detail. The amount of detail you get in the shadows is totally dependent upon your exposure when you shoot the picture.

If your film is *overexposed* and you pull it by reducing the developing time, the reverse effect occurs. Contrast is reduced and there is very little effect on the grain structure of the film.

Contrast: Pushing and Pulling. Frequently photographers intentionally push or pull their film to alter contrast. If you're shooting on a dull, overcast day and want to add contrast to the scene, *underexpose* the film one stop and *increase* the development time to compensate. This will increase the contrast. To reduce the contrast on an extremely bright day, *overexpose* the film one stop and *reduce* the development time accordingly.

These are general rules concerning contrast control that apply to all films. The amount of exposure and development change will vary with the shooting situation. Many photographers have learned through experience the amount of change necessary, but a more practical approach is offered by the zone system, a system of tonal control, created by Ansel Adams, which offers a methodical and logical means for determining how to control contrast problems. For a detailed explanation and directions for use, refer to Ansel Adams's *Basic Photo Series*; Minor White's *Zone System Manual*; or Fred Picker's *Zone VI Workshop*.

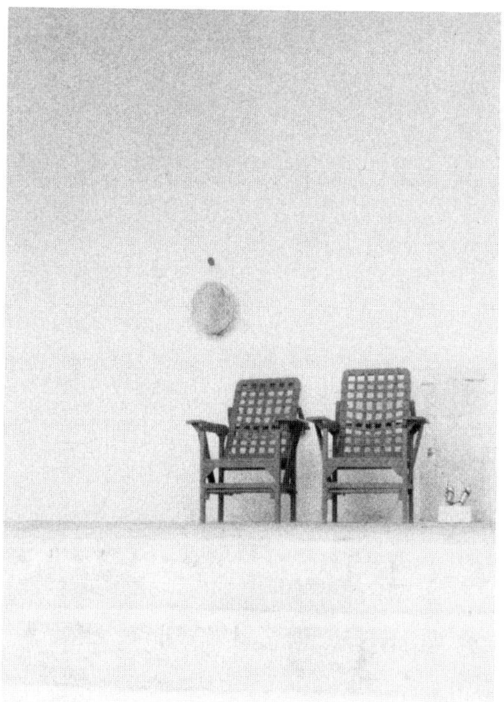

The photograph at left by Ricardo Salcedo was intentionally overexposed and overdeveloped to exaggerate the grain pattern inherent in the film.

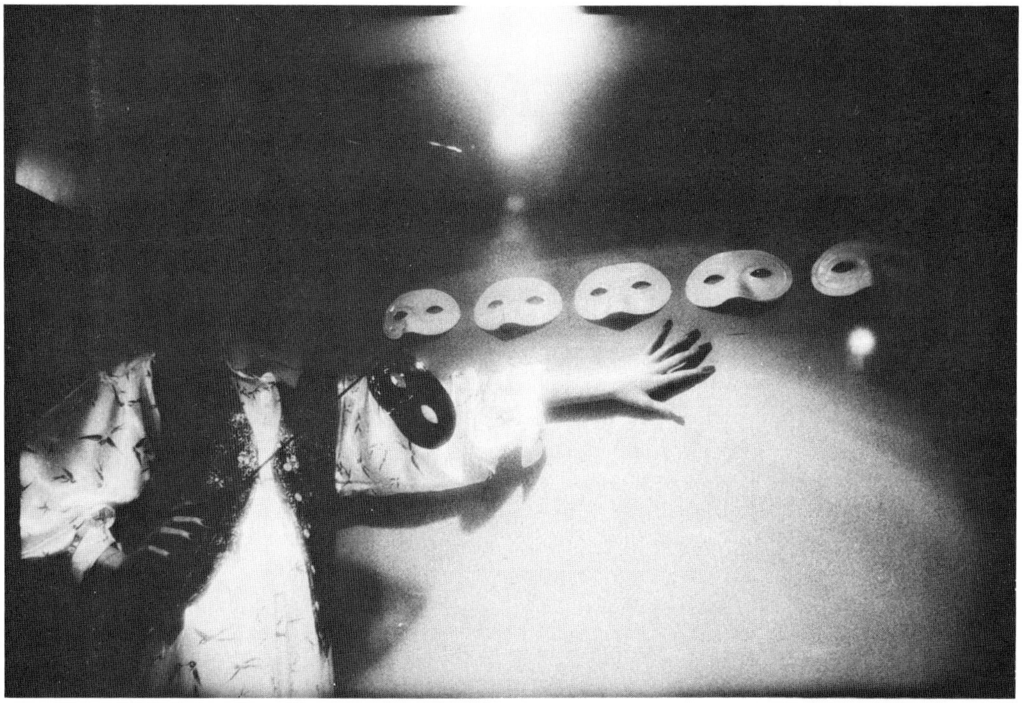

David Dubuque used black-and-white infrared film for this photograph of a window display at night. The grain was enhanced by the infrared film being shot at 100 ASA with no filters and developed normally in Kodak D-19 developer.

The Snip Test

If you're uncertain as to whether your film was properly exposed, a snip test may be the answer. Cut several inches of exposed film off your roll and develop it normally. You will have to sacrifice several frames from your roll of film, but it is worth the effort if you save the rest of the roll.

After processing the snip, evaluate the film and determine whether or not you need to alter the processing time. If it is over- or underexposed, use the preceding chart as a guide for altering the processing.

Processing for Grain and Contrast

Because photographers always seem concerned about grain, manufacturers continue to produce an endless array of new grain-minimizing products. Grain is a constant topic among camera store groupies and most photographers consider it something to avoid but, regardless of your attitude, grain is an inherent part of the photographic process.

Many photographers, such as Ralph Gibson and George Krause, have taken advantage of the unique character prominent grain gives to their photographs. For many years, fashion photographers have also used a combination of excessive contrast and grain to simplify and to add graphic impact to their images.

Controlling Grain. Grain is less apparent if you use slow-speed films. This is true with color as well as black-and-white films. High-speed films (Ilford's HP5, Kodak's Tri-X, or Kodacolor 400) have a much more obvious grain structure than slower-speed films. With slow-speed films, the emulsion is composed of very fine silver particles. To make high-speed films more sensitive to light, it is necessary to use larger particles of silver which create a grainier appearance in the final image.

To make the grain in your photographs more pronounced, start with a high-speed film and use a combination of carefully controlled overexposure and overdevelopment. Grain is increased by too much exposure, excessive agitation during film development, or by extending the developing time.

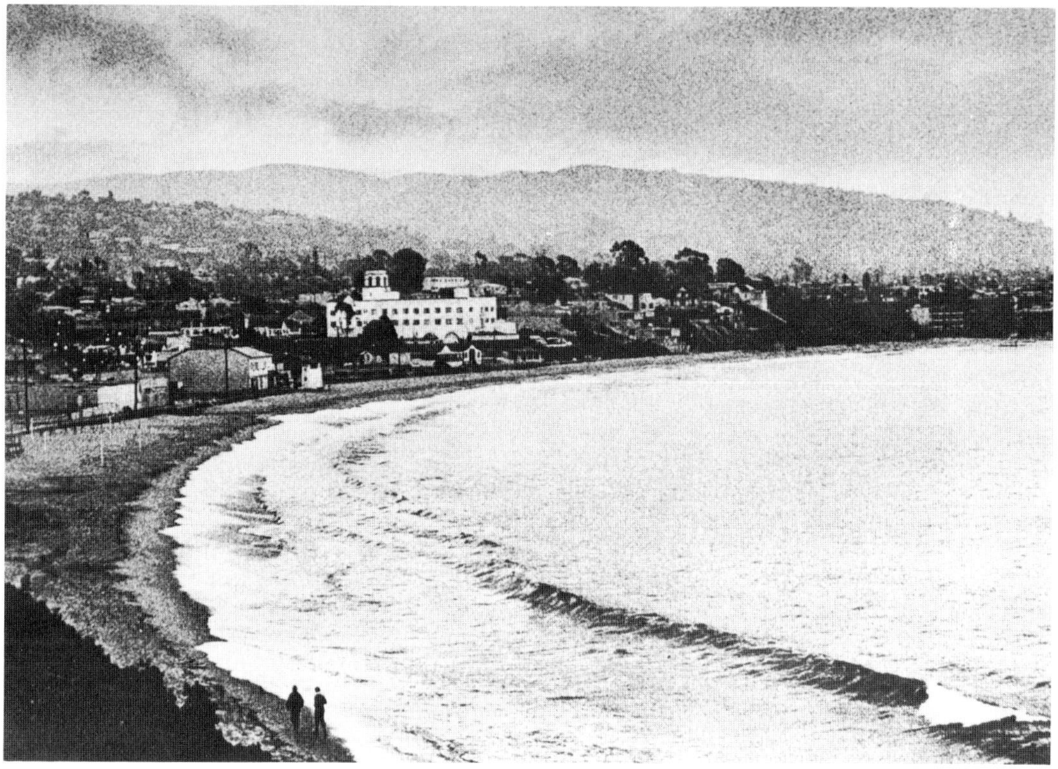

Although extreme grain and contrast are avoided by many photographers, they add to the feeling and graphic quality of these two images by Robert Randall.

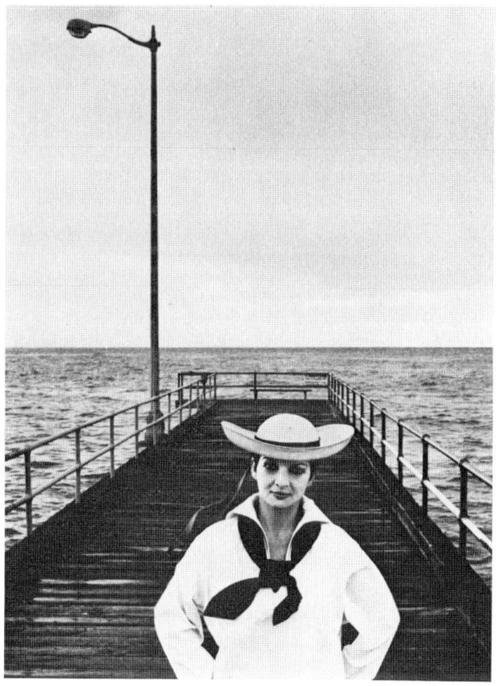

These procedures not only increase the grain, but they also give you more contrast. In prints, shadow areas will be black with very little detail and highlights will be washed out to white. This flattens spatial relationships and emphasizes the graphic character of your images. Such negatives will probably be extremely dense and require long exposures during printing.

Try shooting Kodak's Tri-X film at ASA 800 rather than the normal ASA 400. Once exposed, process the film in undiluted D-76 developer at 75 degrees (24 C) for ten minutes. During the development, minimize the agitation to four times at two-minute intervals. This process results in dense, grainy negatives that are underexposed and push processed. Your negatives will maintain some shadow detail as well as good highlight detail. To exaggerate this process further, decrease the ASA of the film so you overexpose by one or two stops and use the same development procedure.

Printing Dense, Grainy Negatives

Printing dense negatives involves a little more work than you may be used to. Because of their density, long exposures will be necessary.

Controlling Negative "Pop." During these long exposures, you will also be plagued by negatives that pop out of focus due to enlarger heat. Here's how to avoid the problem:

1. Leave the enlarger on once it is focused.
2. Wait for the negative to pop.
3. Refocus and leave enlarger on.
4. Stop down the lens for the proper exposure.
5. Place a red or opaque filter into position under the lens.

The filter enables you to put your paper into the printing easel without fogging it while leaving the enlarger light on. If the enlarger is shut off, even for a few seconds, the negative will probably pop. By leaving it on and using a red or opaque filter, you can alleviate this problem. If you are using color materials, be sure to use an opaque filter rather than a red one, since color materials are sensitive to all colors of light.

When printing dense black-and-white negatives, some photographers increase contrast by printing on a higher grade of paper than normal. This, in combination with the overexposure and overdevelopment, can produce an aura around the highlights. It also causes the blacks to be extremely rich, but totally lacking detail.

Getting More Detail in Highlights. Frequently you will find that the highlights produced by dense negatives need more detail. This can be achieved by burning in these areas during printing, but this becomes a difficult task when exposures are extremely long. To decrease the time necessary to burn in a highlight area, try opening the enlarger lens one or two stops. This

A combination of overexposure and overdevelopment was used by Ricardo Salcedo to achieve the grain evident in this image. Unfortunately, this often results in extremely dense negatives which are hard to print.

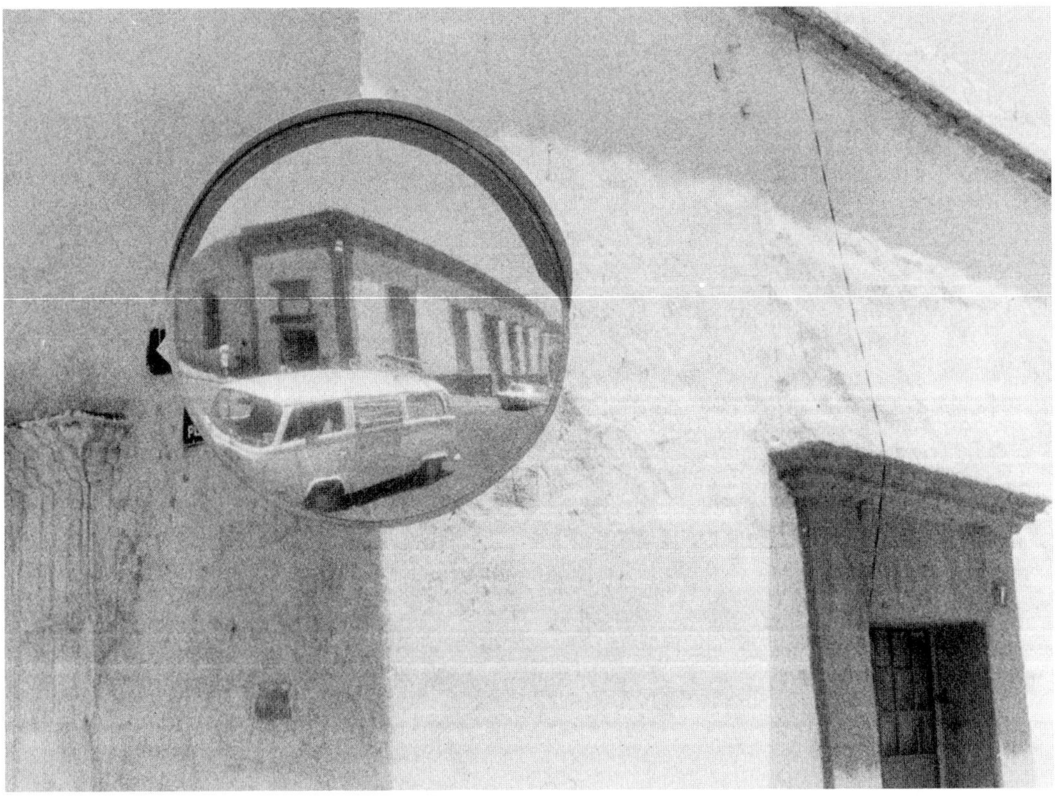

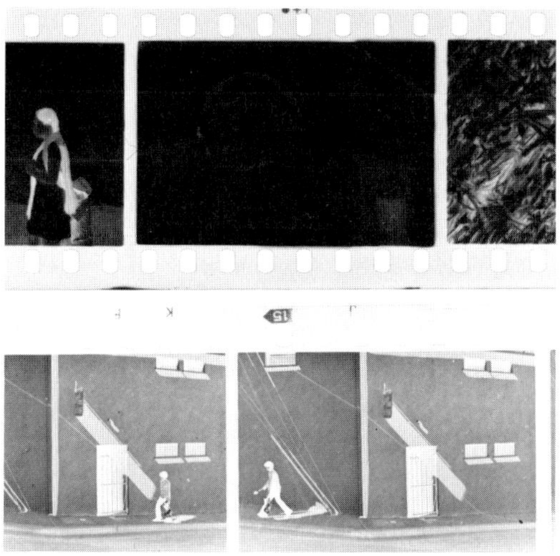

This illustration shows the difference between normal black-and-white negatives (bottom row) and the one used by Ricardo Salcedo for the previous photograph.

may cause a slight difference in definition. However, if you are careful, it shouldn't be noticeable and you can decrease the burning-in time significantly.

If you are already working with the lens wide open, the other alternative is to accelerate the development of the highlight areas. After developing the print for its normal time, take it out of the developer and apply undiluted developer to the highlights. By rubbing concentrated developer lightly into these areas, you create friction which results in a slight increase in detail. To inrease the action, heat the developer. If neither of these approaches seem adequate, try adding a gram of Phenidone (a developing agent which can be purchased at a chemical supply house or ordered through your camera store) to 16 ounces (473 ml) of undiluted Dektol. Use this as a spot developer for washed-out highlights. The Phenidone-Dektol combination can be applied directly to the print surface with a brush, cotton swab, or your fingers. This causes a rapid acceleration of development and brings out detail that was completely lost before. But apply it with care. Staining is possible even when your normal developer in concentrated form is rubbed onto a washed out highlight area.

Positives to Negatives for High-Contrast Color Prints

An easy way to make high-contrast color photographs is to process color transparencies as color negatives. This produces contrasty color negatives equivalent to switching from a grade 2 black-and-white printing paper to a grade 4 or 5. Color negatives made in this manner lack the orange cast (mask) that normal color negatives have and are quite beautiful in themselves. The colors in this type of negative are the complements of the color originally photographed.

To make high-contrast color negatives from transparency film, only use transparency film that is processed in E-6 chemistry. Kodachrome, Agfachrome, and any other film that is not made for processing with E-6 chemistry will not work. You can either shoot the appropriate film at the normal ASA, or increase the ASA and push process the film to exaggerate the grain and make the contrast more extreme.

Process the film in Kodak's C-41 chemistry, which is made for processing normal color negatives, but also works to convert E-6 transparency film into color negatives.

Use the recommended processing time for C-41 chemistry when processing E-6 transparencies as high-contrast color negatives. Only alter the development if you plan to push the film.

Once the film is processed, examine your results. These unmasked, high-contrast color negatives can be quite extraordinary as negative images. Since they lack the orange mask that normal color negative film has, the colors are rich and vibrant. They can be printed as high-contrast positive images on normal color negative printing paper, or as negative images on a reversal-print material such as Cibachrome. They can also be used as negative-image slides for projection.

Printing high-contrast color negatives made from transparency film is no more difficult than printing normal color negatives, except the film has more contrast. The printing procedure is the same in terms of choosing a filter pack and making exposures. A good way to become familiar with the process is to begin by making a proof sheet of the whole roll of film. This enables you to view all of the images at once, and to get a feeling for how they will look. Because of the high contrast inherent in negatives made from positive film, be especially aware of the relationships of highlights and shadows when you photograph. Consider the shadows as shapes since they will have very little detail when printed. Also, expect most of the hightlights to wash out to pure white.

When a Lab Processes the Film. Ordinarily, commercial outlets will not do this special process. If you have it done by a custom lab, be sure that they understand what you want; otherwise you may get conventional slides instead of high contrast color negatives.

Many labs refuse to process transparencies as color negatives because they fear that their chemistry will be contaminated. But, according to Kodak, there is no contamination, nor any need to worry about processing both normal color negatives and E-6 transparencies in the same run. However don't try to process color negatives as transparencies, because it won't work.

Low-Contrast Development

Excessive contrast, caused by extremely harsh lighting conditions, can be reduced by *overexposing* and *underdeveloping* film. The overexposure provides enough light for detail in the shadows, while the underdevelopment decreases highlight density. When film is processed, it starts by developing uniformly. Since the shadows usually receive less light than other areas of the film, they soon stop developing while the highlights and middle values continue to be developed. Consequently, in overexposed film the shadows have extra density and only the highlights and middle values are reduced by underdevelopment. The result is a negative with less contrast that is easier to print.

This approach to contrast control works with both black-and-white and color films. But due to the delicate nature of color films, it is best to process them normally and reduce the contrast by masking (see chapter 2).

A general rule to follow is to overexpose by one stop and reduce the development by one-third. Investigate the zone-system for more specific information on developing a systematic approach to contrast control through alterations in exposure and development.

Two-Bath Development

You can also use a *two-bath development* technique to reduce the contrast of black-and-white films. The simplest form uses a normal film developer for the first stage and water for the second. The *alkaline two-bath technique*, using a developer like D-76 for the first bath and a Kodalk solution as the second bath, is another common approach. Both of these methods allow the shadow areas to develop normally, while reducing the highlights, thus shortening the overall contrast range of the film.

Water-Bath Development. This is the simplest of the two-bath development techniques for reducing the contrast of black-and-white films. The film is partially developed in a normal film developer and partially in a water bath. While the film is in the developer, the highlights and shadows develop uniformly. When the film is transferred to the water bath, the developer which has been absorbed into the emulsion of the film continues to work. The developer acts faster on the highlight areas because they received more light when the film was exposed. This means the developer exhausts quickly in the highlights, but continues working in the shadow areas. This enables the density of the shadow areas to build up while reducing the density of the highlights.

Development by inspection is the best way to determine how many steps you should go through to get adequate density in the film. For fast panchromatic films, development must be started in total darkness. But after the film is in the developer for half of the total development time it can be inspected for a few seconds under the illumination of a dark green series 3 safelight filter, provided you keep the film four feet (1.22 m) from the safelight. At this point, you can make a quick judgment about the density of the film. But the viewing conditions are very poor, and if you leave the film exposed to the safelight for too long you will fog it. However, with a little experimenting and practice, you should be able to determine the proper film density. Without using the inspection technique, you have to rely totally on previous experience to determine the proper amount of development.

Follow these steps:

1. Use a normal developer, such as D-76, full strength for the first bath; use water for the second bath.
2. Bring both solutions to 68F (20C).
3. Try immersing the film in the developer for one minute.*
4. Agitate continuously for the first thirty seconds, then five seconds for every thirty subsequent seconds.
5. After a one-minute development, transfer the film to the water bath without agitation.
6. If developing by inspection, develop the film until the first highlights begin to appear.
7. Then transfer film to the water bath and allow it to stay there for two minutes.
8. Return film to the developer bath for one minute, using constant agitation for the first thirty seconds.
9. Transfer the film back to the water bath for another two minutes without agitation.

It is important not to agitate the film during the water bath, in order for the developer to stay on the film and not become too diluted. The developer which was absorbed by the emulsion of the film continues to work in the water bath. It quickly exhausts in the dense highlight portions of the negative, but continues to develop in the thin shadow areas. By the time two minutes are up, the developer has been completely diffused out of the emulsion layer and the process has stopped.

Repeat the procedure until the film has built up sufficient density. Experience will be your best guide. Inspection will help, but this only serves you properly once you've done it a few times and learned what to look for. Contrast can be controlled by varying the interval; the film is in the developer from a minimum time of thirty seconds to a maximum of two to three minutes. With roll film, reverse (invert) the film reel for each step to avoid uneven development. Initially you should experiment by making tests with film that is not important to you.

Alkaline Two-Bath Development. The alkaline two-bath procedure is similar to the water-bath technique in theory as well as results. But you use an alkaline bath of Kodalk instead of water. With a fine-grain developer such as D-76 full strength, use a one percent Kodalk solution made up of 10 grams of Kodalk Balanced Alkali mixed with water to make 32 ounces (1000 ml) of solution.

*The effect of water-bath development depends on the length of time the film is in the developer. The sooner you transfer the film from the developer to the water bath, the greater the reduction of contrast and the softer the final image will be.

With the alkaline two-bath technique time and temperature are not extremely critical. However, to avoid reticulation, it is best to have both chemicals at nearly the same temperature. For consistency, use 68-70F degrees (20-21C) with this technique.

During alkaline two-bath development, the film emulsion absorbs developing agents in the first bath that are then activated by the alkaline solution of the second bath. Developing agents in the second bath exhaust quickly in the highlight areas, and stop working because there are no new developers to replace them. However, developing agents in the shadow areas continue to work longer since there are not as many exposed silver bromide crystals for them to affect. Thus, contrast is reduced because the shadows receive more development than the highlights.

To use this technique:

1. Immerse the film in the developer for four minutes with continuous agitation for the first 30 seconds.
2. Agitate 5 seconds for each subsequent 30 seconds.
3. Remove the film from the developer.
4. Put film in the Kodalk solution without agitation. When using roll film, reverse (invert) the film reel after the first 15 seconds in the second bath to avoid uneven development.
5. Leave the film in the second bath for three to four minutes. (However this is not critical, since the activity of the developer will decrease the longer the film is in the solution.)

Concentration of the developer in the first bath is usually varied to compensate for the developing speeds of different films. Slow-developing films (those with higher ASA ratings) should have a more concentrated solution so that the developer will continue to work longer once it is in the second bath. For the second bath to be effective, rapid-developing films need a more diluted first bath. To determine whether you are using a slow- or a fast-developing film, compare the developing times given on developer data sheets for specific films and make your judgment accordingly. A thick-emulsion film such as Tri-X works better with alkaline and water-bath techniques than a thin-emulsion film such as Panatomic-X, because the Tri-X emulsion will absorb more developing agents enabling them to work longer in the second bath. However, testing should be done before you attempt to process any important film with this technique.

Black-and-White Transparencies

Seldom do photographers desire black-and-white transparencies unless they plan to make copy slides of existing black-and-white art work. Even then, most make the slides by using color-transparency film. Unfortunately, the quality is never the same. No color-slide film can reproduce a black-and-white image as faithfully and beautifully as can a black-and-white film developed as a positive transparency.

Choosing the Right Film. To make black-and-white transparencies, use Kodak's Panatomic-X film or Kodak Direct Positive Panchromatic Film 5246, and process the film in Kodak's Direct Positive Film Developing Kit. The developing kit comes with instructions for shooting the film as well as processing it. When using Panatomic-X film, Kodak suggests using an ASA of 80; but this may result in overexposure, so an ASA of 125 is preferable.

Processing for Black-and-White Transparencies. After shooting the film, follow the kit's instructions and mix the chemistry. Everything, except the redeveloper, can be mixed in advance and reused. The redeveloper exhausts very quickly and should be mixed just before use. The redeveloper comes in a number of small packets to facilitate preparing the amount you need.

Summary of Processing Procedure

Step	KODAK Outfit Solution	Time at 68 F (20 C)*
1.	First Developer†	8 Min.—Small Spiral Reels 8 Min.—Small Noninvertible Tanks 9 Min.—Rack and Tank 6 Min.—Reel and Trough
2.	Water Rinse	2 to 5 Min.‡
3.	Bleach Bath	1 Min.
4.	Clearing Bath	2 Min.
5.	Redeveloper	8 Min.
6.	Water Rinse	1 Min.
7.	Fixing Bath	5 Min.
8.	Wash	20 Min.§

*Includes drain time of 10 to 15 seconds at end of each step.
†The time in the first developer must be adjusted to the effective rate of development obtained with the apparatus used and the degree of agitation employed.
‡A 2-minute time is sufficient with a running water wash with good agitation.
§Kodak Hypo Clearing Agent may be used, if desired, to shorten wash time and conserve water. Use as directed on the label.

Black-and-white transparency processing is similar to color-transparency processing in a number of steps. Also, the timing and temperature control are just as critical. During processing, the film is chemically reversed from a negative image to a positive one, just as with color-transparency processing.

Panatomic-X and Direct Positive Panchromatic Film 5246 are processed identically with the Kodak Direct Positive Film Developing Kit. A quart kit will process eight 36-exposure lengths of 35 mm film.

The processing time during the first developer is variable, depending upon your processing procedure. With Panatomic-X film shot at ASA 125, a six or seven minute first developer time has proven to be the best. As with all film processing, agitation is extremely critical. Agitate continuously during the first 30 seconds of each step, then 5 seconds for every minute thereafter.

Film Reticulation

The striking textural effect of reticulation is created by repeated switching of the film from hot to cold solutions during processing. The abrupt temperature changes cause the film emulsion to swell and then shrink, creating stress that forces the silver grains in the emulsion to break apart and clump together in rather regular patterns. The amount of hot and cold stress can be varied to control the degree of reticulation and the resulting distorted-texture pattern. By using extremely hot water, the emulsion can be made to slide around on the film base, causing very bizarre distortions.

In the past, reticulation was a fairly common accidental problem. But with current films, to get the textural effects caused by reticulation, you have to make a special effort.

Reticulation can be done during the initial film processing, or it can be done with already processed film. Both color and black-and-white films can be reticulated. However, once your film has been reticulated, it cannot be returned to its original condition. So be sure to make a final commitment before you reticulate any irreplaceable shots. You may want to make duplicate negatives or transparencies and reticulate them rather than the originals.

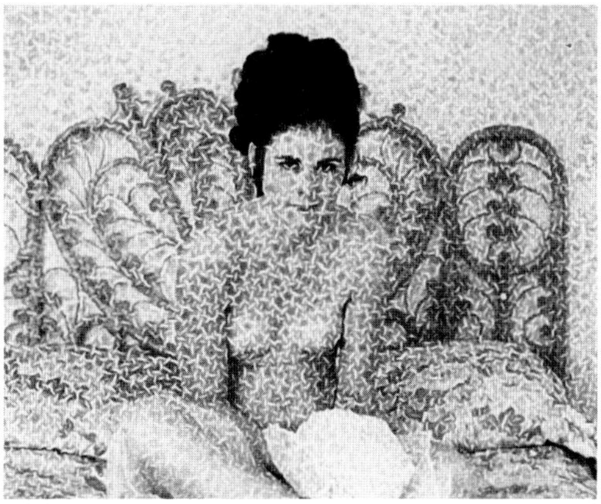

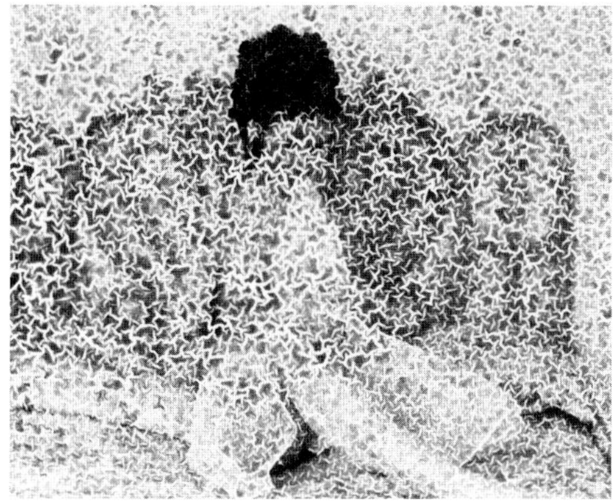

These photographs show the effect of film reticulation. In the photograph on the left the figure is recognizable, while in the one on the right the reticulation has almost obscured the subject. The two negatives were subjected to differing amounts of hot and cold stress.

Reticulating Black-and-White Film During Initial Processing. To reticulate black-and-white film, begin by processing it normally in the developer. Then rinse the film for one minute in an acetic-acid stop bath heated to 140–150 degrees (60–66 C). Following the acetic-acid stop bath, immerse the film in a water bath chilled to about 40 degrees (4 C) for one minute.

Reticulation can vary from a fine, regularly textured pattern to a coarser, more variably textured pattern by either reducing or increasing the temperature stress the film is subjected to. If you want a coarser reticulation pattern, increase the temperature extremes and alternately immerse the film in the hot and cold liquids several times. Because you will be working with a daylight processing tank or in the dark, it will be impossible for you to visually judge your results. Only after experimenting a few times will you be able to anticipate the results.

When you think the film has reticulated enough, fix and wash the film. Be sure to use a fixer with a hardening agent to help set the emulsion. After washing, do not use a wetting agent or try to squeegee the film, because its surface will be extremely delicate. Hang the film to air dry.

Reticulating Color Film During Initial Processing. Like black-and-white films, color films can be reticulated to produce either fine or coarse patterns. With color-negative films, a fine pattern occurs when the reticulation is done before beginning the actual film processing. A coarser pattern results when the reticulation is done later during the processing. With transparency films, whether you want a coarse or fine pattern, the reticulation should be done prior to the processing. To alter the degree of reticulation with color-transparency films, vary the degree of temperature stress.

Reticulating Color-Negative Films. To get a fine reticulation pattern:

1. Begin in total darkness with the color-negative film loaded on the developing reel.
2. Immerse in hot water at 135 degrees (57 C) for two minutes with gentle agitation.
3. Transfer film to a bath of ice water without agitation for one or two minutes.
4. Finally, bring the film to the proper processing temperature by soaking it for 15 seconds in a water bath at the same temperature as the normal processing chemicals.

At this point, the reticulation has occurred and the film should be processed according to normal procedures.

For a coarse reticulation pattern:

1. Process the color negative film through the normal developer and bleach steps.
2. In total darkness, immerse the film in hot water—approximately 135 degrees (57 C)—for two minutes.
3. Plunge the film into ice water for two minutes.

4. Bring the film back to the proper processing temperature by giving it a normal wash for the prescribed time and continue the processing with the fixer step.

Reticulating Color-Slide Films. Color-slide films should be reticulated before beginning the normal processing steps:

1. Load the film onto a developing reel, immerse it for one minute in a hot water bath at 130 degrees (55 C) with continuous and gentle agitation.
2. Soak the film in ice water for one minute.
3. Finally, bring the film back to normal processing temperature by placing it in a water bath at the proper temperature.
4. Process the film according to normal procedures, only dry it as quickly as possible afterwards with a hand-held hair dryer in order to avoid water spots.

Note: to vary the degree of reticulation, alter the amount of temperature stress you submit the film to.

Reticulating Already-Processed Films. To reticulate already-processed color or black-and-white films:

1. Begin by soaking the film for 10 minutes in a 70 degree (21 C) water bath to soften the emulsion.
2. Put the film into a hot alkaline bath at 130 degrees (55 C) for 3 minutes.
3. To make the alkaline bath, dissolve three level tablespoons of sodium carbonate, not bicarbonate, in 8 ounces (250 ml) of water.
4. Following the alkaline bath, transfer the film to a cold water bath at about 40 degrees (5 C), and let it soak for several minutes.
5. Visually check the film to determine whether the reticulation pattern is obvious enough to suit your needs. If not, repeat the procedure until you are satisfied.
6. Once you have arrived at a satisfactory result, wash the negatives at 70 degrees (21 C) for 5 minutes and let them dry.

An advantage to reticulating already-processed films is that you can work in the light and make visual judgments as to the amount of reticulation you want. Also, you can make duplicates of important shots and reticulate them rather than the originals.

The Sabattier Effect on Film

The Sabattier effect is often surrounded by a kind of mysticism, like a magic darkroom trick that is unpredictable but great if it turns out right. Yet, if used properly, it is a controllable process that can yield a variety of exciting results. The process was discovered more than a century ago by the French doctor and scientist Armand Sabattier, who described it as a pseudo-solarization reversal effect. Today, it is commonly called solarization, but there is a distinct difference between solarization and the Sabattier effect.

Solarization vs. the Sabattier Effect. *Solarization* is the reversal of an image on film or paper caused by extreme overexposure. This used to be a problem in the past, but not today with modern films. *The Sabattier effect* is the reversal of an image that occurs because film or paper has been exposed to light during development. Only a partial reversal occurs with the Sabattier effect, creating an image that is part negative and part positive.

Mackie Lines. What distinguishes the Sabattier effect from solarization is a narrow band, called a Mackie or bromide line, that forms between the highlight and shadow areas of an image. These Mackie lines usually appear as white outlines in a print.

When the print or film is re-exposed during later stages of development, those parts of the image that received the most light (the dark areas) are already significantly developed, while the rest of the photograph still has light-sensitive areas that will react to more light. These low density areas redevelop rapidly when re-exposed to light during this stage. This creates an excess of waste materials (bromide ions)

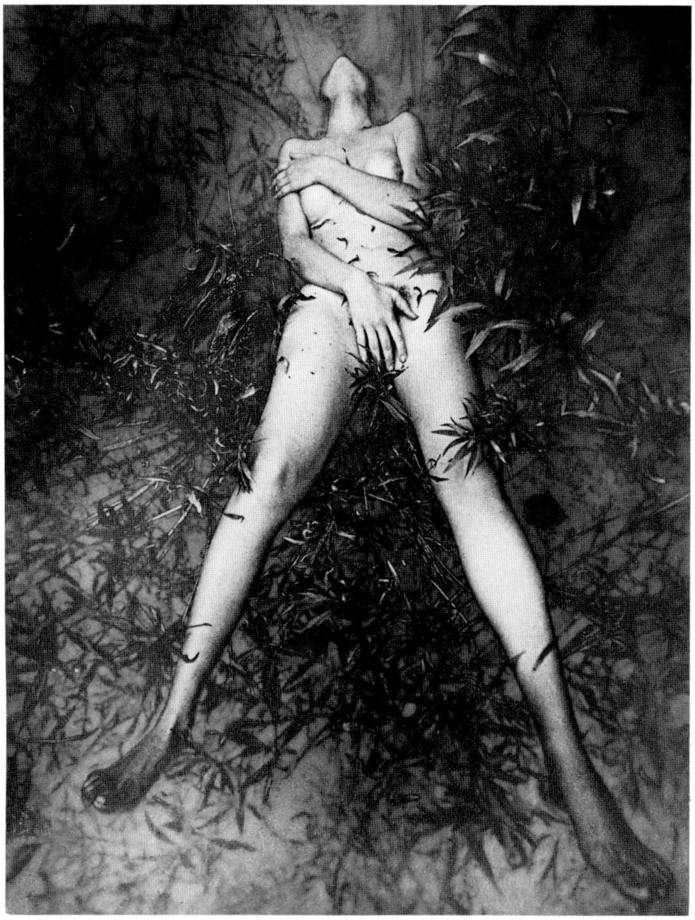

The Sabattier effect, or solarization as it is commonly called, produces unique results but is hard to control. However, when done to film it enables you to make many identical prints.

that collects between areas already completely developed and those beginning a redevelopment phase due to the re-exposure. The concentration of waste materials impedes development and causes Mackie lines, which appear as outlines around areas of density in the image.

The Advantage of Using Film. The Sabattier effect can be used with either film or paper, but there is an important advantage in using film. Once a satisfying result is achieved, the negative or slide can be used to make as many identical prints as you like. Duplicating results is much more difficult when using prints. However, you should think twice before trying the Sabattier effect on your film because it is an irreversable process. To preserve original film, make duplicates of original shots and work with them. Then if your re-exposure during development is incorrect, you have only lost a replaceable duplicate.

It is easier to produce the Sabattier effect with sheet films than roll films, since sheet films can be developed individually in a tray. With roll film, try cutting it into small strips and processing them separately in trays. You may have to sacrifice a few frames, but it enables you to work with the film more easily than you could with a long roll.

If you plan to make duplicates of your original black-and-white negatives or positives, make them on orthochromatic sheet film. Then you can use a red safelight during processing and visually judge the process as you work. The Sabattier effect works with most films, whether black-and-white or color, negative or positive. However, it is easier to get dramatic results with negative films than positive films since positive (transparency) films become lighter when they are exposed to more light.

Sheet Film. To produce the Sabattier effect:

1. Expose your film as you normally would, except for transparency film which should be underexposed about one stop to counteract the effect of the re-exposure lightening it.

One characteristic of the Sabattier effect on film is black mackie lines. (When a print is Sabattierized the mackie lines are white.) DeAnn Jennings, who took both these photographs, used Tri-X film for the image on the facing page, and exposed it to window light for five seconds after development. The film was then immediately immersed in fixer, skipping the stop bath. Because this procedure reduces contrast, a grade 6 paper was used for the print.

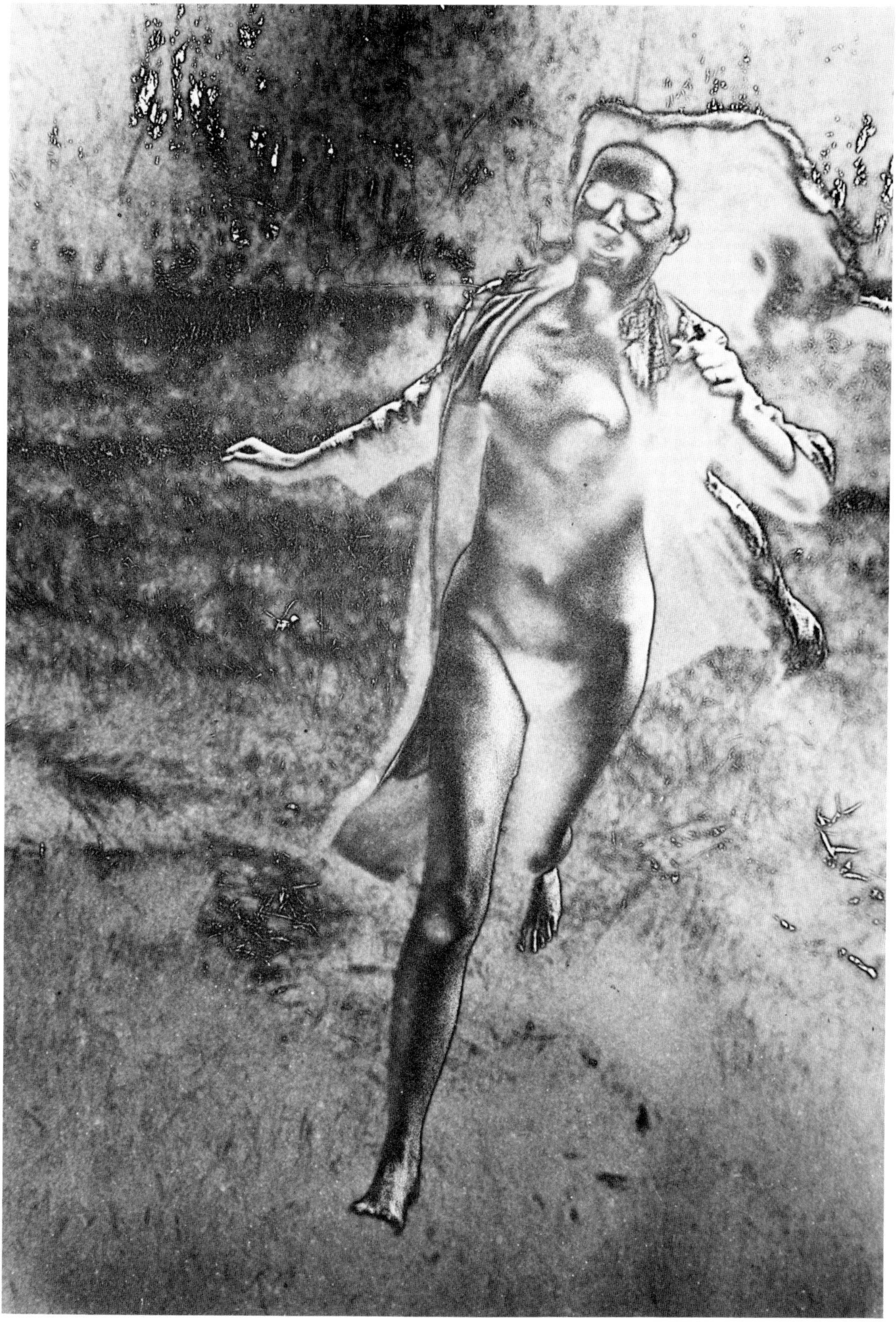

2. Process sheet film in a tray using your normal developer at the recommended temperature and development time. (Plan to re-expose the film to light halfway through the development stage).

3. Cease all agitation of the film 30 seconds before you re-expose it so the waste materials can build up to produce dramatic Mackie lines.

4. When the film reaches the halfway point in development, re-expose it to a dim light source while it rests at the bottom of the developing tray. (The light source should be directly over the tray, no stronger than a 7½ watt bulb, and at least four feet [1.22 m] away from the tray.)

Re-exposure should be very brief, no more than one or two seconds. It will take some experimenting and testing to determine the right amount of light suitable for your taste and needs.

Roll Film. With roll film:

1. Develop roll film on a reel in a daylight processing tank as you normally would.

2. Halfway through development, take the reel of film out of the tank and rinse it with water to slow the developer's activity. (Do this in complete darkness and be sure to leave the developer in the tank so it can be used again after the re-exposure.)

3. Carefully take the film off the reel and hang it from a clip so the whole roll can be re-exposed to light.

4. The re-exposure should be done with the same sort of light source suggested for the sheet films.

5. Re-expose the film for one or two seconds and then carefully wind the film back onto the reel.

6. Once the film is back on the reel, put it into the film developing tank and complete the rest of the developing.

Whether you're working with sheet or roll film, after the re-exposure begin agitating the film again, complete the rest of its development, and finish processing as you normally would. After the film is dry, evaluate your results and determine whether you need to alter the re-exposure time or not. If you're using negative film and the image is too dark, reduce the re-exposure time. With transparency film, give it more light if it is too dark and less light if it is too light. Black-and-white films can be bleached if they are slightly too dark. This is frequently done to make the Mackie lines stand out better. (For bleaching, see the section in chapter 2.)

You can get color variations by changing the color of the light source when re-exposing color films. Use colored light bulbs or color filters over the light source.

You'll discover many variables that influence the outcome of the Sabattier effect. A series of test re-exposures are necessary to determine the exposure that works best with your images and working conditions. By alternating the amount of re-exposure and the point in time chosen to re-expose the film, you can make the reversal effect more or less evident. By developing a consistent procedure to minimize the variables, you can accurately judge your results.

Alternative darkroom effects, such as the Sabattier effect, are fun and offer an opportunity for you to use your photography and imagination in ways that go beyond the reality the camera captures. Whether you find them merely a novelty or a means to express your feelings, special-effect techniques can open new doors.

2

Creative Alternatives with Processed Negatives and Slides

This chapter deals with the problems and creative considerations you face after your film is processed. To take full advantage of your pictures, it may be necessary to alter your film by bleaching, intensifying, or contrast masking before you start to print. You may want to try alterations to change the visual effect of the final image. For instance, color can be added to both black-and-white and color films to enhance their statement. You can also draw on the film, scratch through the emulsion, and subject the film to heat to change the character of the images.

Intensifying Black-and-White Negatives and Positives

Intensification is a process used to add density and contrast to black-and-white negatives and positives. Normally, photographers intensify their film in an attempt to save an underexposed or underdeveloped image. But it is also used to heighten contrast and grain and the graphic impact of the photograph.

Intensifiers increase the existing density of black-and-white films by chemically adding either more silver or other metals, such as mercury, chromium, or copper to the film. This makes it possible to make an acceptable print from a negative that was originally too thin (lacking density) or too flat (lacking contrast).

Intensification works best where density exists, but is insufficient. The intensifier cannot add detail to film that lacks it in the first place. Very thin, underexposed images receive little help from this procedure. But slightly underexposed or correctly exposed but underdeveloped film will show a definite improvement. Very thin film reacts poorly to intensification because it has little density for the intensifier to react on. It still helps to intensify very thin film, but the results may not be as satisfactory as you'd like. Slightly underexposed, or correctly exposed but underdeveloped, film has enough existing density for the intensifier to affect.

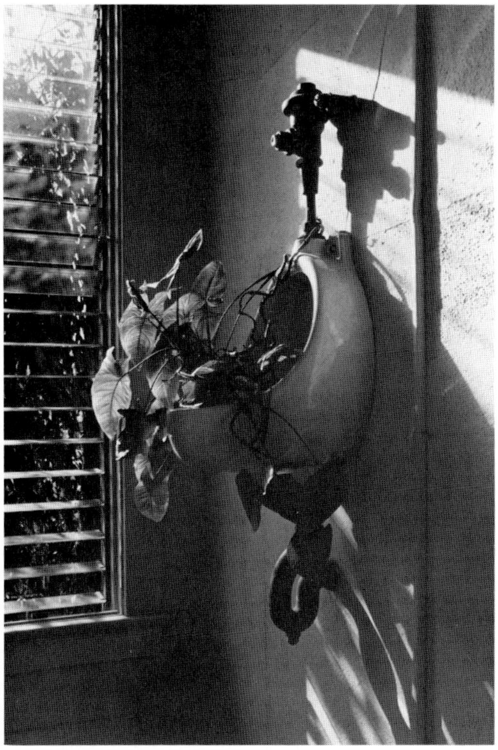

A slightly underexposed negative produced this print on a grade 2 paper.

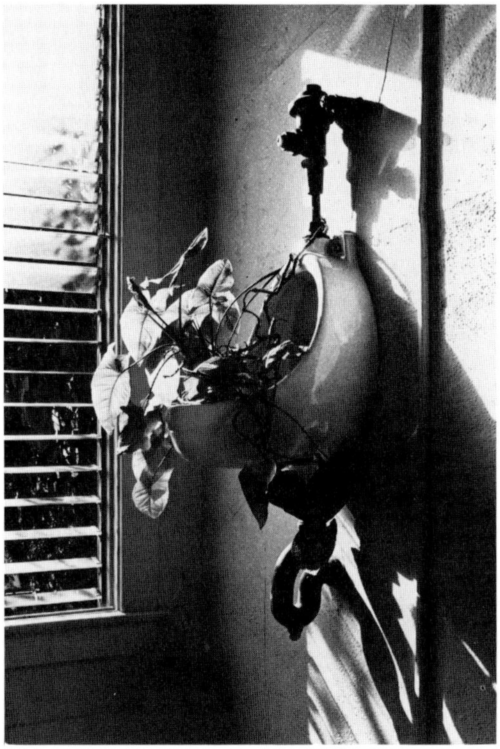

A similar negative, shot at the same time and exposure, was intensified and used to make this print. Note the dramatic difference in grain and contrast.

Intensification helps correctly exposed but underdeveloped film because it increases the contrast lost due to the underdevelopment. Because increases in density from intensification are proportional to the existing density of the image, highlights are intensified more than shadows and the overall contrast of the film is increased.

Intensification causes an increase in grain size, and it also affects permanence. Many intensification processes stain the film and limit its life. Permanence can usually be increased by treating the film in a black-and-white developer such as Dektol 1:3 for several minutes after intensifying and then thoroughly washing it.

Chromium Intensification. You can use a variety of methods to intensify black-and-white films. One of the more popular methods is chromium intensification. The chromium intensifier reacts with the silver in film emulsion and increases contrast as well as grain. With normally exposed and normally developed film, chromium intensifier can be used to exaggerate grain and contrast. With underexposed and/or underdeveloped film, it can only be used as a corrective tool.

Chromium intensification is a two-step process beginning with bleaching the film and then redeveloping it. You can either mix your own solutions or purchase Kodak's prepackaged Chromium Intensifier—two packets of powder that make 16 ounces (473 ml) of bleach and 16 ounces (473 ml) of clearing solution. You will also need a metol-hydroquinone developer, like Dektol, to redevelop the image. Mixing your own intensifier lets you alter the proportions of the chemicals and control the amount of intensification. The formula is shown in the accompanying chart.

The strength of the working solution can be altered to suit your needs as shown in the accompanying chart.

If you use Kodak's prepackaged Chromium Intensifier, follow the package directions. However, if you mix your own intensifier from the formula given in this chapter, follow this procedure to intensify your film:

1. Soak the film in water for 10 minutes to soften the emulsion.

2. Immerse film in bleach solution for 3 to 5 minutes, or until the blacks have changed to a yellow color.

3. Rinse the film in running water.

4. After rinsing, put the film in a 2.5 percent solution potassium metabisulphate for 2 minutes or until the yellow stain completely disappears.

5. Rinse again in running water for 30 seconds.

6. Then transfer the film to a 3 percent borax solution for one minute.

7. Redevelop the film in a metol-hydroquinone developer, such as Dektol, diluted 1:3, until the white image darkens completely.

8. Then wash the film for 15 minutes in running water, soak in a wetting solution, squeegee, and dry.

If more intensification is necessary, repeat the process.

Toning for Intensification. Another intensification method to improve a negative for easier printing is toning the film. Unlike chromium intensification, this procedure does *not* increase the grain and it has less effect on contrast. But toned negatives produce prints with better detail and more contrast than they would without toning. The addition of color to your black-and-white negatives may also stimulate you to consider new ways to use your images.

By changing the color of a black-and-white negative to yellow, orange, or red the density is not physically increased, but, for practical purposes the printing density increases as these colors reduce the amount of blue light passing through the film.

A variety of toners are available which add color to both film and prints. Most commercial dyes, such as food coloring, can also be used to add color to film. Red dye provides the most intensification.

Among toners, uranium (which is hard to find) produces an effective red color. Cop-

FORMULA FOR CHROMIUM INTENSIFIER

Stock Solution A	Potassium bichromate 0.5 oz. (14.2 g)	Water to make 10 oz. (295.7 ml)
Stock Solution B	Concentrated hydrochloric acid 0.5 oz. (14.2 g)	Water to make 10 oz. (295.7 ml)

CHROMIUM INTENSIFIER PROPORTIONS

Amount of Intensification	**Solution Proportions**		
	Stock Solution A	***Stock Solution B***	***Water***
Slight	**10 parts**	**10 parts**	**5 parts**
Medium	**10 parts**	**4 parts**	**11 parts**
Strong	**10 parts**	**2 parts**	**13 parts**

per toners, available in prepackaged form at photography stores, produce a reddish color that is also a good intensifier. Sepia toners produce a yellow color which also works.

Reducing Black-and-White Films

When black-and-white negatives and positives are too dense (due to overexposure or overdevelopment), the emulsion density can be chemically reduced to make the film easier to print. There are three types of reducers:

1. *Subtractive (or cutting) reducers* uniformly decrease the density of the film. Because there is less silver in the shadow portions of a negative, the shadows are lightened more than the highlights, causing an increase in contrast. This is the best type of reducer to use with overexposed negatives lacking in contrast.

2. *Porportional reducers* decrease the emulsion density in proportion to the amount of silver present. Highlights are reduced at a greater rate than the shadows, and thus contrast is reduced. Slightly overdeveloped film benefits from this type of reducer.

3. *Super-proportional reducers* have little effect on the shadows while greatly reducing the highlights. These reducers should be used with film that is underexposed and overdeveloped (as when push processed).

The most common and popular reducer is Farmer's Reducer. You can buy it prepackaged at camera stores, or you can buy the ingredients and mix your own. Farmer's Reducer can be used as both a subtractive (or cutting) reducer and a proportional reducer by varying its strength.

The formula for Farmer's Reducer is shown in the accompanying chart.

Mixing Cutting Reducer. Mix 1 part of solution A with 5 parts of solution B and add water to make 30 parts. Once parts A and B are mixed together they deteriorate very rapidly, so after 15 minutes you should toss the solution out and mix a new batch.

Soak the film in water before immersing it in the reducer. The degree of reduction should be judged visually. To check the progress of the procedures, take the film out of the reducer and rinse it in water. This does not stop the reducer, but dilutes it and slows it enough for you to evaluate your progress. If the film needs more reduction, return it to the reducer. When the reduction has gone far enough, remove the film from the reducer and rinse it with water. To stop the action of the reducer permanently, refix the film and then wash and dry it as you normally would.

Proportional Reduction. Farmer's Reducer acts as a proportional reducer when the working solution is mixed with about only one-tenth the amount of potassium ferricyanide normally used. The reducer can also be used in two separate baths. First immerse the film in a bath of potassium ferricyanide and then in the sodium thiosulfate. The second, separate fixer bath stops the action of the reducer immediately

FORMULA FOR FARMER'S REDUCER

Stock Solution A	Potassium ferricyanide 2 oz. (57 g)	Water to make 20 oz. (591 ml)
Stock Solution B	Sodium thiosulfate 8 oz. (227 g)	Water to make 40 oz. (1172 ml)

Formula for Ammonium Persulfate

(A super-proportional reducer)

Chemical	Amount	
	U.S. Customary Amount	Metric
Ammonium persulfate	60 gr.	3.3 g
Sulfuric acid (10 percent)	3.3 fl. dr.	12.3 ml
Distilled water to make	4 fl. oz.	120.0 ml

and enables you to inspect your results. If you want additional reduction, repeat the process until you are satisfied. This two-bath method has several advantages. First, it is the safest reduction procedure because immersion into the sodium thiosulfate stops the reduction completely. Secondly, the individual solutions keep longer when used separately.

Super-proportional Reduction. Ammonium persulfate is used to make a common super-proportional reducer. To make the working solution, use the accompanying formula.

When mixing the reducer, make sure that the ammonium persulfate crystals crackle as they dissolve. Make only the amount you need, since the solution does not keep and must be used immediately. The reducer turns a milky color when exhausted.

Presoak the film in water, then immerse it in the reducer. When the reduction is sufficient, transfer the film to an acid fixer, such as Kodak's Rapid Fixer, for five minutes. Then wash and dry the film as you normally would.

Reducers help minimize problems with fogged film, and make it easier to print overexposed and overdeveloped film. These methods will also remove the anti-halation layer from color films accidentally processed in black-and-white chemistry.

This print by P. W. Derby, was made from a negative altered by the Sabattier effect. The Sabattier effect works well with film, but frequently the image is too dense to print properly. When this is the case, try bleaching the film to bring out the contrast and Mackie lines.

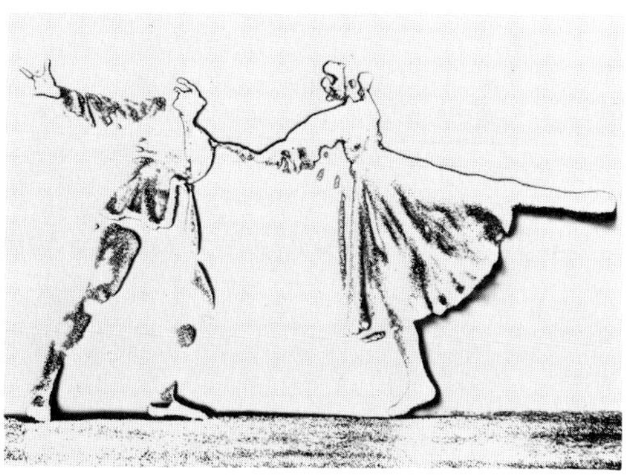

The negative was bleached before this print was made. The bleaching altered the effect of the image in a way which couldn't be achieved otherwise.

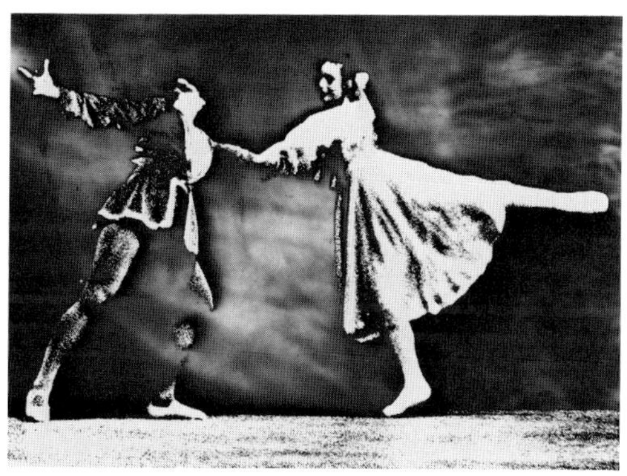

Rescuing Color Film

There are a number of procedures for altering a color bias or compensating for an incorrectly exposed color transparency. Unfortunately, there is no quick-and-easy method. Most procedures are technically involved, time-consuming, expensive, and only worth the trouble if there is no other alternative. Each transparency presents its own problems, and a variety of different approaches can be used to try to save it.

Corrective Duplicating. The simplest and least expensive way to improve or save a transparency is by corrective duplicating. Underexposed transparencies (too dark) can be lightened several stops by increasing the exposure during the duplicating process, while overexposed transparencies (too light) can be improved by decreasing the exposure. Color biases can be altered by filtering. Even old, faded color transparencies can be improved through duplicating procedures.

You can improve an original transparency by duplicating it yourself or by sending it to a custom lab. Duplicating techniques vary, but adequate results can be achieved at home with a minimum of equipment and expense. A slide-copier attachment can be used in conjunction with a macro lens, with a bellows, or with a normal lens mounted in reversed position to make duplicate slides that are the same size as your original.

When making duplicate slides, use color filters to match the color of your original, or to alter its color. These filters, available in glass or gelatin, can be purchased at camera stores. (Three-inch [7.62 cm] gelatin filters are the most economical and convenient.) There are two types of filters available: color-compensating (CC) and color-printing (CP). Color-compensating filters are designed to be used in front of the lens, while the thicker color-printing filters are made to be used in the head of an enlarger between the light source and the film. Both types of filters will make color corrections, but the color-compensating filters give better definition when shooting through them.

Filters are indexed in degrees indicating their density. The larger the number, the deeper the filter. For instance, a 5-degree filter has a very slight effect, while a 20-degree filter makes an obvious difference. The filtration you use depends on the type of original film, the type of duplicating film you use, and the light source. Testing is necessary to determine this. Thus, unless you plan to do a lot of duplicating, you will find it's less expensive and time-consuming to have a custom lab do it.

If you plan on doing your own slide duplicating, one of the biggest problems you will run into is contrast control. Any regular film used to duplicate another film will increase the contrast unless you compensate by flashing or overexposing and underdeveloping. Both flashing and exposure/development compensations require extra considerations which complicate your job. But, you can avoid this problem by using films designed for duplicating slides. These films are made to produce less contrast.

One such film is Kodak's Ektachrome Slide Duplicating Film 5071. This film produces the best results when used with tungsten light; but it can also be used with electronic flash and corrective filtering (refer to the film-data sheet). Among tungsten lights, quartz or tungsten-halogen lights are recommended, because they fade less and maintain a more constant color temperature than regular photo floods.

To sufficiently lighten extremely dark underexposed transparencies, you may need as much as four times the exposure necessary for a normally exposed slide. For instance, if you normally expose duplicate slides at *f*/8 for half a second, open the lens two stops to *f*/4 to lighten a very dark slide. While overexposed transparencies cannot be completely corrected, a reduced exposure will help a little; but it is hard to replace what is not there.

Color biases can be altered or improved through filtration. Use color-compensating filters and determine the amount of filtration necessary by viewing each transparency together with various filters. See if adding a certain color improves the original. A 5-degree correction is fine tuning, a 10-degree correction is obvious, and a 20-degree correction is significant. Sometimes it is necessary to use two colors at the same time, but try to use as few filters as possible to avoid any loss of image definition. Subtract filters to make a correction whenever possible, rather than adding more. In the end experience will be your best guide.

To determine what correction to make, use the accompanying chart as a guide:

For color corrections, the primary filters—red, blue, and green—must be used individually. When any two are combined, they create black and block the light. However, any two secondary filters—cyan, yellow, and magenta—can be combined for correcting color casts. Avoid using three secondary filters together because the combination creates neutral density (gray) and reduces the light intensity. To determine what filtration to use, refer to the accompanying table and experiment. After you have worked with color correcting for a while, it should be easy to make color judgments, and improve problem slides.

Reducing and Bleaching Color Transparencies. Unlike black-and-white films, color films cannot be reduced or bleached successfully. Color-negative films and most slide films should not be reduced or bleached at all. Former E-3 and E-4 Ektachrome films could be bleached for a specific color cast, or reduced overall with a product called Colorbrite. Unfortunately, the newer E-6 Ektachromes (the only ones available today) cannot be easily bleached or reduced. Colorbrite doesn't work with E-6 films, and there is no commercial product to take its place. But chemicals are available that can be used to bleach specific color casts and there are dyes that can be added to E-6 Ektachromes to intensify or alter colors.

These chemicals are expensive, and to use them adequately requires time, patience, and a lot of practice. Normally, only professional retouchers attempt reducing and bleaching color transparencies. Further information on adding dyes or bleaching E-6 transparencies can be obtained by writing to the Eastman Kodak Company. Request pamphlet E-68, *Retouching Ektachrome Transparencies.*

Applying Color to Film

People have been coloring and drawing on photographic prints since the beginning of photography, but applying color to film is seldom done. It is almost impossible to apply color or draw on film with the same finesse one can use on a print. The color

COLOR CORRRECTIONS FOR TRANSPARENCIES

If a transparency is too	Add	Subtract
green	magenta	green (yellow & cyan)
magenta	green (yellow & cyan)	magenta
blue	yellow	blue (magenta & cyan)
yellow	blue (magenta & cyan)	yellow
red	cyan	red (yellow & magenta)
cyan	red (yellow & magenta)	cyan

looks applied and subtle details and colorations are hard to handle when drawing on a small piece of film, like a 35 mm slide.

Yet coloring film is an area worth exploring because there is a unique character to prints made from film that has been colored and/or drawn upon. The enlarging process alters the scale of the drawing and the results are therefore unlike those normally obtained when drawing on a print. Also, once the film is altered you can easily make as many prints as you like, while alterations on a print have to be repeated each time a new print is made.

Toning Film. Toning is a quick and easy way to add overall color to film. Most people think toning is only done to prints. But black-and-white film can also be toned and toning can add a new twist to slide shows, film strips, or movies. Toned black-and-white film can also be used to make color prints by printing directly on a positive print material such as Cibachrome or Kodak's Ektachrome 2033 Type R color paper.

One of the easiest toners to use, Edwal Color Toner, gives dramatic results with both film and prints. This liquid toner comes in five colors: blue, brown, red, yellow, and green. Intermediate colors can be obtained by toning the film first with one color and then with another. Edwal Toner converts the silver image in black-and-white negatives, prints, slides, and movie films into permanently colored images.

These toners come in four-ounce (125 ml) bottles that make 64 ounces (1.9 litres) of working solution, enough to tone about 120 4×5 prints. The toner is in one solution, and comes with very complete directions. Inside the cap of each bottle of toner is a small plastic cup containing a red powder. This powder must be mixed with the liquid part of the toner to make it active. Prior to mixing, the toner will last indefinitely; but once the ingredients are mixed, the toner lasts only six to eight weeks.

Before using the toner, make sure your film has been thoroughly fixed and washed. Any residual fixer not washed out will interfere with toning. Then immerse the film in a working solution (one part toner to fifteen parts water) and tone it for three to four minutes with gentle agitation. Prolonged toning, for 15 or 20 minutes, bleaches the silver out and produces chalk-like tones with very little depth. Once the film has been toned to your satisfaction, wash it in running water for ten minutes, then squeegee and dry.

If you want to tone only part of the film, try using maskoid or rubber cement to cover the part of the film you don't want toned. These can be applied with a small brush or toothpick. Because toner reacts to the silver in the emulsion, mask the film on the emulsion side only. Once the image is toned, remove the mask by rubbing it off. This process will give you an image that is partially black-and-white and partially toned. The process can be repeated to get multiple colors in an image. (See chapter 10 for information on toning prints.)

Hand Coloring and Drawing on Film. You can use oil and acrylic paints, felt pens, and most other types of pigments

This image was produced by drawing on the original 35 mm color slide with a black felt pen. Drawing directly on slides is a good way of abstracting the image, deleting information, and adding texture.

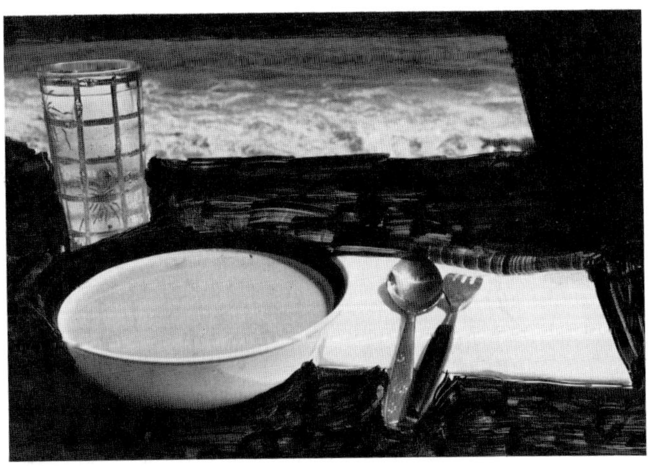

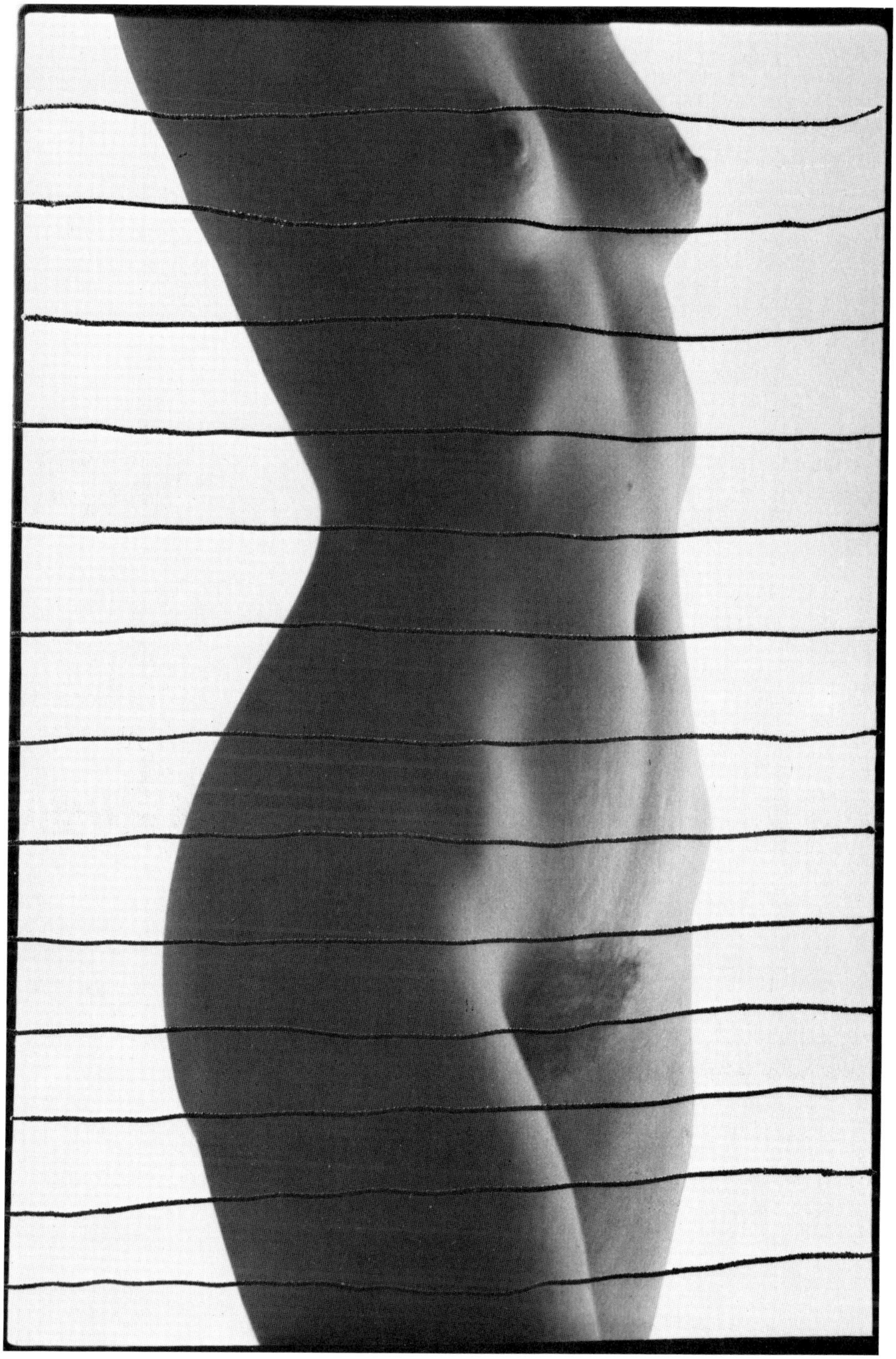

The black lines in this Caged Nude *photograph were created by scratching the emulsion of the negative with an X-acto knife.*

and dyes to add color and to draw on the surface of film. Drawing can be done on either negative or positive film. With color slides, you can add color directly to a positive original, making it easy to visualize the final result. With color negatives, the colors you apply to the film will print in reverse. By adding color to black-and-white negatives and then printing on a positive color-print material, such as Cibachrome, you create an illusion of a positive image where the color was added and still retain negative black-and-white elements in the picture. This can result in a visually interesting photograph that comments on the relationship between painting and photography, color and black-and-white, and negative and positive images.

India ink and the dyes used in most felt pens work well on both black-and-white and color films. Felt pens produce an obvious, blotchy effect that is enhanced when the image is enlarged. They can be used to provide overall color effects, or to accent specific parts of a picture. Fine-line pens can be used, but generally the effect is far from subtle, and should be used to make an obvious statement about the act of coloring, rather than trying to integrate it as part of the photographic process. Depending upon the type of film, the color device used may adhere better to either the emulsion or the base side. Try it first with some scrap film, then when you feel confident switch to the film you want to color.

There is a major drawback to drawing or painting on film—once you have started, there is no turning back. You've made a commitment and you're stuck with it. Also, once you've colored the film, handle it very carefully because the dyes or ink used may flake or wear off the surface of the film.

Etching or scratching through the emulsion is another way to alter and draw on film. This technique, though rough, can be dramatic and draws attention to the precious nature of the film itself by the act of violating it. Once again, it is an approach that allows no turning back. Remember that an unusual or novel technique alone may not justify itself, unless the technique works with images to make them more effective.

Altering Images with Heat

Ordinarily, you protect your films from the elements, but for bizarre effects, try applying heat to selected images. Hold a frame of black-and-white or color film with the emulsion side down over a small flame, and let it heat slowly. When the emulsion begins to bubble, pull the film away from the flame and inspect it. If you are satisfied, let the film cool completely. If not, expose it to the flame again until you get the desired effect.

The bizarre distortions in this image were produced by heating a color transparency with a match until the emulsion started to bubble. The transparency was then sandwiched with a black-and-white negative, and used to produce this print.

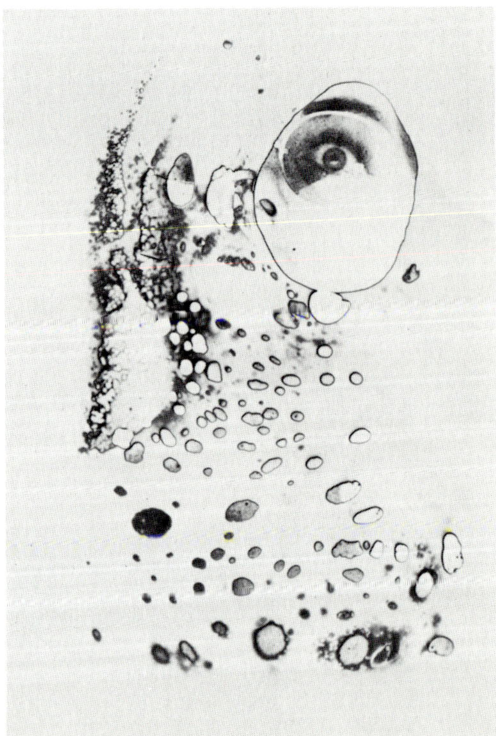

The distortion caused by melting the emulsion can be very dramatic, especially with color films. But once again, this process is irreversible. Because results are hard to control, begin by experimenting with scrap film, and even later only use film you are willing to sacrifice. Too much heat can cause the film to burn completely, creating large holes in the emulsion. Limited heat, applied with patience and control, produces distorted effects that can be quite unusual. Experiment with both black-and-white and color films, but color slides usually produce the most dramatic results.

Altering Images by Freezing Film

Freezing film also creates unusual textural effects. When wet film is frozen, a frost forms which alters the emulsion and creates permanent patterns that show up when the film is printed. These patterns, random ice-crystal forms, can add a pleasing effect to figure studies, scenics, and other images.

Prior to freezing film, soak it in water for ten minutes to get the emulsion soft. Then,

The delicate texture pattern in this photograph by David Dubuque was created by placing wet film in a freezer.

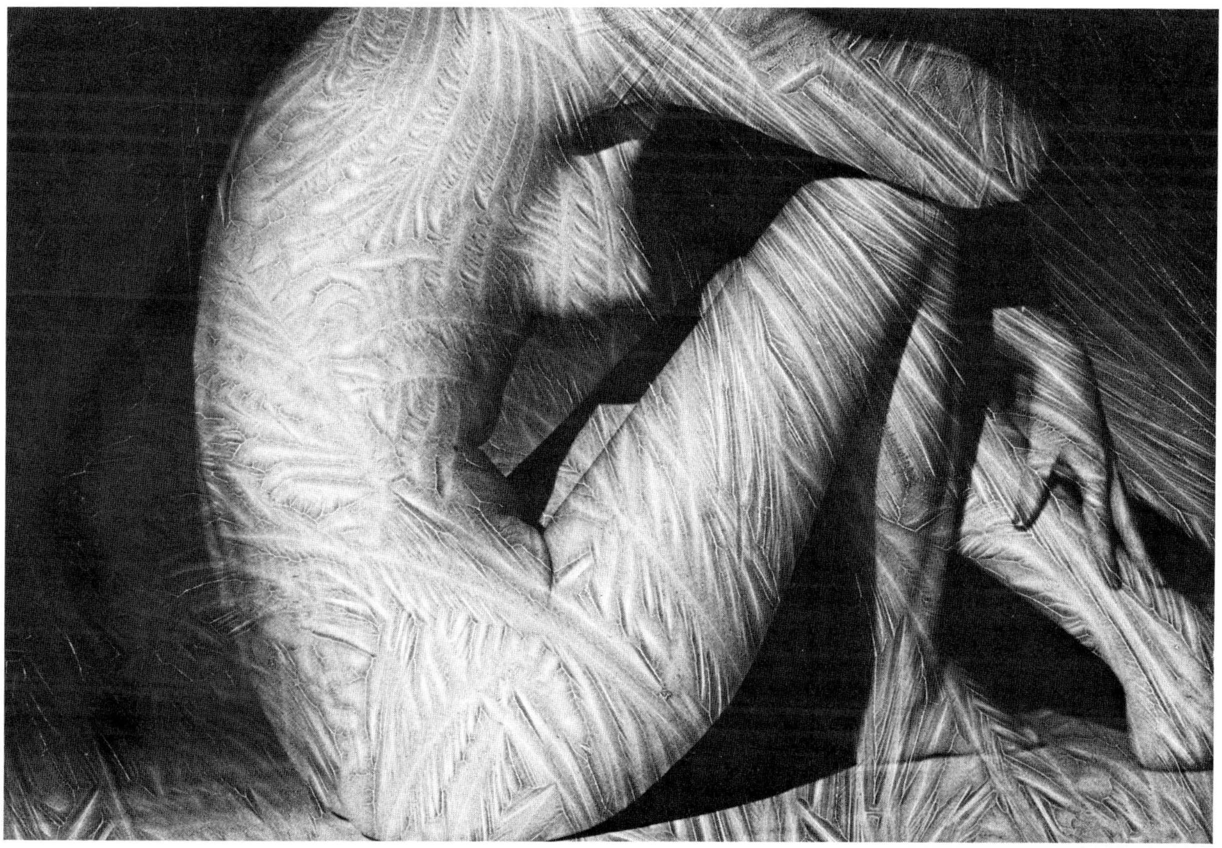

without squeegeeing, put the wet film into the freezer compartment of your refrigerator. Several hours later, take the film out and hang it up to thaw and dry.

To avoid destroying a good film that has images on it, try freezing some clear film. The frost patterns will be just as apparent on clear film. Then, once dry, the resulting texture pattern can be sandwiched with another image you desire to print.

Internegatives

Internegatives are often used to make prints from color slides. Even though positive-to-positive printing materials exist (such as Cibachrome and a variety of Type R-color processes), internegatives are necessary to make black-and-white prints from slides. They also simplify contrast control when making color prints.

Transparencies have more inherent contrast than color negatives, because they are designed for projection, not printing. Color negatives have less contrast and are easier to control in printing. Traditionally, direct-printing processes using transparencies have been plagued with contrast problems; but improvements in materials and chemistry have helped tame these problems. Even so, many photographers still prefer to make internegatives from their slides to achieve satisfying prints.

The internegative process gives the photographer more control. This control can make the difference between a good print and a really fine one. Some photographers make internegatives by using a 1:1 duplicating system with their camera. But a better approach, providing more control, is to enlarge your transparencies in the darkroom onto 4×5 sheet film. This enables you to dodge and burn on the internegative to lessen printing problems. It also makes it easier to control the contrast of an individual image by altering the exposure and development of the internegative.

Black and White Internegatives. To make anything but a negative black-and-white image from a color slide, you must first make an internegative. Most black-and-white films can be used for this purpose, but it is best to use a panchromatic film (sensitive to all colors) with a fine grain structure. Kodak's Ektapan, available in sheet sizes only, is an excellent film to use. This film is panchromatic, has moderately fine grain, and an ASA of 100.

To make a black-and-white internegative, put your transparency in the negative carrier with the emulsion side up. The film used to make the internegative can be held in place several ways. The best method is to use a 4×5 film holder attached to the baseboard of your enlarger. This provides a secure, dust-free method to hold the film flat and eliminates the need for glass to hold it down flat. To focus the image, just put a piece of 4×5-inch white paper in the holder. (Remember to take it out when you are finished.) If a film holder is unavailable, tape a piece of 4×5-inch black paper to your baseboard. Then put the film, emulsion side up, on top of the black paper and cover with a piece of clean glass. (The black paper prevents the light from bouncing back through the film when exposed.) By taping the paper to the baseboard you can determine in the dark where the film should go.

Once you've worked out the logistics, it's time to begin testing. Since transparency films have more contrast than negative films, you have to reduce the contrast when making an internegative. With black-and-white films, you have to control contrast by overexposing and underdeveloping. For instance, normally exposed black-and-white Ektapan film has a development time of nine minutes at 68 degrees (20 C) in D-76 undiluted. To reduce the contrast for internegatives, overexpose the film by one stop so as to have a normal density when development time is reduced to five minutes rather than nine minutes. This will give you excellent shadow detail, while holding the highlights within a printable range.

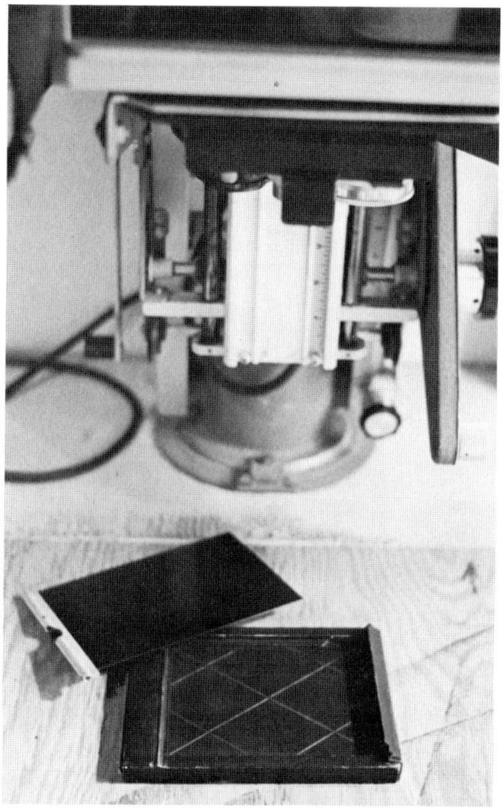

A 4×5 inch film holder (attached to the enlarger baseboard) is excellent for holding film when making internegatives.

The amount of overexposure and underdevelopment varies with each working situation. Run a series of tests with your own equipment according to your working habits to establish what suits you best. Try to establish a standard working procedure and reduce as many variables as possible. Always use the same film, developer, enlarger height, and exposure procedure. Alter your exposure and development only if needed. Increase the exposure time when making internegatives from dark, more opaque slides; reduce it when working with light, overexposed slides. Don't be afraid to dodge and burn wherever it seems necessary. The better the internegative, the easier it will be to print. Remember that you are working with a panchromatic film that's sensitive to all light, so complete darkness is a must, and safelights cannot be used.

Color Internegatives. While the film is more expensive, color internegatives are made in basically the same manner as black-and-white internegatives. However, the film must be filtered when exposed, and needs to be processed in C-41 color-negative chemistry. Unless you plan to consistently make a large number of internegatives, it is not worth the time, money, and energy to produce them yourself. Send them to a custom lab that's set up to handle them efficiently and under controlled circumstances.

If you do plan to make color internegatives, get Eastman Kodak's pamphlet E-24. It will give you most of the technical information needed. Use either Kodak Vericolor Internegative Film 6011 (roll) or Kodak Vericolor Internegative Film 4112 (sheet). If you use other color-negative films, expect them to have too much contrast. You will also need a Kodak Three-Point Transparency Guide, a densitometer, and the capacity to process the film in C-41 chemistry.

Establishing the proper filter pack is the difficult part. Color-internegative film must be filtered to achieve the proper color balance. The filtration will vary from one darkroom working situation to the next, so testing is necessary. If your filtration is off, you'll find unwanted colors appearing in shadows or highlights, while the rest of the picture looks great. This means a color crossover has taken place from one layer of the internegative film to the next, making it impossible to get a correctly balanced print.

To avoid this problem, make your initial tests with the Three-Point Transparency Guide; read them with the densitometer, and consult your local Kodak Technical Representative. Once you reach the proper filter pack and exposure, your results should be fairly consistent. It's wise to run occasional control strips (which can be purchased from Kodak), to make sure there's been no shift in the chemistry or film.

Masking for Contrast Control in Color Prints

A color print made from a color slide never looks the same as the projected slide. The eye adapts to the overall balance of a projected slide so that both the highlights and the shadows show good detail and rich color. In a print, the colors don't seem as rich, and the highlights and the shadows lose detail. This is partly due to the difference between transmitted and reflected light. Light going through a projected transparency brings out all of the richness of the slide. In comparison, a print is less radiant when viewed by reflected light.

Contrast control is a frequent problem with prints made from slides. Film has a greater contrast range than printing paper. A slide with bright sunlight and deep shadows may look beautiful on a screen, but it will probably be hard to duplicate the same feeling in a print. A Type R or Cibachrome print will increase the contrast to the point where shadow details are hard to maintain without completely sacrificing the highlights. Even with an internegative, many slides are impossible to print correctly. Most photographers try to cope with this problem by becoming very adept at dodging and burning the print. But even the most skillful printer occasionally runs into slides that cannot be properly printed.

The answer to this problem is contrast masking. Black-and-white film masks can be made to sandwich with your original transparency. These masks help reduce the contrast range of the print so that dodging and burning won't be necessary. With a mask, a slide that took a tremendous amount of manipulation to print without a mask can frequently be printed in a single exposure. A print made this way will maintain both shadow and highlight detail.

Contrast Masking. Low-contrast masks made from black-and-white sheet film reduce the density range in the highlights of a transparency, making it more suitable for printing. With a properly made mask, a print should be able to record a full range of highlight and shadow details. If the mask is not strong enough, the print will be too contrasty. If the print is too flat, it means the mask was overdone. The best masking procedure involves two steps: first, a highlight mask, and then an overall-contrast mask.

The Highlight Mask. A highlight mask prevents the overall-contrast mask from becoming too dense in the highlights. Without a highlight mask, important highlight areas would be lost. The highlight mask is a contrasty negative with density in only the highlight areas of the image. It is made from the original transparency by contact printing, and is used in combination with the original transparency to make the overall-contrast mask.

A highlight mask keeps the highlights in the photograph crisp when masking to reduce contrast. These two masks were used to make the print on page 41.

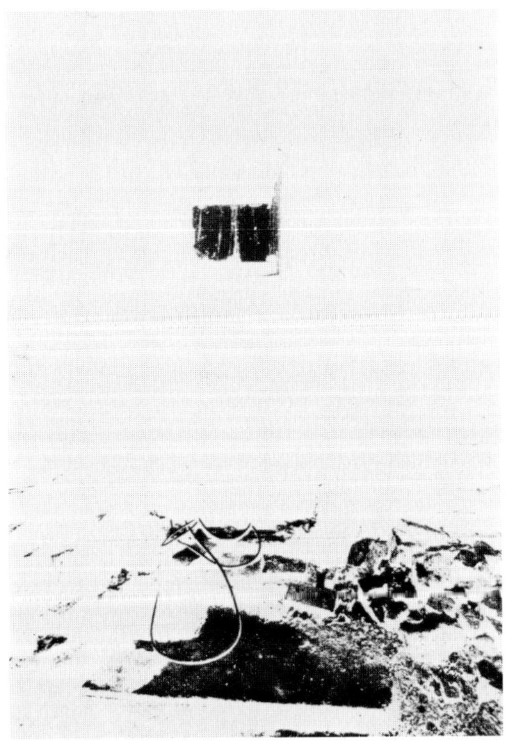

The density of the highlight mask will vary with the original picture and the effect you desire. To get more detail in the highlights, increase the density of the highlight mask. Normally, the maximum density of the highlight mask is about 0.40.

To make a highlight mask, use Kodalith Pan Film 2568 (Estar base). It is normally only available by special order in sheet-film sizes. Kodalith Pan is sensitive to all colors of light, unlike the more common Kodalith Ortho film, which is sensitive to all colors but red. Because of this safelights cannot be used.

Contact print the original transparency with its emulsion side facing the emulsion side of the Kodalith Pan film. Place a .003 Kodak diffusion sheet, or a 0.10 mm thick piece of clear film, between the transparency and the masking film to produce a slightly diffused image on the mask.

A soft-focus overall mask is made from a sandwich of the highlight mask and the original transparency. The highlight mask is then discarded.

Use your enlarger as a light source and make the exposure on the enlarger baseboard. First attach a piece of 4×5-inch black paper to the baseboard to make it easier to position the film in the dark. This black paper will also absorb excess light during the exposure, while a light-colored baseboard could reduce contrast and sharpness by reflecting light back through the film during the exposure.

The exposure of the highlight mask is fairly critical, and it takes some testing to determine what is right for your equipment and transparencies. Each transparency will vary in its needs and should be treated individually. After some experience, you'll find it easier to judge if the exposure of the highlight mask is correct. If the mask is overexposed, contrast will be increased rather than reduced, resulting in harsh tones in the print. Underexposure will not cause enough of a change to make any noticeable difference.

To determine what exposure to use, put the enlarger at a height so the light easily covers the area of the baseboard. Stop the lens down completely and make a series of test exposures at two-second intervals. Since Kodalith Pan film only comes in 4×5-inch sheets, expose several transparencies at the same time. (Four to six 35 mm transparencies can be exposed simultaneously on one sheet of 4×5 film.) You can cut them apart later for individual use.

Develop the film in a tray with Kodak Developer D-11, full strength with continuous agitation, for 2½ to 3½ minutes at 68 degrees (20 C). After development, immerse the film in an acid stop bath for ten seconds, then fix the film for five minutes. Wash the film for ten minutes, then treat it in a wetting solution (such as Kodak's Photo-Flo), squeegee, and dry.

Align the finished highlight mask, emulsion-to-emulsion, with the original transparency. Use small pieces of tape to hold the two pieces of film in register. Be careful to only use the tape on the edges of the transparency, so the adhesive doesn't per-

Contrast Masking Sequence

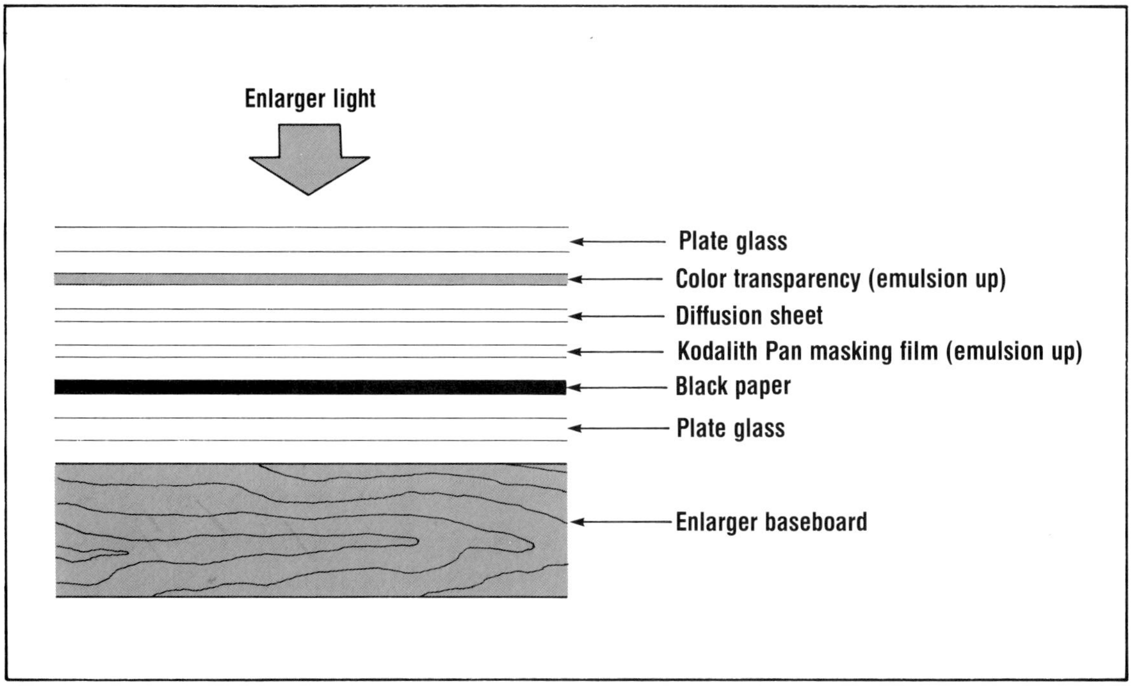

The above diagram shows the arrangement of the elements necessary to make a contrast mask. First put a sheet of black paper on the enlarger baseboard. Then place the unexposed Kodalith Pan masking film emulsion side up on top of this black paper and cover it with a diffusion sheet, or piece of clear film. Place the original transparency emulsion side up on top of the diffusion sheet, and cover the whole thing with a piece of clean glass. You are now ready to expose the contrast mask.

Contrast Mask Easel

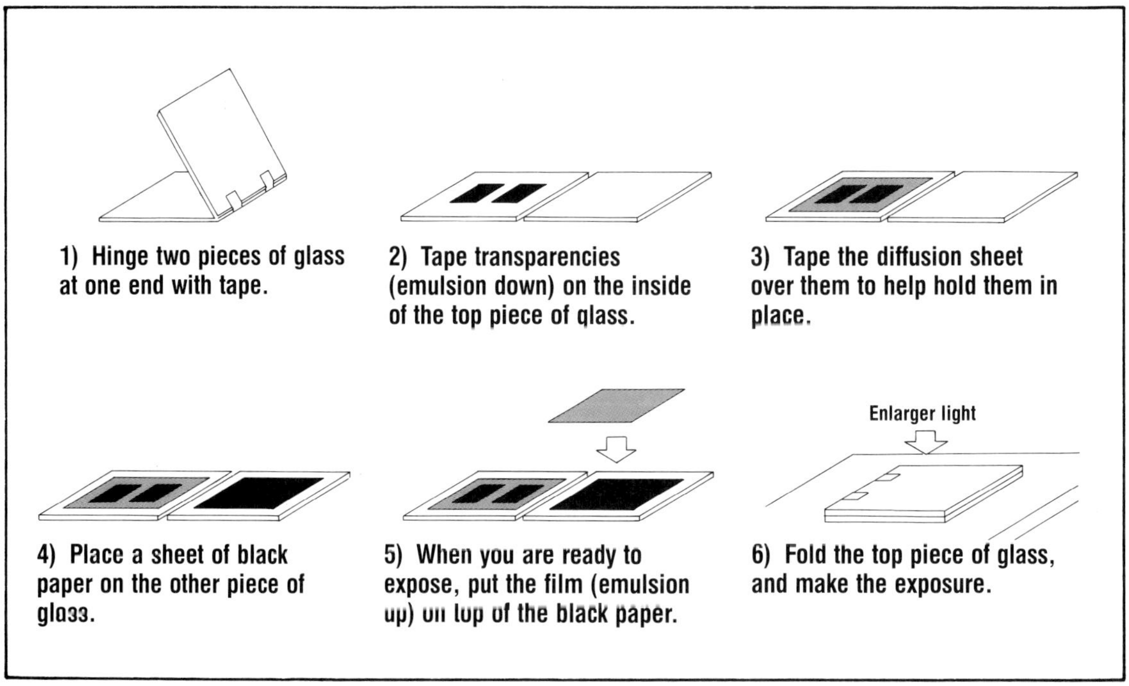

If you are going to make a number of contrast masks you may wish to make an easel like the one above. It's easier to use in the long run.

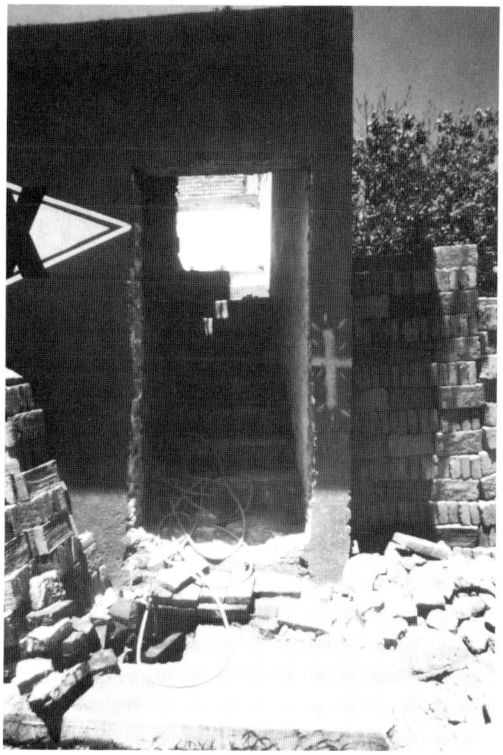

The contrast in this print is excessive, making masking a necessity. The original was a 35 mm transparency printed on Cibachrome.

A highlight mask and an overall mask were both necessary to reduce the contrast in the transparency enough to make this print without dodging and burning.

manently damage your original slide. This combination of the highlight mask and transparency has a rather strange appearance, but this is normal. When the highlight mask is replaced by the overall-contrast mask, the reversal of the highlights will disappear.

The Overall-Contrast-Reduction Mask. The overall-contrast-reduction mask is made in the same basic manner as the highlight mask. It is made from the sandwich of the highlight mask and the original transparency on Kodak Pan Masking Film 4570. You can make the overall mask without using a highlight mask, but normally the results will be much better if a highlight mask is used.

The overall mask is a low-contrast black-and-white negative that reduces the contrast of the original transparency when the two are combined together. The harder and denser the mask, the more contrast is reduced. However, if the mask is overexposed and its tones extend into the darker middle-values and shadows of the transparency, the resulting prints may be too flat.

You make the overall-contrast-reduction mask by contact printing in a manner similar to the procedure used to make the highlight mask. Make sure the sandwiched highlight mask and original transparency are emulsion-to-emulsion. When the overall mask is made, the base side of the original transparency should be facing the Pan Masking film. The exposure will be through the film support of the transparency, causing the mask to have a slight unsharpness that makes subsequent registration easier. A piece of Kodak Diffusion Sheet (.003) can also be used between the transparency and the unexposed masking film to further diffuse the image. With film larger than 35 mm, use a piece of 1/8-inch (0.31 cm) plate glass in combination with the diffusion sheet to further reduce sharpness.

Because the masking film is panchromatic, color filters can be used to lighten or darken colors in the original transparency. A yellow filter will slightly lighten dark-blue tones in the final enlargement. A magenta filter will lighten green, while a cyan filter will lighten red.

The exposure for the Pan Masking film varies with individual transparencies and equipment. Make a series of intitial exposure tests at two-second intervals, the lens set at *f*/16. It's impossible to determine which exposure is best until you make some masks at various exposures, sandwich them with the original, and make a print. The mask should be soft in focus with low contrast and a density similar to an underexposed negative.

Develop the exposed Pan Masking film for three minutes at 68 degrees (20 C) in Kodak Developer HC-110, working dilution F. If your results are underexposed (too thin), increase the exposure time rather than the development time so that contrast is not increased. Stop, fix, wash, and dry the film according to the instructions packed with the film.

When the overall mask is finished, remove the highlight mask from the original transparency and replace it with the overall mask. Mount the overall mask with its emulsion side against the back of the original transparency in accurate registration. This combination, with the overall mask on top and the emulsion of the transparency facing down, is then enlarged.

3

Photograms

A photogram is a light drawing made without a camera. It is the result of manipulating light and time with sensitized materials. The making of photograms is generally overlooked by photographers in our gadget-oriented society where the emphasis is on new lenses, fast films, and automatic cameras. Yet there is excellent creative potential in cameraless photography.

Most beginning photography students are given assignments to produce photograms. Not only do these assignments provide them with a better understanding of light and photographic materials, but they require beginners to compose images. Unlike working with a camera, where you react to something that is already there, when making photograms you generally start with only a blank sheet of unexposed photographic paper.

Historically, some of the first photographic experiments were photograms. The first photographic images made by William Henry Fox Talbot, the inventor of the negative-positive process, were photograms. But it wasn't until the 1920s that artists such as Christian Schad, Man Ray, and Moholy-Nagy started experimenting more systematically with the possibilities of photograms. Each of them had their own name for the process: Schad referred to his images as Schadographs; Man Ray called them Rayographs; and Moholy-Nagy called them light drawings or photograms.

These early experimenters were concerned with creating their own reality by going beyond objectivity into the subtle nuances of abstraction. Moholy-Nagy described photograms as images having no real relationship to subject matter, consisting solely of design elements and the play of light in space.

These early photographers were confined to working with black-and-white materials. But today's new color processes, designed for home darkroom use, make it possible to take advantage of the potential color offers for abstract expression in photograms.

The techniques for making photograms are basically very simple, but the results can be very sophisticated. Many contemporary artists find the photogram to be a versatile and stimulating medium. Most photographers use traditional black-and-white or color-print materials, but many work directly on film or with non-silver processes such as cyanotype and Van Dyke. Some photographers have even made life-sized photograms of people on mural paper or cloth that they've sensitized with an emulsion like cyanotype (blue printing).

Making a Photogram

It's easy to make a photogram. All you have to do is go into the dark, place something on a piece of photographic paper, turn a light on and off (any light source can be used), and develop the paper. The results vary depending on the photographic materials used, the direction and intensity of light used to expose the paper, and the objects selected to make the image.

Almost any light source and light sensitive material can be used to make photograms. An overhead room light, a penlight or regular flashlight are worth trying, but your enlarger light provides the simplest means of control since it's already hooked up to an interval timer. However, a light source such as a penlight flashlight allows you greater flexibility in varying the angle of light used when making a photogram. Shadows and shapes are altered in a way that's impossible with the stationary overhead light from an enlarger.

Most beginners tend to make photograms that are fairly obvious black-and-white silhouettes of the objects they use. They fail to take advantage of the range of tones in between black and white that can give the photogram form, depth, and feeling.

If you make a photogram with a curved object like an egg, the effect you get will vary depending on the amount of light used for your exposure. A short exposure produces a silhouette of the egg. A longer exposure allows the light to bleed around the edges of the egg creating an image with blacks, subtle shades of gray, and white at the point where the egg was in contact with the printing paper. Whatever object you use in your photograms, the visual effect

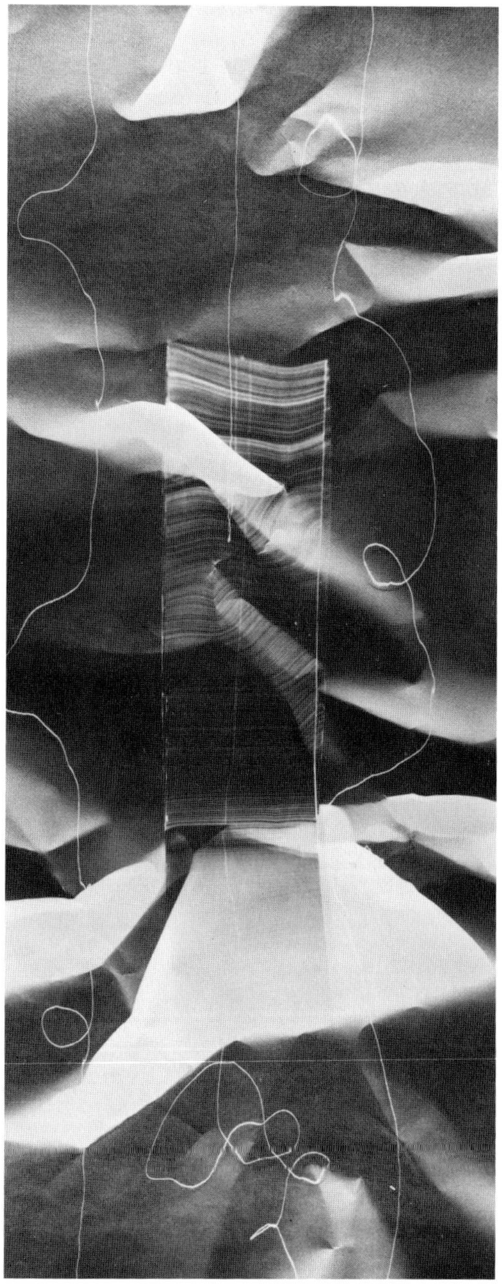

By crumpling photographic paper and then exposing it to light, Sheila Pinkel created a photogram which is the result of the interaction of light and a light-sensitive material. The only alien ingredients are threads which caused the white lines. This piece deals with the essence of photography—the phenomenon of light.

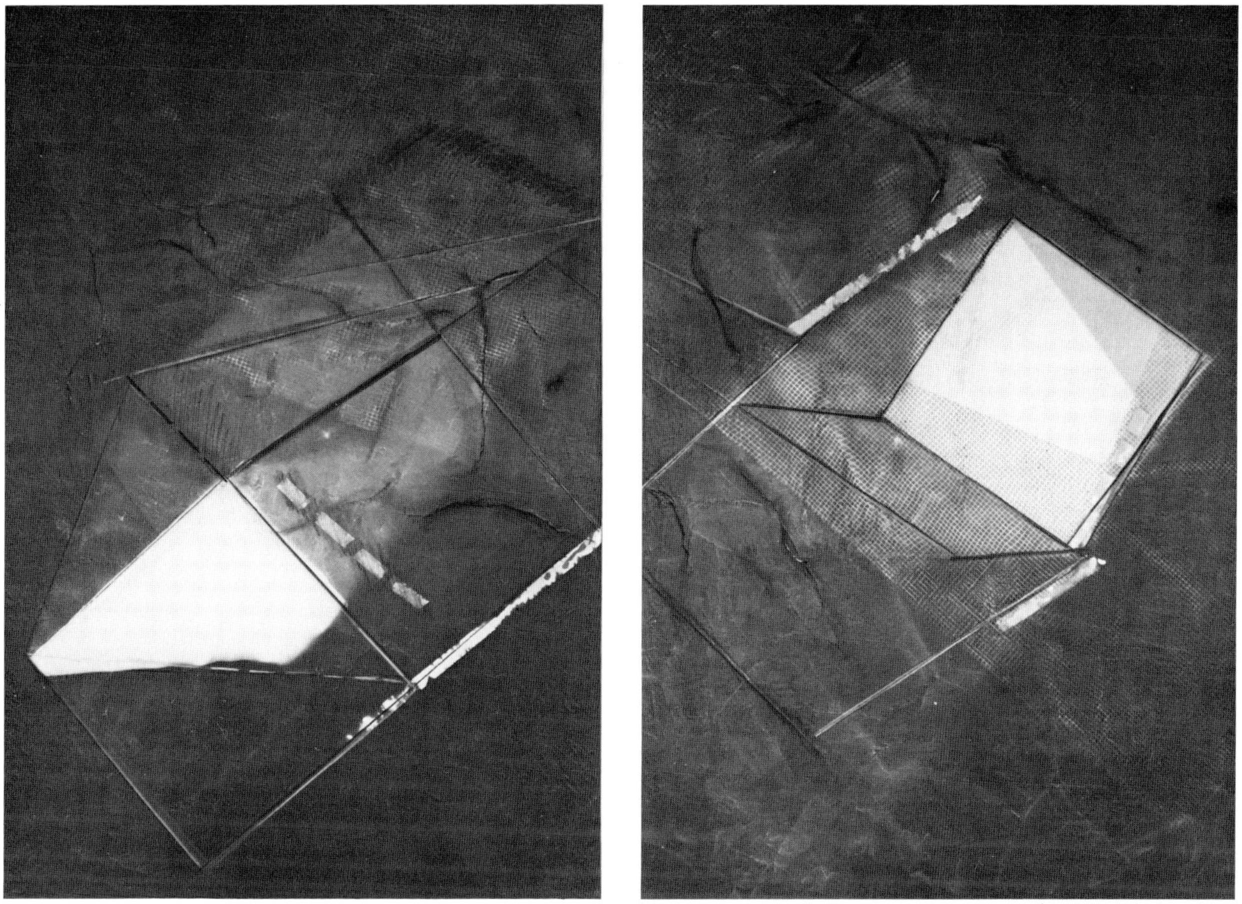

This large 69 × 49½ inch two-panel piece by Barbara Kasten is a combination of painting with light and pigments. She begins by making large photogram images on print paper which she attaches to canvas. She then applies oil pastels and oil paints to the print surfaces to complete the piece.

will vary depending on the angle and amount of light you use when exposing the printing paper.

A few simple exposure tests in the beginning will save time and give you the data needed to reproduce any tonal values desired.

When making a photogram, first determine the light source you plan to use. If it's the enlarger light, raise the head so the light covers the size paper you plan to use. Place an empty negative carrier in the enlarger and focus on the edge of the carrier. Then place several pieces of masking tape on the baseboard of the enlarger to let you know where the unexposed printing paper will be placed when you're ready to make your exposure. Next do a test strip to determine what exposure will give you a strong black. Then you'll know the maximum exposure necessary to get a black background as well as a variety of different gray tones. These data apply as long as you use the same light source without altering its intensity or the distance of the light to the paper. With most photograms, this data can be used as a starting point. However, individual objects vary in their opacity and you may need to make additional exposure tests.

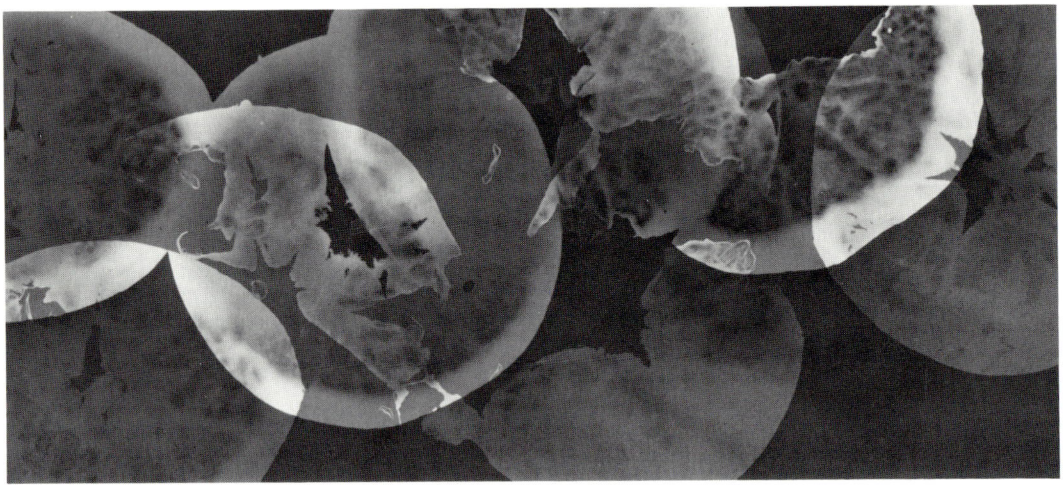

This photogram was made with orange slices. Two exposures were made, with the slices moved between exposures to create the overlap. The original image was in color.

To make a test strip, stop the lens down to *f*/8 or *f*/11 and make a series of three-second exposures. Then develop the test strip. If the test strip is too dark overall, stop the lens down further and make another one. If it's too light, open up the lens. When using a light source other than an enlarger, vary the light intensity by moving the light closer to, or farther away from, the printing paper.

Some Photogram Techniques

There's more than one way to make color or black-and-white photograms. The normal procedure is to place objects, either opaque or transparent, on unexposed photographic paper, and expose them to light. Literally anything can be used to form a design—cellophane, bent wire, string, kitchen implements, body parts, feathers, paper of varying degrees of translucency cut or torn into different shapes, organic materials like plants or foods. Polished objects reflect light and produce spots and lines of light on the print. Glassware reflects and refracts light in unexpected ways, producing unusual shapes and patterns.

Transparent objects in direct contact with the paper produce sharp-edged silhouettes unless enough exposure lets the light pass through them. Objects that don't come in complete contact with the print surface, such as eggs, allow the light to flow around them. This creates subtle but usually directional tonal values, depending on the exposure time. Multiple flashes of light from several directions also produce variations of tone, shape, and texture.

Photograms are considered one-of-a-kind images because it's hard to rearrange objects in the dark exactly as they were before. But many times the image is awkward and needs refinement. I overcome this problem by making my arrangements of objects on a piece of thin glass, then placing the glass over a piece of unexposed paper. After the exposure, I remove the

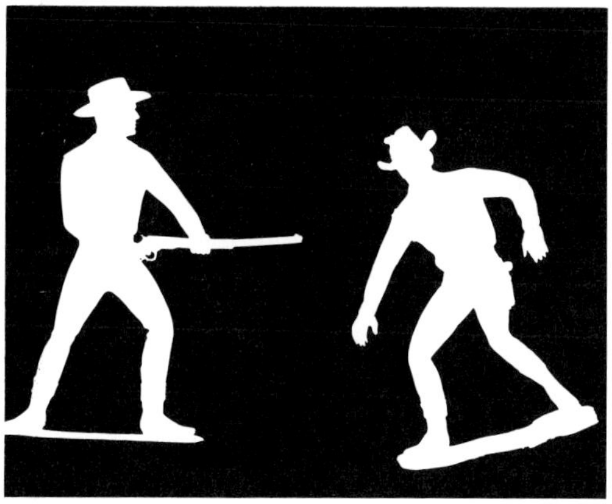

Plastic, three-dimensional, toy cowboys were used to make the basic photogram silhouette above.

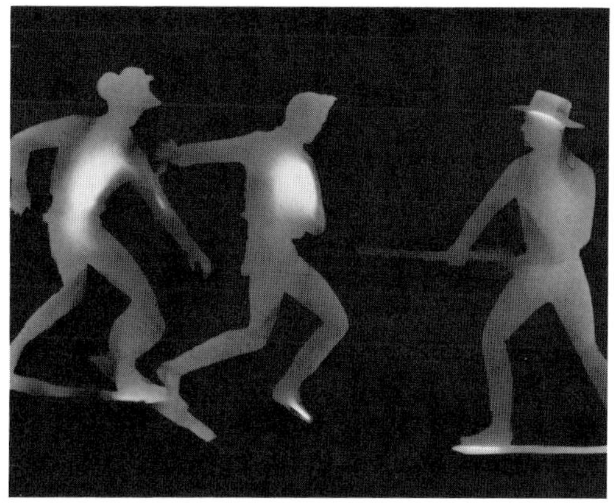

When the exposure was increased from 3 seconds to 60 seconds, the light bled around the objects, giving form and dimension to the photogram.

By changing the angle of the light source, the toy figures became comically distorted. The photogram below was exposed with a penlite rather than the enlarger.

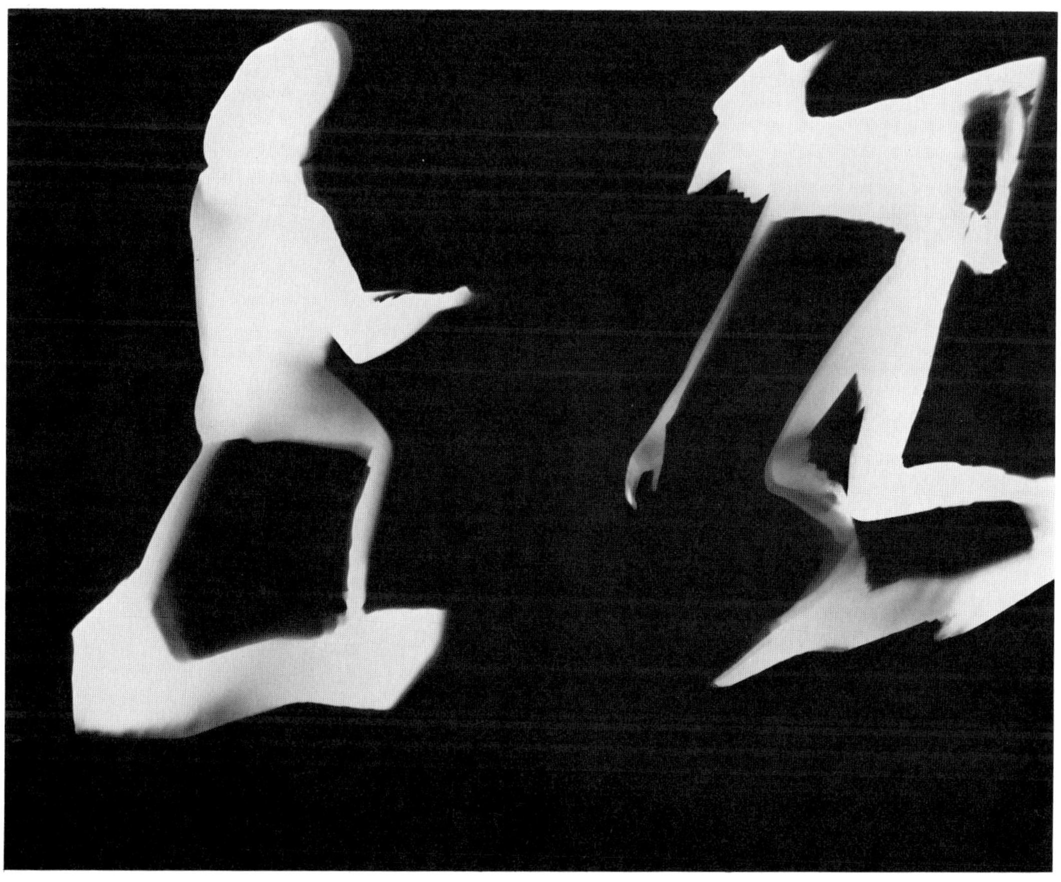

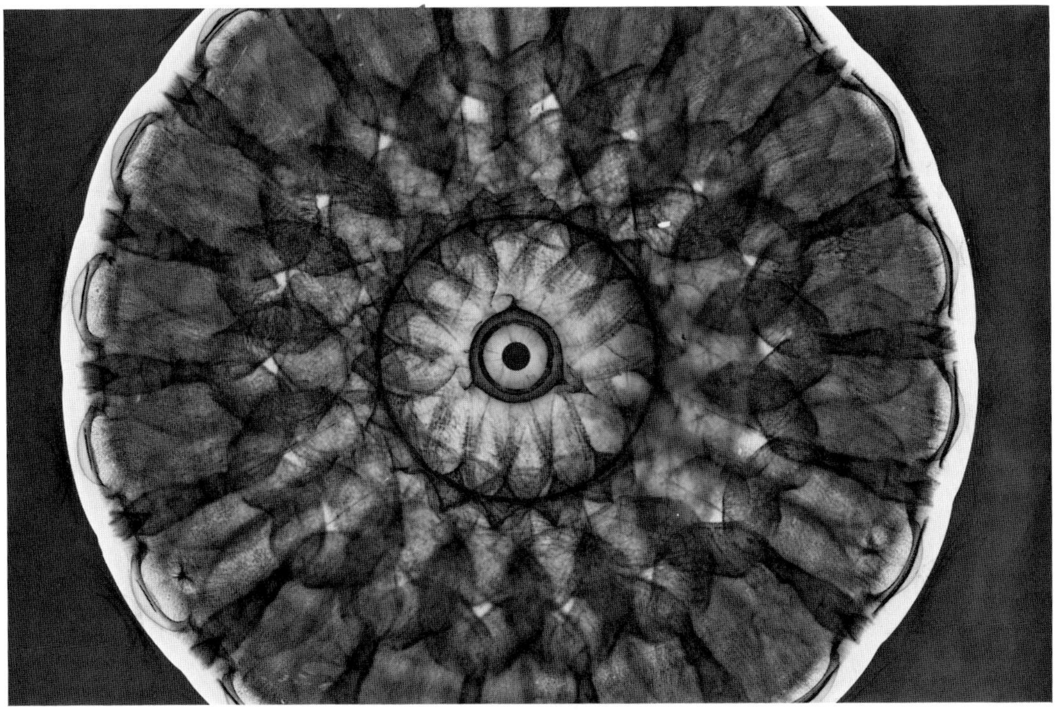

The same crystal dish was used to make these two photograms. When the dish was turned over, the light refraction created a totally different pattern.

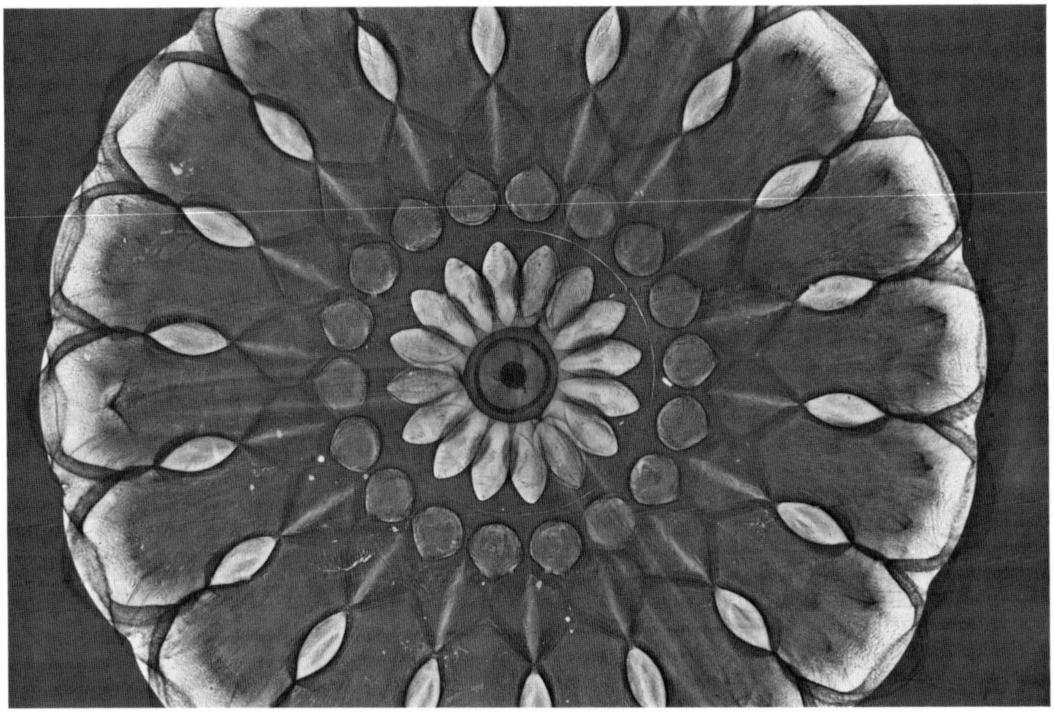

glass without disturbing the objects. When the print is processed, I determine if changes have to be made and if so, expose another print.

You can also use a glass to raise objects above the paper. Use a glass that's larger than the printing paper so that it can also be supported above the paper surface with some handy, sturdy objects. The space created diffuses the image and allows light to bleed around the edges of the object.

You can also use layers of glass to control multiple exposures. Support several pieces of glass above the printing paper, with several inches between each layer. Place objects on each layer of glass so that some overlap. Make an exposure and remove the top piece of glass. Then make another exposure. After removing the second layer of glass, make another exposure. Continue the process until all the glass layers are removed. When using this process, it's very important to calculate your exposure times before you begin. Refer to your exposure tests to determine not only what colors you want but what will happen with the repeated buildup of exposure in the same area.

Varying the Light. You might want to try varying your light source. The shadows cast by sidelighting give a completely different effect. However, when you change the light source your initial exposure tests are no longer valid. You'll have to make a new series of tests or else guess.

Color Photograms

Color photograms, although a little more involved than black-and-white ones, are made in the same general manner. If you have a black-and-white darkroom, you can make color photograms with very little extra trouble and expense.

You will need color paper, color chemistry, color-safelight filters, and color-printing filters. There are two color-safelight filters available, a number 10 and a number 13. You can use either filter but the number 13 is a newer and slightly brighter filter than the number 10. There are two types of printing filters available, the subtractive and the additive. Subtractive color-printing filters are cyan, yellow, and magenta. These are used for most color printing, since the filters can be combined and a single exposure used to make a color print. Additive filters, which are red, blue, and green, have to be exposed separately to make a color print. This makes them less practical than subtractive filters for normal color printing. But, the additive system is the most functional for computerized color-printing systems. It is also the easiest to use when making color photograms, because the color relationships are more direct and easier to determine.

Red, blue, and green are the primary or additive colors of light. Their complements—cyan, yellow, and magenta—are subtractive or secondary colors of light. An exposure through any primary filter, such as red, will give you its complement (in this case, cyan). When you expose through blue, you get its complement yellow. Green produces magenta. Exposures can only be made through one primary filter at a time. Combining any two primary filters produces black because no light can pass through the filters to expose the paper. But, by exposing two primaries separately, one after the other with equal amounts of light, you can produce the third primary on the print. Thus equal amounts of exposure through red and green produce blue. However, separate but equal exposures with three filters produce black on the print.

You can use either *Color-Compensating* (CC) or *Color-Printing* (CP) gelatin filters for color photograms. Color-Compensating filters are used in front of a camera or enlarger lens and are more expensive than Color-Printing filters, which are used between the light source of your enlarger and the negative carrier.

When making color photograms the filters must be between the light source and the printing paper. When you use an enlarger to make an exposure, it's easiest to hold the filters under the lens. The quality of the filter doesn't matter as long as it alters the color of the light. You may find these filters in camera stores, but they're generally available by special order only. Red filters are a number 25A or number 29, blue a number 47B, and green a number 61.

An enlarger is the easiest light source to control for making color photograms, though other light sources are possible. Position the enlarger head all the way up, and place an empty negative carrier in it. Focus on the edge of the negative carrier and then stop the lens down two stops. Make a series of six separate test sheets, one for each primary color (red, blue, green) and one for each secondary color (cyan, yellow, and magenta). To make these tests, hold the filters under the lens and expose the paper through each of them. To get secondary colors, make a test strip of 10 to 15 one-second exposures for each color by exposing through each primary filter. Be sure to record all data, including enlarger height, *f*-stop, exposure times, and filters. You will need to refer to it in the future.

To get the primary-exposure tests, you'll have to make separate but equal exposures through each of the three combinations of two. In other words, you'll have to use red and blue to get green, red and green to get blue, and green and blue to get red. The color scales from these tests let you predict the proper exposure for any color value, provided the light source is the same.

P.W. Derby made this photogram by coating the sides of his hands lightly with Vaseline, and then putting them in contact with the surface of the printing paper. The sunflower image was printed separately, and dodged while the rest of the paper was exposed to light. Vaseline impedes development, and thus the hand images stayed white. However, the Vaseline must be removed during the fixer bath for the whites to be permanent.

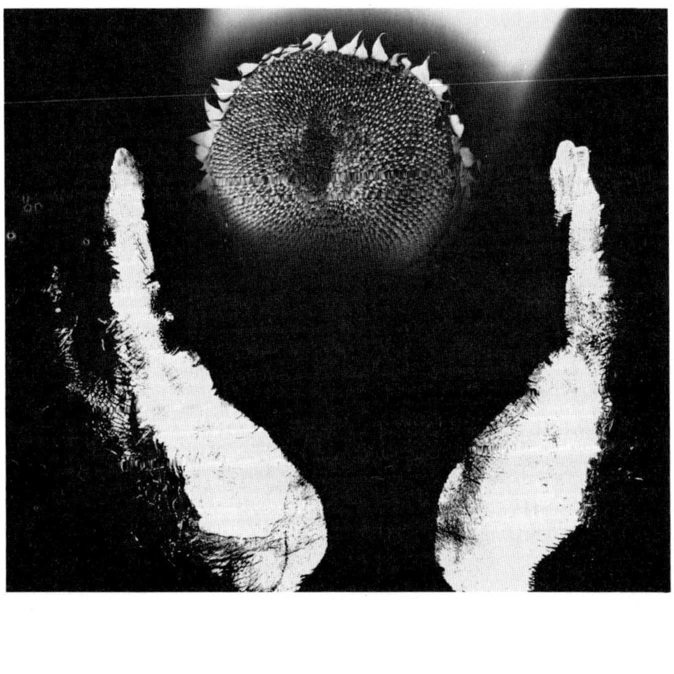

You can get a variety of color effects by moving the objects between exposures with different colored filters. If you expose through a red filter when making multiple exposures, the uncovered areas of the print become cyan. Then if you expose through a blue filter after rearranging the objects, you'll get yellow in the areas of the print which weren't exposed previously. Where the two exposures overlap, you'll get green in the print—the one primary color which wasn't used when exposing. This is because separate but equal exposures through any two primary colors gives the third. Where the two exposures didn't overlap, you'll get either cyan or yellow depending on which color of light struck the paper in that particular spot. If there's any white in the print, it means light didn't strike that part of the paper at all. Then, if you made an additional exposure through the green filter, the part of the print where all three colors were exposed equally will go black. These color relationships are for color-negative print materials, such as Kodak's Ektacolor 74RC paper. If you use a direct-positive print material such as Cibachrome, the color relationships will be exactly the opposite.

This life-size photogram was made by Sheila Pinkel. She placed an old deteriorated bedspring on photographic mural paper. Then during the exposure, she jumped on the bed springs. The blur was caused by her movement.

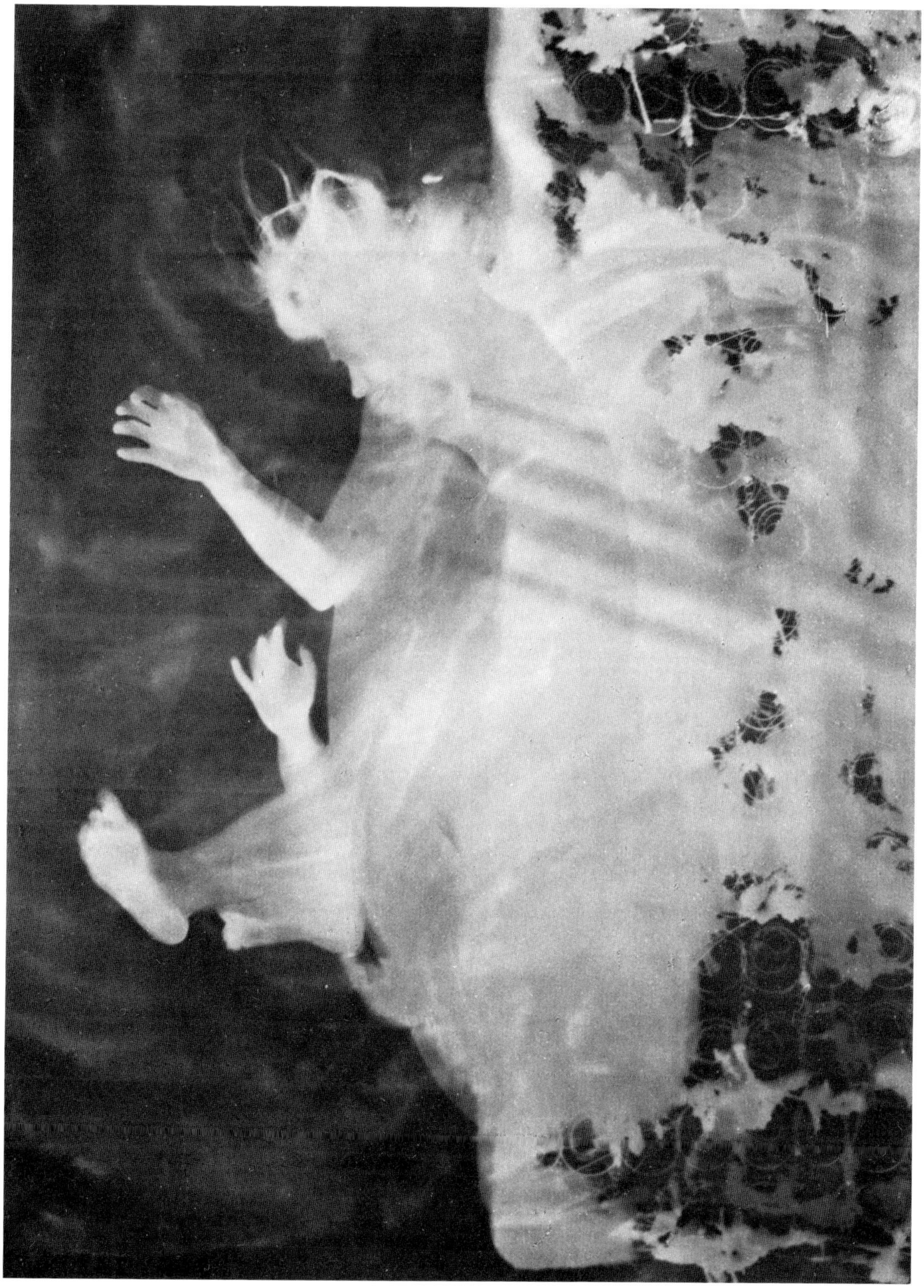

More Photogram Variations

For some interesting effects, lightly coat objects with petroleum jelly and put them in contact with the paper surface. The petroleum jelly impedes development, and the areas of the print which come in contact with it remain white. When coated this way, surfaces with textures, such as skin, leaves, or flower petals produce amazing results.

You can use pages out of magazines and newspapers to create unusual images. By using them as paper negatives and contact printing them, the image includes what's printed on both sides of the page. Furthermore, through the use of color variation, you can create a totally new reality.

Lifesize prints can also be made, on mural paper, or by making a non-silver emulsion and coating it on cloth or other appropriate material.

Combining Camera Images with Photograms

You can combine regular photographic images from your negatives with photograms by multiple printing. To do so, first make your photogram and develop it. Then rinse the print in running water for several minutes and squeegee the surface. This will momentarily stop the action of the developer. Then put the print back on the enlarger baseboard. If you're using black-and-white materials, place a red safelight filter under the enlarger lens and project your negative onto the photogram. With the red filter you can adjust the size of your image, or move the photogram around to a better position, without having to worry about fogging the print. When everything is ready, remove the filter and make the exposure. With color materials you can't use a red filter and will have to guess at the proper positioning. Redevelop, stop, and fix the print as you would normally.

The Addition of the Sabattier Effect

You can also use the Sabattier effect to add color to a photogram. With color-negative print materials, re-exposing a print through a colored filter after development but before the bleach-fix, produces its complementary color in the areas of the print that would otherwise be white. With positive-color print materials the opposite effect occurs. Hence, with the Sabattier effect you are able to add color to, and alter the visual effect of, your photograms. For more insight on how to apply this technique refer to chapter 6.

All of the effects discussed in this chapter can be applied to color as well as black-and-white materials. They can be controlled and predicted if you are methodical and consistent in your approach. Light-drawing can be an exciting, challenging experience. It is an area of photography that's totally unlimited.

4

Basic Print Variations

Once you get over the excitement of printing photographs for the first time, you'll probably be amazed at how easy it can be. But, after working in the darkroom awhile, most people realize there's a big difference between printing a photograph and making a good print. The ability to make an excellent print has to be learned through experience. It represents a great achievement in photographic craftsmanship.

You can use many different approaches to achieve quality prints, but control is really the key. You must know the variables to learn how to control them. It's impossible to make good prints unless you know how to control the shooting and film processing as well as the printing. They are all dependent upon each other.

This chapter deals with basic print variations, methods that will enhance your images and improve your printmaking ability. You'll find information on a variety of techniques that add to your control of printing, and lead to finer prints.

Resin-Coated vs. Fiber-Based Printing Papers

Since the introduction of resin-coated papers, the variety of surfaces, tints, and emulsions available for black-and-white printing has steadily diminished. This is due both to increasing costs and the general acceptance of resin-coated (RC) materials. To overcome this limitation, you must learn how to take full advantage of the limited materials available.

Conventional fiber-based papers provide the most permanent and greatest variety of prints. In some cases, they contain more silver and produce richer prints than RC papers. However, they're generally more expensive and more time consuming to process and dry than RC papers. Good prints can be made with either type of paper, but photographic artists and fine printmakers still tend to prefer fiber-based papers. Resin-coated papers are preferred for commercial purposes. However, if you expose and process your film properly and consistently, you should be producing negatives that are easy to print on either fiber-based or RC papers.

Contrast Control for Black-and-White Prints

To get the most out of a particular negative, you may find that your normal procedures aren't enough. When more contrast might help, simply switching to a higher grade of paper may not give the desired result. Contrast masking and print flashing are exotic techniques for contrast control, but subtle changes in contrast can also be achieved by altering or by changing your paper developer.

For example, try using a packaged developer designed to give either more or less contrast than conventional paper developers. You can also alter the dilutions of your developer to change its strength. Mixing your own "custom" developers is another option. Then the developer's contrast can be made to suit your needs. But, for the majority of photographers, varying packaged developers is easier and provides enough control.

This photograph, shot in harsh light, depends upon rich tones and contrasting values for much of its impact.

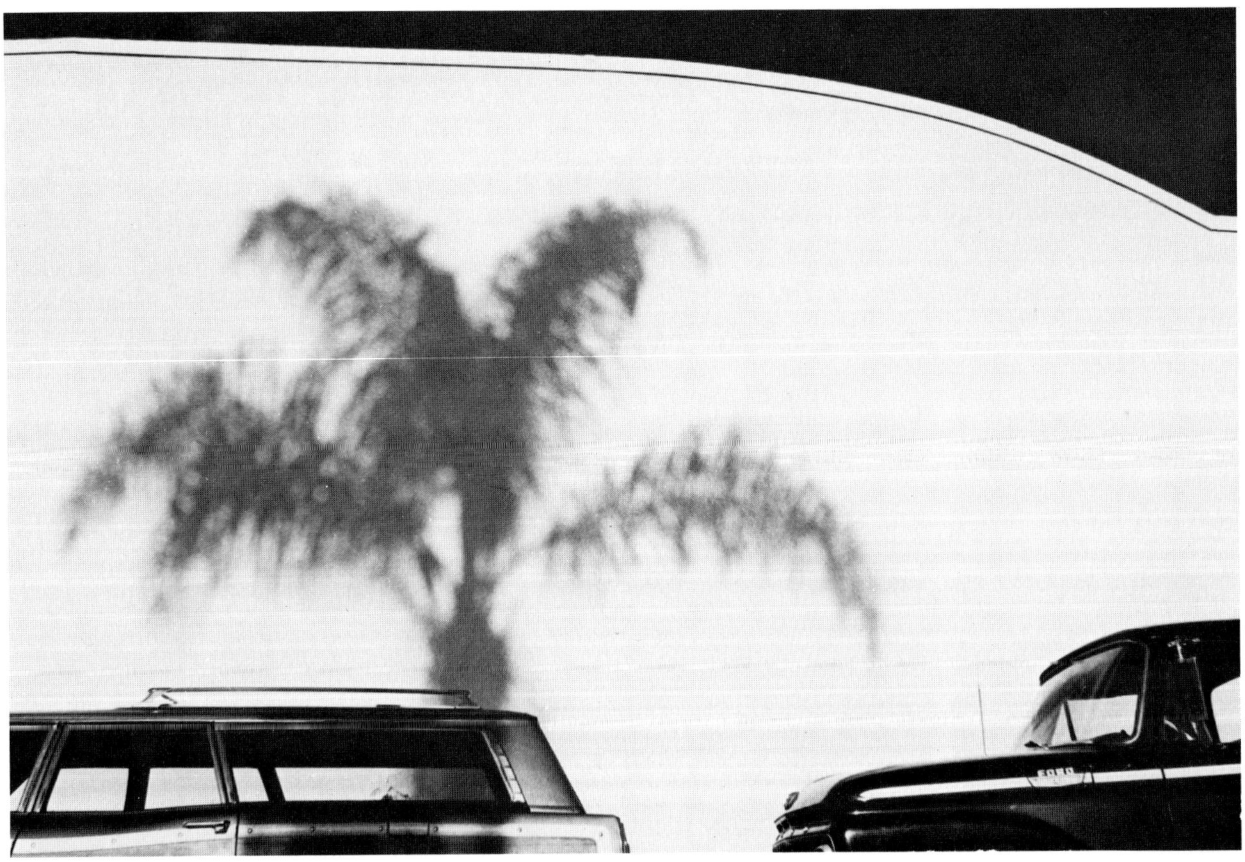

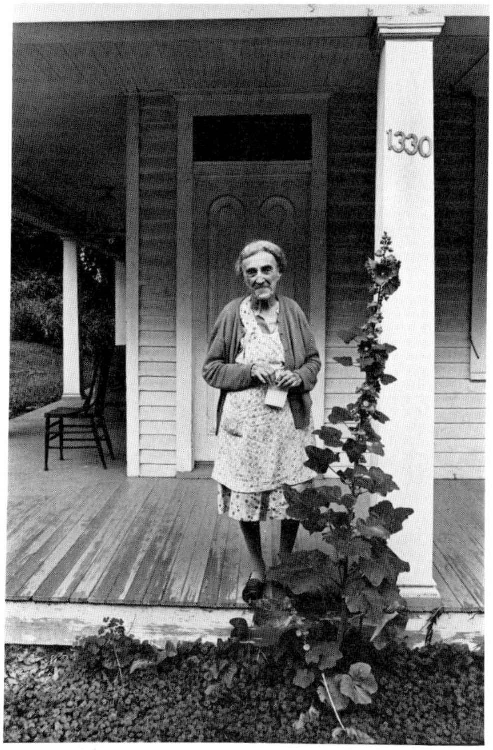

Subtle tonal values and delicate detail made it necessary for the photographer, Mark Chamberlain, to use variable developers when printing this photograph of a home-town friend.

Variable Developers. A three-developer setup makes subtle contrast changes and may produce the feeling you want in your prints. Use Kodak's Dektol 1:2 for normal print contrast.

Selectol-Soft will reduce contrast and produce soft tones with warm-tone portrait papers. When used with cold-tone papers such as Agfa-Brovira, Kodabromide, or Oriental, it reduces the contrast almost a full grade. Yet the result has a different appearance than you would get by just changing paper grades.

For increased contrast, use undiluted Dektol. This increases the contrast almost a full contrast grade, but, like the Selectol-Soft, the feeling produced is different.

To get intermediate contrast ranges, develop your print partially in one developer and finish it in another. This way you can subtly alter the range between shadows and highlights, while maintaining detail that would normally be lost.

This third method works well if you're printing a negative that looks best on a grade 3 paper processed normally, but lacks detail in the shadows. Instead of trying to save the shadow detail by dodging, try altering your development procedure. Use Selectol-Soft at its normal dilution as your initial developer. Remove the print from the Selectol-Soft after it has developed for one-third the normal time. The image should be barely visible. Then put it into a tray of Dektol diluted 1:2. Continue the development in the Dektol until the normal processing time is completed. This should reduce the contrast slightly, give better shadow detail, and maintain the feel-

A slightly underexposed, flat negative produced this print on a grade 3 paper.

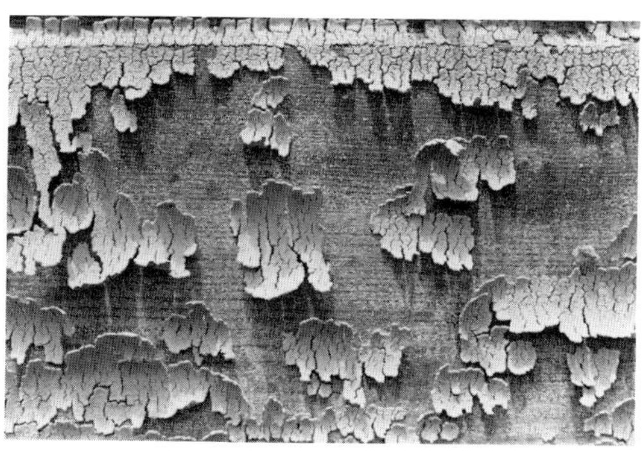

However, when the same negative is printed on a grade 6 paper the whole feeling of the image is altered.

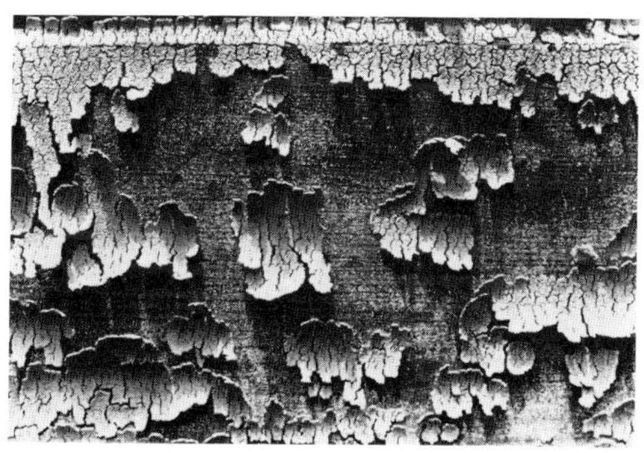

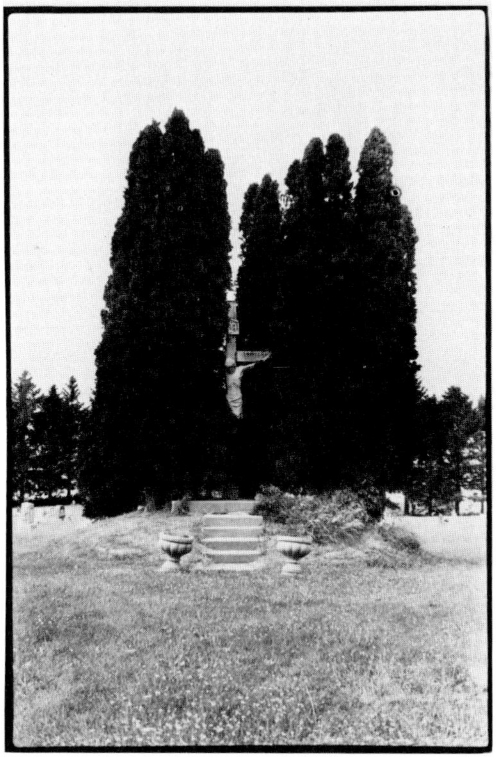

Although this print on a grade 3 paper looks good, it presented problems for the photographer, Mark Chamberlain. It was too flat when printed on a grade 2 paper, while a print on grade 3 lost too much detail.

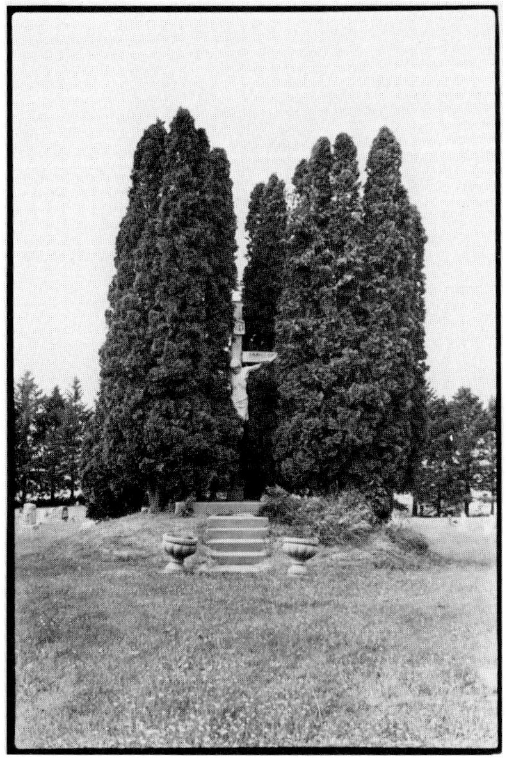

This print was also made on a grade 3 paper, but variable development provided more detail without sacrificing the contrast.

ing that a grade 3 paper gives to this type of negative. If the difference is not enough, then increase the time in the Selectol-Soft and reduce the time in the diluted Dektol. If the contrast is still too high, use only the Selectol-Soft.

If the image lacks contrast when developed normally in Dektol 1:2 and printed on a grade 3 paper, the alternative is to partially develop the print in diluted Dektol and then complete the development in undiluted Dektol. This causes a subtle increase in contrast, while still preserving better shadow detail than you would get on a higher grade of paper. How much time you should allow for each chemical will vary and must be individually determined. If splitting the development doesn't seem to be enough, then try developing the print for the full amount of time in undiluted Dektol, before switching to a higher grade of paper.

Differences in Negatives. Every negative varies in its demands and must be individually tested to determine the optimum developing procedures. If you're serious about your work, you should be willing to take the extra steps necessary to get the most out of your images. Some photographers test print a negative for several days, trying different papers and developer combinations until they find the right combination that gives the feeling they want from that negative. While this may be a bit extreme, it's important to keep in mind that photography is a subjective medium, and that your prints can stir strong emotions when handled properly.

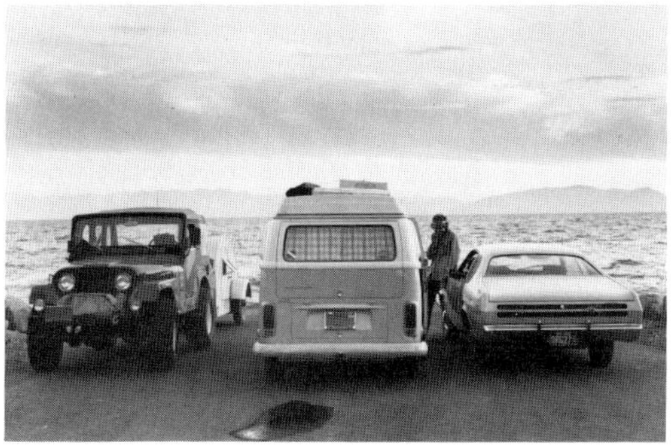

This image, by Gejar, was printed on a grade 3 paper. Although the detail is fine, the print is flat and lacks contrast.

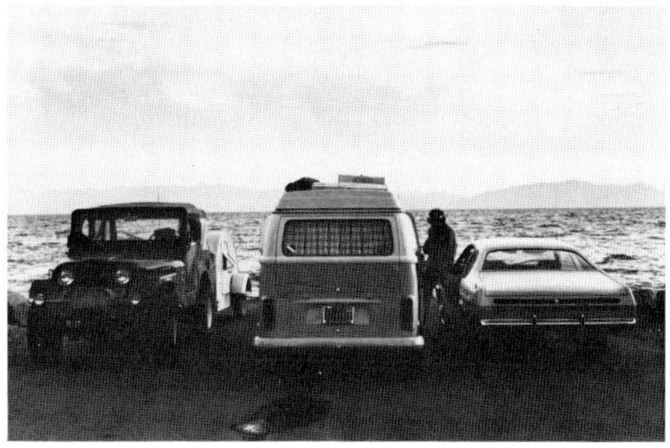

A grade 4 paper made the print too contrasty and lacking in detail.

Differences in Papers. The printing paper you use determines how well the variable developing procedure works. Most conventional fiber-based papers (Kodabromide, Ilfobrom, Oriental, and Agfa-Brovira) respond well to variable development. With these papers, try a three-minute development time for a strong black. Resin-coated papers generally don't respond as well to manipulation techniques as fiber-based papers do. In addition, the processing time of RC papers should not be extended beyond the recommended time of one minute to a minute and a half. With RC papers, extended processing times have little effect on the final results. Every type

The problem was solved by flashing a grade 4 print. The flashing added a slight overall fog that brought out detail without reducing the contrast as much as a lower grade of paper.

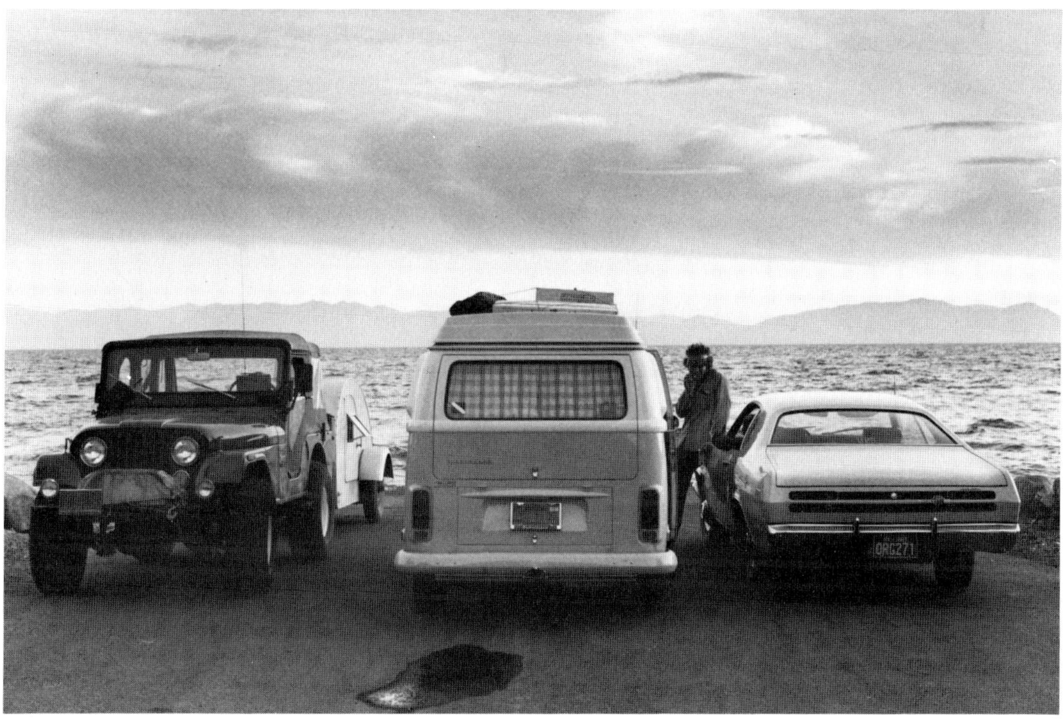

and brand of paper has a different response to these techniques and should be tested with that in mind.

Custom Developers

As mentioned earlier, you can gain even more contrast control by mixing your own "custom" developer.

Early photographers often mixed their own chemistry to get personal formulas, but today few photographers bother. Even though it costs less money to mix your own chemistry, our convenience-oriented society influences most photographers to buy packaged developers. Aside from reduced cost, the most important fact is that you can alter the contrast-producing properties of your developer to suit your own particular needs.

Though more time consuming, custom mixing gives you more complete control of your results. A good scale is the only equipment you need to mix your own chemicals. A triple-beam balance scale is best, but expensive. The Balancing Act scale is an inexpensive and adequate model.

Developer Components. Developers are made from a variety of ingredients, and changes in the proportions of these ingredients produce different effects on photographic printing paper. The ingredients of a developer generally include developing agent, accelerator, preservative, and restrainer. Normally, these are dissolved in tap water.

The developing agent, sometimes called a reducing agent, makes the image visible. It reduces the exposed silver salts in the emulsion to metal and thus forms the image. Most modern developers use two developing agents, Hydroquinone and Elon (or Metol). Elon produces a low-contrast black image. Hydroquinone is a high-contrast developing agent that produces a brownish-black tone. Hydroquinone is less active than Elon and does not work below 60 degrees (15 C). That's why the recommended developing time for most developers is 68 degrees (20 C).

The accelerator activates the developing agent which is too weak to react by itself. The accelerator is an alkaline chemical (sodium carbonate is most commonly used).

The preservative is normally an alkaline. It increases the life of the developer by removing oxygen. Sodium sulfite is generally used for this.

The restrainer (usually potassium bromide) controls development. It prevents the unexposed silver in the emulsion from developing, while allowing the exposed silver to develop. Without the restrainer, the print or film would have an overall grayness or fogging. The restrainer can be used to alter contrast by increasing or decreasing the amount.

The way these ingredients are mixed together determines the character of a black-and-white developer. A low-contrast developer normally has an equal quantity of Elon and Hydroquinone; while a high-contrast developer contains less Elon than Hydroquinone.

Considering the effects made possible by varying black-and-white developers, it's surprising that the use of variable developers to alter contrast has not become more common with color-print materials. This is mainly due to the complicated nature of color emulsions which have three light-sensitive layers, rather than just one like black-and-white emulsions. However, contrast can be affected by varying the formulas of color developers and altering development time. A number of technical books go into much more detail on this subject. For further information on alterations and alternative formulas to use with color materials, contact Dignan Photographic, Inc., 507½ South Normandy, North Hollywood, California, 91606. They have a publication called *Simplified Color Processing Formulas*, as well as other material on the modification of color processes.

For alternatives to try with black-and-white materials consider the well-known

Formulas for Custom Paper Developers†

Chemical	Developer			
	D-72 (Dektol)	Amidol*	Beers Formula** "A"	"B"
Elon (Metol)	12.4 g	———	32.0 g	———
Sodium sulfite	180.0 g	29.0 g	92.0 g	92.0 g
Hydroquinone	48.0 g	———	———	32.0 g
Amidol	———	8.8 g	———	———
Sodium carbonate	320.0 g	———	94.0 g	126.0 g
Potassium bromide	76.0 ml	6.0 ml	44.0 ml	88.0 ml
BB Stock	———	60.0 ml	———	———
Water (total)	4.0 l	1.0 l	4.0 l	4.0 l

†Mix all chemicals in the order listed. Start with three litres of water (except for Amidol) at 125 F (52 C), add the chemicals, and then add water to make four litres.

*This formula is for one litre only as it decays in approximately one hour and must be mixed as it is used.

**The two stock solutions of the Beers Formula are mixed together in different ratios and then diluted with water to make a working solution.

Beers Formula Contrast-Control Dilutions

Dilution*	1	2	3	4	5	6	7
Stock "A"	500	435	372	310	250	190	128 ml
Stock "B"	0	65	128	190	250	310	872 ml
Water	500	500	500	500	500	500	0 ml

*These different dilutions give contrast control equivalent to about one full paper grade.

Beers formula and Edward Weston's favorite developer, Amidol.

The chemicals needed to make your own developers can be purchased or specially ordered through most photographic stores. However, if your store cannot supply your needs, you can order from the following mail order companies:

Lauder Chemical Co., 350 Peninsula Ave., San Mateo, CA 94401

Porter's Camera Store, P.O. Box 628, Cedar Falls, IA 50613

Zone VI, 291 Buckminster Rd., Brookline, MA 02146

Mixing your own developers not only lets you vary the formulas, but also saves you money in the long run. But, it is less convenient than buying packaged developers, and some of the chemicals can be harmful if not handled according to their instructions. *With Amidol, avoid contact as much as possible because severe staining of skin and clothing may result.*

Local Development for Black-and-White Prints

Once in a while, even if you are an expert at dodging and burning, you may find that the highlight areas of a print need to be accented. Many professionals try local development, especially if the print is in the developer and they want to try to save it rather than make a new exposure. If, as your print is developing, you notice a par-

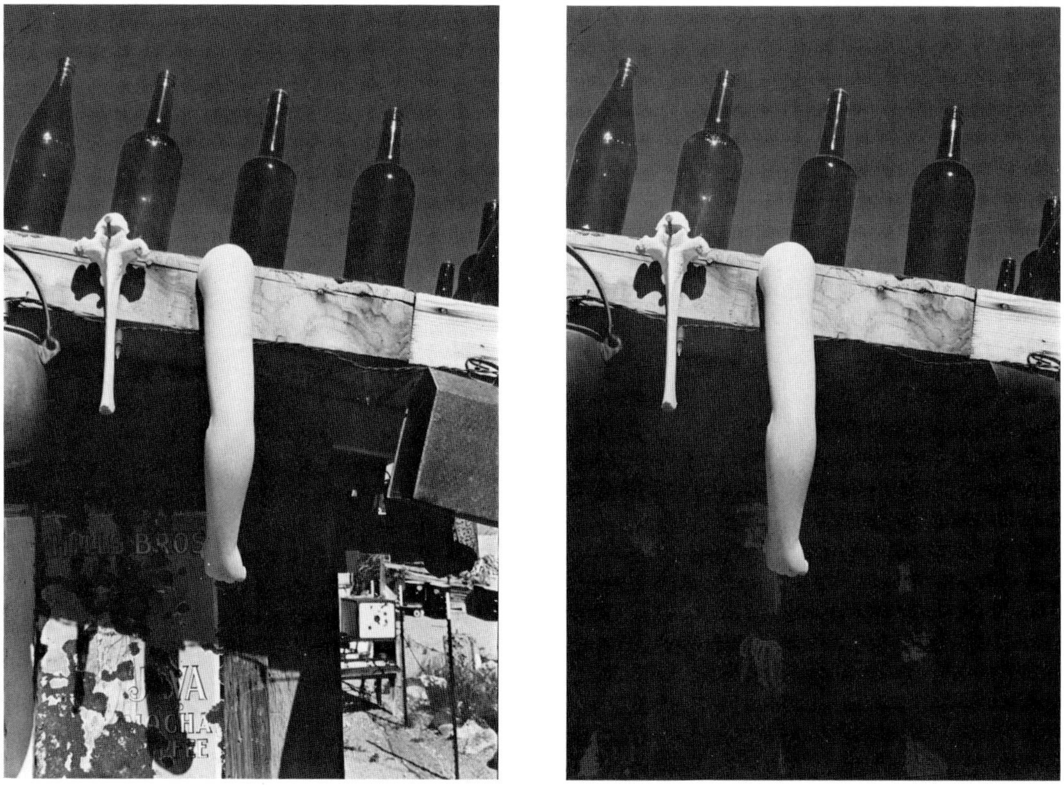

Selective burning can be used to eliminate unwanted detail in a print. The bottom portion of the photograph on the right was burned-in to a complete black to make the plastic arm stand out.

ticular highlight area isn't showing its subtle detail, apply a little undiluted developer or hot water directly to this area. Use your fingers to rub it in. The friction from your fingers generates heat which speeds up development. The effect is subtle, but it works and can save a print.

If this is not enough, try using Phenidone to accelerate the development of washed out highlight areas. Phenidone is a developing agent that must be special ordered from Ilford. It is used to bring out highlight detail by photographers who prefer contrasty prints. Take ½ teaspoon (2.5 ml) of Phenidone and add it to 16 ounces (480 ml) of undiluted Dektol. Then apply this highly active developer directly to washed out highlight areas by rubbing it into the print with your fingers. It brings out detail where none existed previously, and saves you from the frustration of having to remake a print with excessive burning-in.

Whether you use hot water, undiluted print developer, or Phenidone, be careful not to overdo it. Too much friction from rubbing the print surface can cause problems, and rubbing in developer or Phenidone can cause staining. Experience is your best guide. Practice first on scrap prints before trying it on important prints.

While local development works well with black-and-white print materials, it is not a recommended procedure for color-print materials. With color-print materials, highlight details can be controlled by burning and dodging, print flashing, and contrast masking. These techniques are discussed elsewhere in this book.

Print Flashing

Print flashing is commonly employed to reduce the overall contrast of a print. It can also be used selectively to reduce or burn out unwanted detail in extremely bright areas that don't respond to normal burning-in techniques. Flashing works with both black-and-white and color-print materials.

With black-and-white materials, flashing is most effective when printing a negative that falls between the contrast ranges of graded and variable-contrast papers. Variable developers, which we have already discussed, provide one option; print flashing is another answer.

As the name implies, print flashing involves exposing the print to additional light. But, unlike the Sabattier effect or solarization, the flashing is done before the print is developed. The simplest procedure is to expose your negative normally on a paper grade that gives too much contrast. Then, with the negative still in the enlarger, take a glassine sleeve (the type used for storing negatives) and hold it under the lens of the enlarger. Re-expose the print through the negative sleeve for the same amount of time as the original exposure. The double thickness of the glassine sleeve reduces and diffuses the light, adding an overall light-gray tone to the print. This additional tone should reduce the contrast about a half a grade, giving you richer print values than you would get if you went to a lower paper grade.

Variations of this technique may be necessary with some negatives. However, in most situations this approach is quite successful with graded papers. With variable-contrast papers, try exposing the print with one filter for part of the exposure. For the rest of the exposure, use a filter of lower contrast. This should alter the contrast so that it falls between conventional contrast grades.

With color-print materials, flashing is extremely difficult and normally avoided. However, it can reduce contrast with prints made from either negatives or transparencies. The same general procedure used for black-and-white prints is used for color prints, except that the light source must be filtered so the color of the print isn't altered. Use the same filter pack used to make the print. This will enable you to reduce the contrast of the print while having a minimal effect on the color balance.

Selective Flashing

Selective flashing can eliminate distracting background details, or add detail to bright highlights too dense to burn in conventionally. A convenient and inexpensive tool for this is a penlight flashlight. First put several layers of cellophane tape over the light bulb to reduce its intensity. Then tape a piece of black paper over the end of the penlight forming a cone-shaped snoot. Make the opening small enough so you can easily regulate the beam of the light and not expose areas of the print that don't need flashing.

To use a penlight with black-and-white prints, first expose the print normally. Then, with the paper still in the easel, place a red filter under the lens of your enlarger. Next, take your penlight and burn in the areas of the print that need additional exposure. Process the print normally.

Try a few tests before exposing a whole sheet of printing paper. The tendency is to over-burn. You may find it necessary to use more tape over the end of the penlight to further reduce its intensity. The important thing is to develop a sense of how the materials will respond to the light. This skill develops with practice.

This approach applies only to black-and-white prints; with color prints it is much more involved. The light source has to be filtered for a particular color effect and it's almost impossible to match colors with those already in the print. The procedure is complicated further because you can't see the image projected onto the printing paper as you can when using a red safety filter with black-and-white prints.

Image Diffusion

Diffusion softens an image and minimizes minor negative defects such as scratches and coarse grain. In portraiture, diffusion helps to hide retouching, and can minimize wrinkles and facial blemishes without retouching. Some photographers also use it

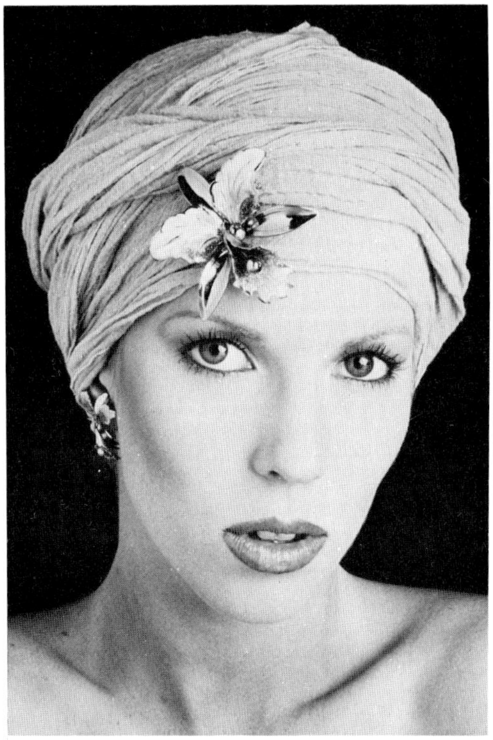

Diffusion is frequently used to soften an image and flatter the subject. In this photograph by Jim Koch, the grain of the 35 mm film makes the skin texture of the model's neck and shoulders seem rough and mottled.

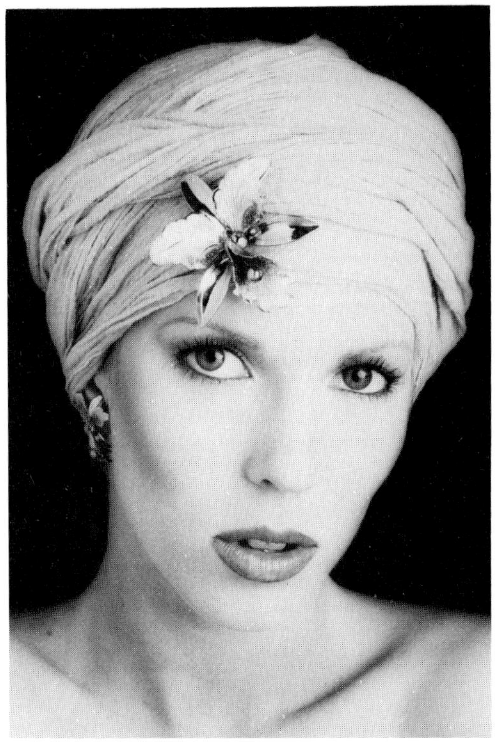

A diffused print of the same negative has a softer feeling. The skin tones now appear even and smooth.

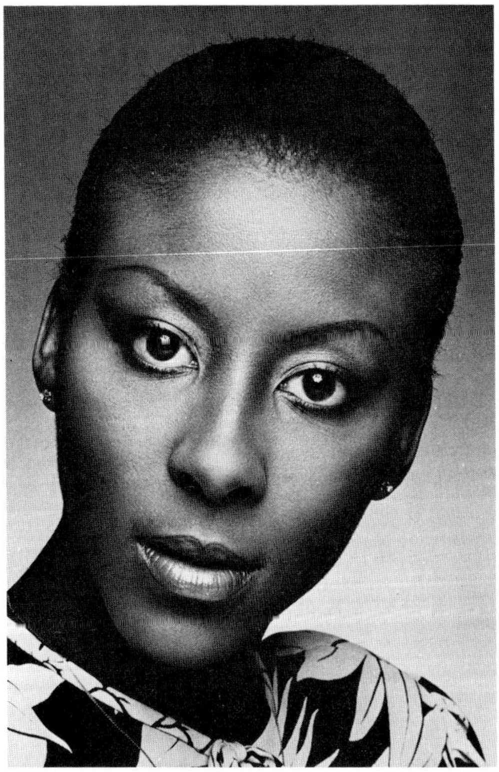

to create a hazy, dream-like pictorial effect.

If diffusion is done in the camera, highlights are affected most because they reflect the most light. During the enlarging process the shadows are affected more. Fortunately, shadow areas are normally too dark to show the exaggerated effect this produces. The disadvantage of diffusing an image during the shooting is that the negative is permanently diffused. Diffusing during printing gives you the option of changing your mind, and varying the amount of diffusion to alter the effect.

Diffusion devices vary from commercially made glass diffusers to homemade varieties, like crumpled cellophane, gray or black nylon hose, transparent negative sleeves, window-screening material, or petroleum jelly on glass.

The portrait on the left by Jim Koch wasn't diffused. The skin texture is distinct.

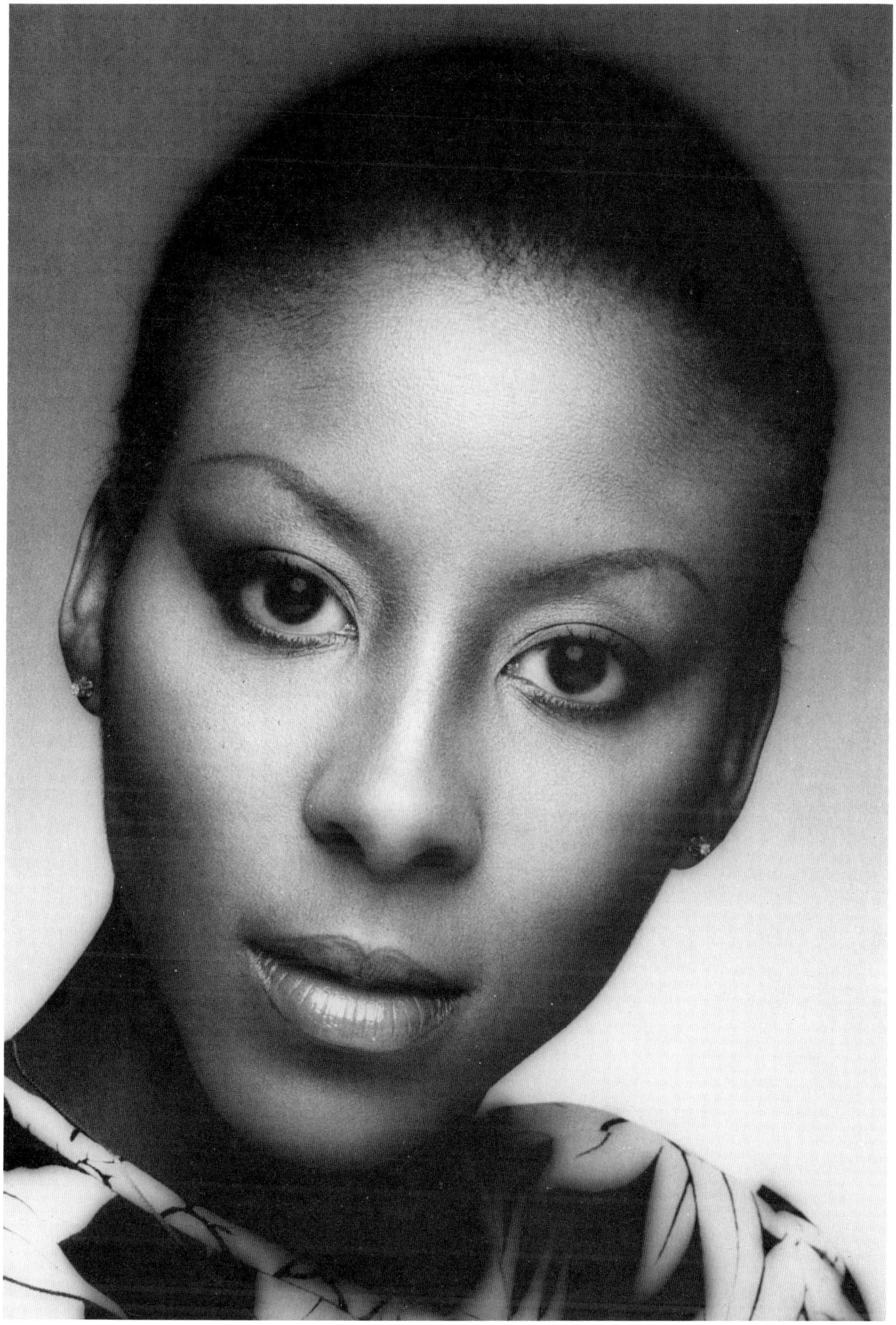

Notice the difference in this diffused print. The contrast and harshness due to the lighting is decreased, and the skin appears smooth. A slight veiling effect occurs along the edges of the darker portions of the image.

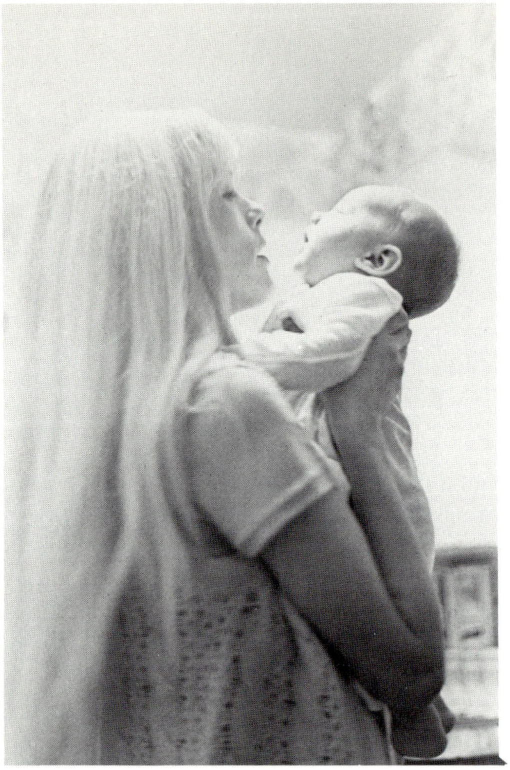

The photograph above has a snapshot quality that distracts from the relationship between mother and child.

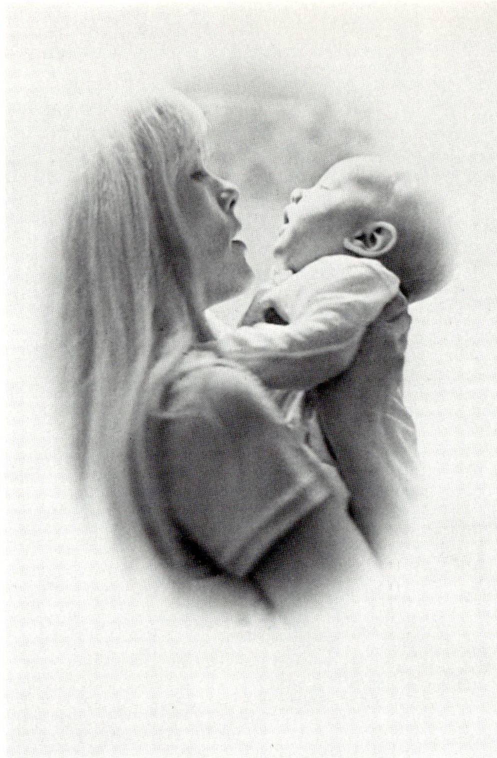

The same image when vignetted has much more impact. The background is eliminated, and all attention is given to the interaction of mother and child.

Diffusing a Print. Hold the diffusion material under the lens and move it slightly while exposing the print. The diffuser's distance from the lens affects the amount of diffusion; the nearer to the lens, the greater the diffusion. Avoid too much diffusion or the print will have a veiled effect, especially in the highlights.

Many photographers prefer to diffuse the image for only a portion of the total printing time. Diffusing the image for one-third of the exposure provides some diffusion while leaving the highlights clear and sparkling. Since diffusion tends to reduce contrast, it may be necessary to use a higher grade of paper than you would use to make an undiffused print.

Local diffusion is something you should also consider. Small diffused areas of the print can accent the subject and make the image more impressive. To do this, selectively smear petroleum on glass. When you hold it under the enlarger lens, it will diffuse only part of the image. Other materials, such as wrinkled cellophane, can also be used; or you can buy specially made diffusion devices with clear centers.

Vignetting

Vignetting is a printing technique primarily used in portraiture to accent the subject by having the distracting background fade out to white.

Vignettes are done in a manner similar to burning-in. Take a piece of opaque cardboard with a hole in it and place it under the enlarging lens for the exposure, allowing only the part of the image you want isolated to hit the paper. Hold the cardboard midway between the enlarger lens and the print paper. Move it continuously during the exposure, allowing the image to fade gradually into a white background.

You can change the size and shape of the hole in the cardboard to suit the needs of the image you're printing. Cut the edges of the hole into a small sawtooth pattern as this makes it easier to get a soft-edged fadeout to white.

Vignetting an image to a pure white surrounding usually works best if the image has a white or light background to start. A portrait shot against a dark background may look awkward if you try to vignette it. In such a case, it's normally better to darken the area around the subject rather than lighten it. This can be done by printing the image normally, and then burning-in the area around the subject to black. Selective flashing with a penlight works well for this. You can also use a dodging wand to hold back the area you wish to save, while gradually burning-in the rest of the image to black.

Perspective Distortion—Corrective and Deliberate

Perspective distortion can be either corrected or induced during printing. Photographers normally are more concerned with correcting distortion than they are in creating it. However, by adding perspective distortion to an image, you may make an ordinary picture more dramatic.

The photograph on the left shows the typical distortion that occurs when parallel vertical lines are shot with the camera pointing down. In the middle photograph, the enlarging easel was raised several inches on the bottom end of the print to help counteract the distortion. To maintain sharpness, this image was focused in the middle, and an aperture of f/22 was used for maximum depth of field. The easel was tilted even further for the print on the right. Notice the elongated door, and the lack of focus at the top and bottom of the image; the angle was too great for focus to be maintained.

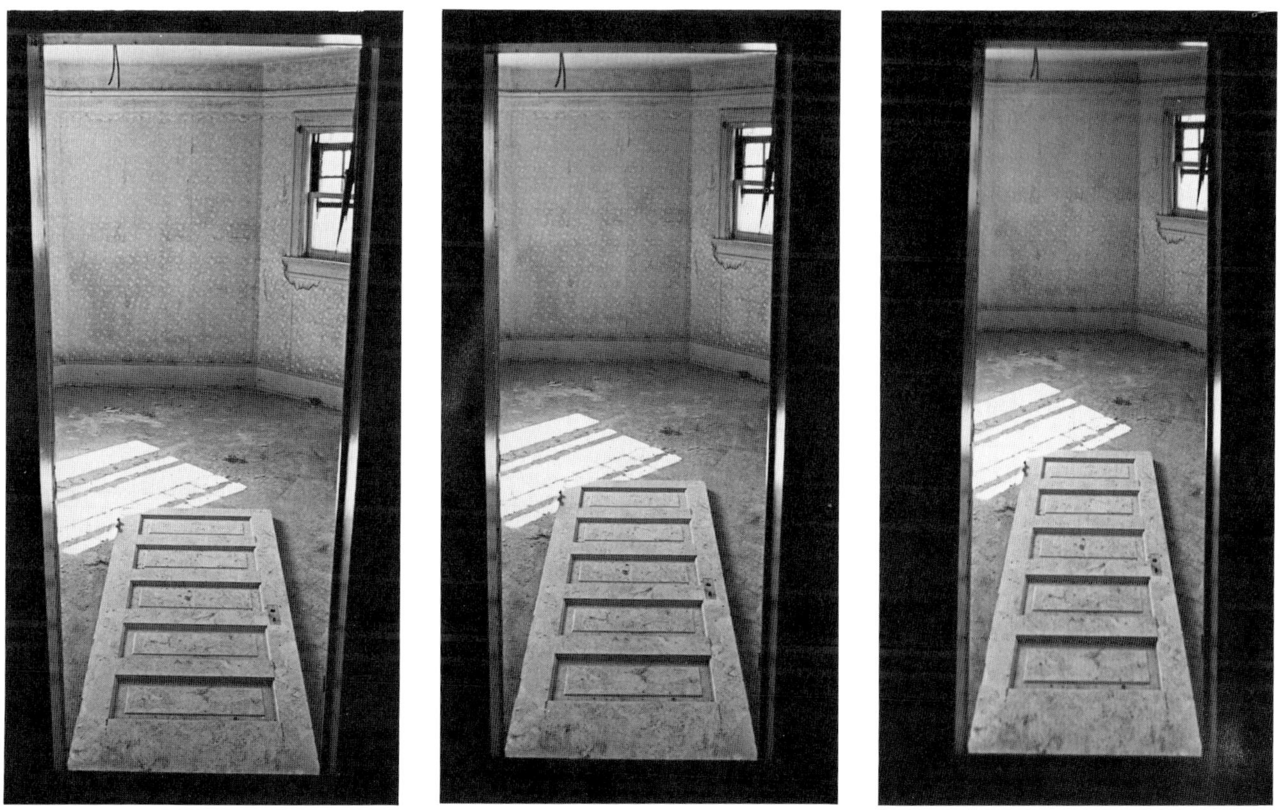

Generally, the perspective distortion produced during the shooting of a photograph is the result of pointing the camera up or down. When photographing a tall building, the camera is pointed up causing the vertical lines of the building to converge. This can be corrected during shooting by changing your vantage point. You can also use the adjustments of a view camera to compensate for distortion. But most of us who work with small hand-held cameras correct the problem in the darkroom.

There are several ways to correct perspective distortion when printing. You can tilt either the enlarging lens or the negative carrier, but the easiest method is to tilt the enlarging easel until the converging lines of the projected image appear parallel. Neither of these approaches completely corrects severe distortion, but they lessen the problem.

Begin by lifting one edge of the enlarging easel until the converging lines appear parallel. Then support the easel in place with something solid, and focus the image at a point one third of the way in from the higher end. To maximize the depth of field stop the lens down to a small aperture. The elevated portion of the picture will need less exposure than the part furthest away from the lens; therefore dodge the higher end during part of the exposure, and/or burn in the lower portion so that the density is uniform.

Tilting the easel can also create distortion or exaggerate elements of a picture. Bending or twisting the enlarging paper so that it's not flat during the exposure is another technique to create exaggerated distortion. The image will elongate if you bend the paper towards its base side, and it will shorten if bent towards the emulsion. To maintain focus, always use a small *f*-stop.

To abstract and minimize detail a grade 6 paper was used for this print. The easel was moved slightly during exposure to produce the blurred-motion effect.

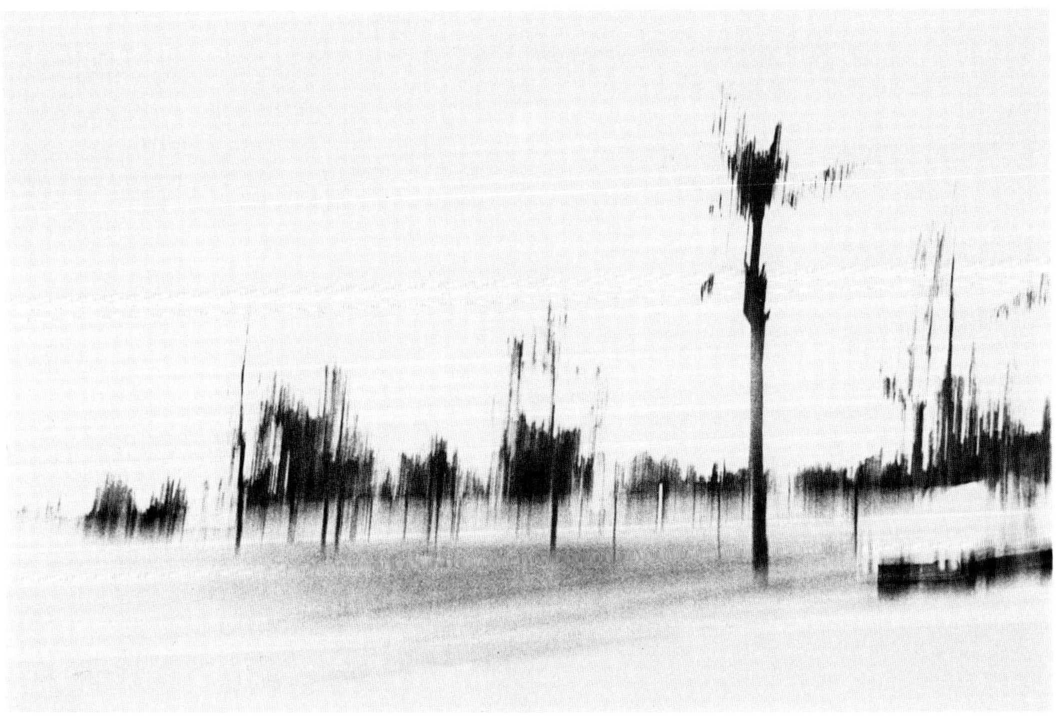

You may have to do some dodging and burning to produce an image with uniform density.

Implying Motion

You can create a feeling of motion or time passing by moving the easel during exposure, or by making a series of multiple exposures while moving the easel slightly each time. Both of these procedures are easy. The results depend on your finesse.

The way you move the easel varies the effect. A slow, staggered movement results in the image appearing out of the blur created by the movement. A smooth, continuous movement abstracts the image until the motion is stopped. The speed and exposure to use must be determined through experimentation, and will vary with materials and circumstances.

To get a smooth, continuous feeling of motion place the easel on top of several small dowels and slowly move the easel over the dowels during exposure.

Print Borders

Through conditioning, people have come to accept the standard 1/4-inch border and borderless prints commercial labs generally produce. But many photographers prefer different borders around their prints.

Large Borders. A white border of several inches around all four sides of the image sets the photograph off in a clean, professional manner.

Also, a border one inch (2.5 cm) or wider preserves the print longer than a smaller border. Contamination normally begins at the edge of a piece of printing paper and works inward. If the print has a large white border around the image area, it is protected from outside contamination because all chemicals that could be affected were bleached out of the white area by the fixer. In addition, borderless prints are prone to damage from handling as well as contamination.

An easel that's adjustable on four sides makes larger borders on prints easy, but these easels are normally quite expensive. An alternative method of producing large borders is to cut a mask out of black cardboard. This mask can be taped onto your regular easel, making it easier to use.

Borderless Prints. Borderless prints can also be produced at home. Most commercial products are expensive and unnecessary. To make borderless prints (11×14 inches or smaller) get a piece of 13×16 inch masonite. Mark off an 11×14 inch area in the center, then tape two one-inch strips of double-weight matte board to two sides of the masonite, forming an L shape. This provides you with an edge to put the paper against. Spray an adhesive (such as 3M Photomount) onto the area of the easel where the paper will be. Let it dry several minutes. The adhesive should be tacky, but not too sticky. If it's too sticky, you'll have trouble getting your prints off.

Black Borders. Many photographers like a thin black border around their images. This black border acts as a frame to set the image off, and sometimes is even necessary to hold the image together.

Several methods can be used to produce black borders. The simplest method is to file down your negative carrier so that the strip of clear film that surrounds the image on the film is showing on all four sides. When the negative is enlarged, this clear area prints as a black border around the image, while the rest of the border remains white.

This procedure works well, unless you want to crop a picture and still have a black border around it. If cropping is necessary, you will need to make a mask, and do what is called a "double-burn" to produce a black border.

To make the mask, cut a piece of opaque matte board the same size as your printing paper. Decide what size image area you want, and how wide the borders should be. Once this is determined, cut the rectangular image area out of the matte board. Then

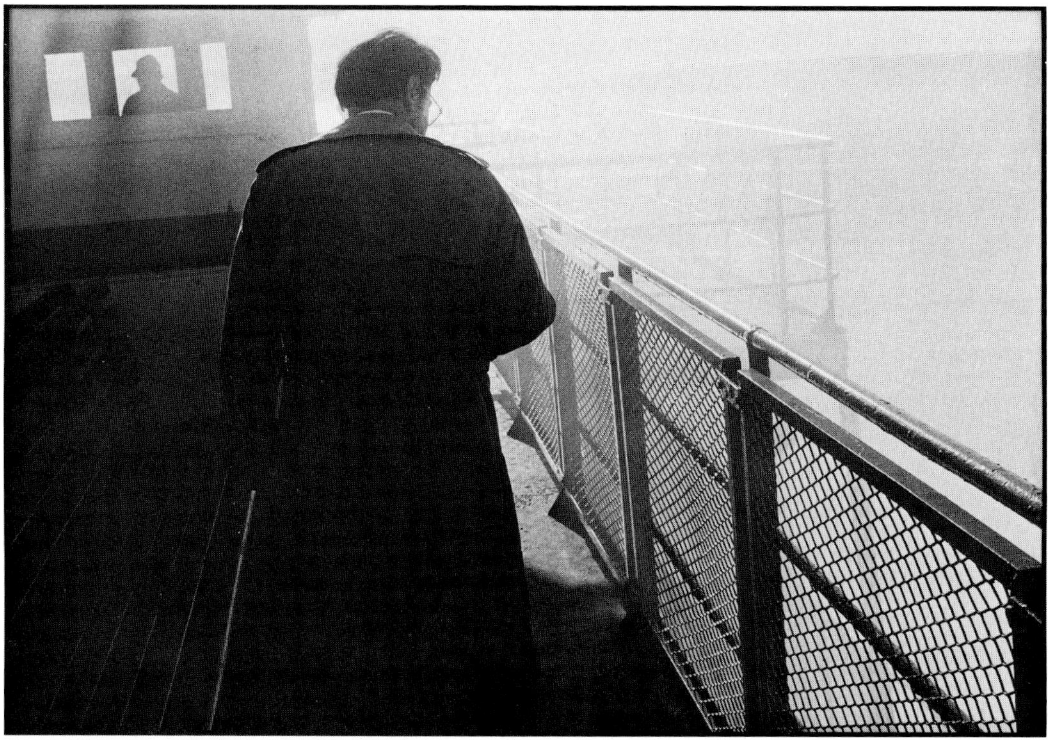

Photographers often use a thin black border as a framing device for their prints. Jim Koch used a border on this print in order to attract attention to the central portion of the photograph.

trim 1/8 inch (0.31 cm) off all sides of the cutout piece. This is your mask. The outer piece covers the print borders, while the inner piece covers the image area.

When you're ready to begin printing, tape the outer mask to the edge of your print easel so it can be flipped up or down. With the outer mask down, focus your negative so that the image fits within the cutout space. Make exposure tests to determine the proper paper grade and exposure. Then lift the mask and insert a piece of paper into the easel. Lower the outer mask, resting it on top of the printing paper. Make your exposure, and any local contrast-variations, with the outer mask in place.

Now take the inner mask and position it in the center of the outer mask. Try to make sure that the inner mask is centered so that there is a 1/8-inch (0.31 cm) space separating the masks on all four sides. Take the negative out of the enlarger and expose the print to white light. This second exposure, with both masks in place, will produce the black border. Be sure both masks lie flat on the surface of the paper and that no light leaks under them. You may have to test to determine how much white-light exposure is needed. Too much exposure can cause the light to bleed under the edges of the masks.

Texture Effects

Some photographers use texture to enhance their photographs. Texture can relieve monotony in prints with large areas of the same tone. While the addition of texture can detract from images dependent upon tiny or suble detail, texture patterns are used widely in portraiture, and for pictorial effects.

Texture can be achieved by using a textured paper, or by using a texture screen when printing the photograph. Textured papers are limited in variety (especially resin-coated papers); therefore, most photographers use either commercial or homemade texture screens.

There are two methods of using texture screens. One is the "screened print," which is done by contact printing. In this case the texture screen must be as large as the printing paper (or larger), and is placed on top of the printing paper during exposure. To keep the screen in contact with the printing paper, use either a vacuum easel or a piece of glass to hold the screen down.

Texture screens designed for the "screen print" method come in a variety of sizes and are much larger and more expensive than the smaller screens for the "screened negatives." But many photographers prefer the larger screens, because there is no enlargement of the pattern.

The "screened negative" method is an easier way to add texture to prints. This is done by sandwiching the texture screen with the negative (black-and-white or color), and printing them together. The screen may be a commercial one, a thin fabric like silk or muslin, a lens tissue, or some special-texture negative that you made by photographing a pattern.

Commercial screens for "screened negatives" are designed to be enlarged up to 20×24 inches, but give the most satisfying results when used on 11×14 or 8×10 paper. The texture pattern on these screens has been reduced, so that when the screen is enlarged, the texture isn't so large that it dominates the image. Commercial screens made on film are inexpensive and easy to use.

Homemade Texture Screens. You can make your own texture screens by photographing textured surfaces. These negatives can then be sandwiched with other negatives and enlarged, or printed onto large pieces of litho film for contact printing. (If you print your texture pattern on litho film, be sure to use a continuous-tone developer (such as Dektol) so the screen doesn't develop to black. Otherwise, the

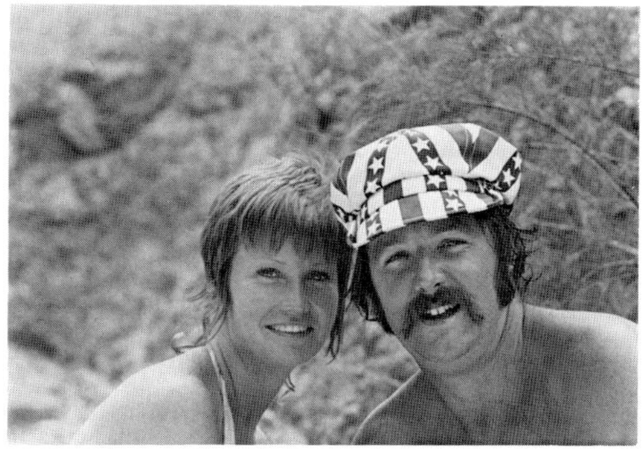

Texture screens can add to a photograph, but they can also dominate and distract from the subject.

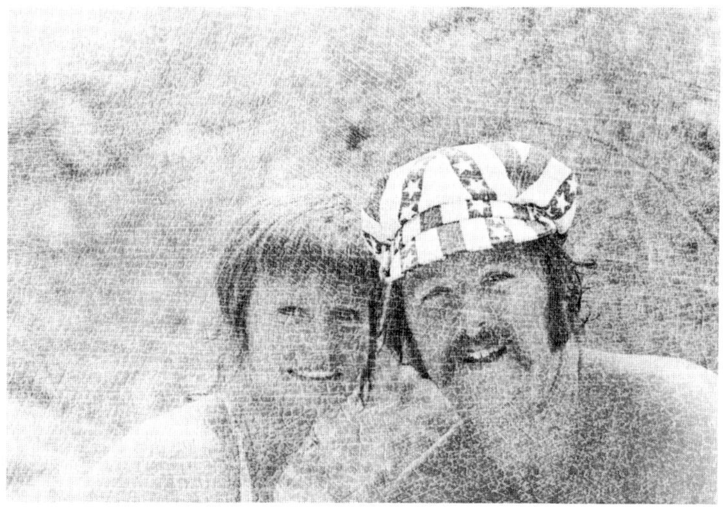

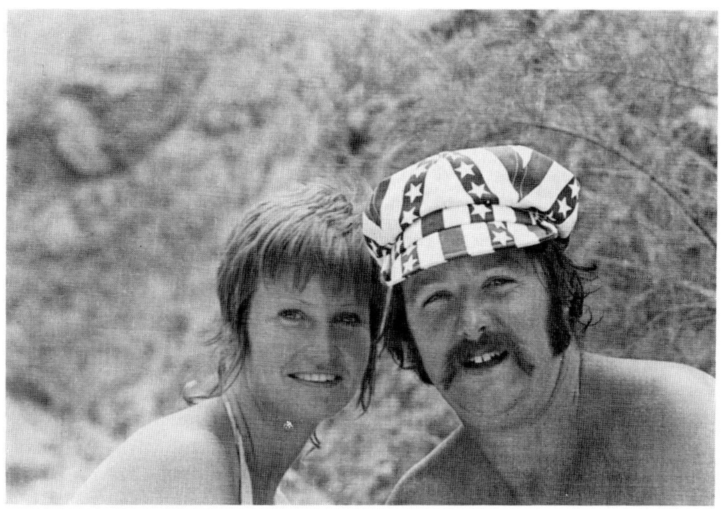

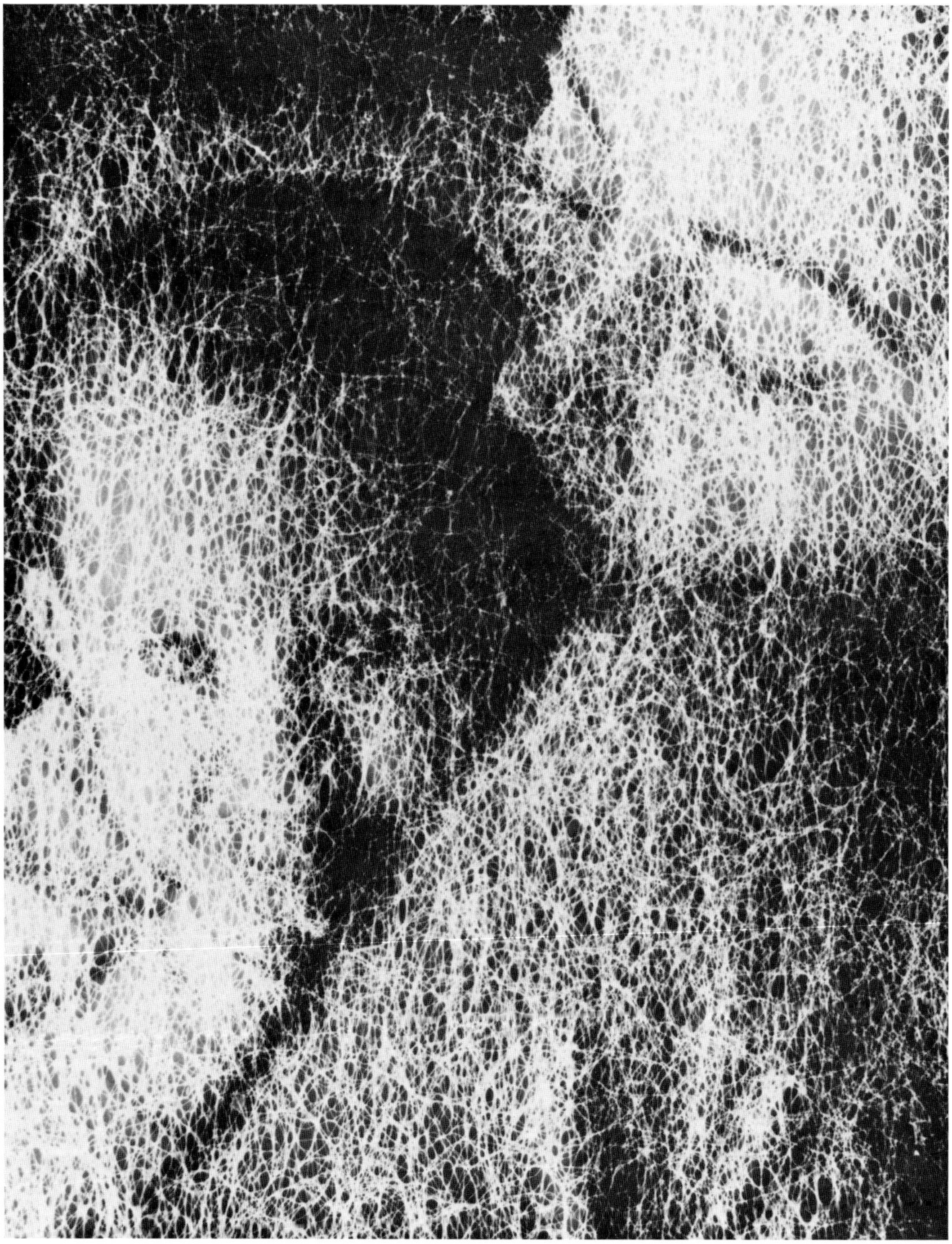

Mark Chamberlain sandwiched lens tissue with the negative to make this interesting print. Many different objects can be used to add texture to an image. Some photographers even draw their own texture screens.

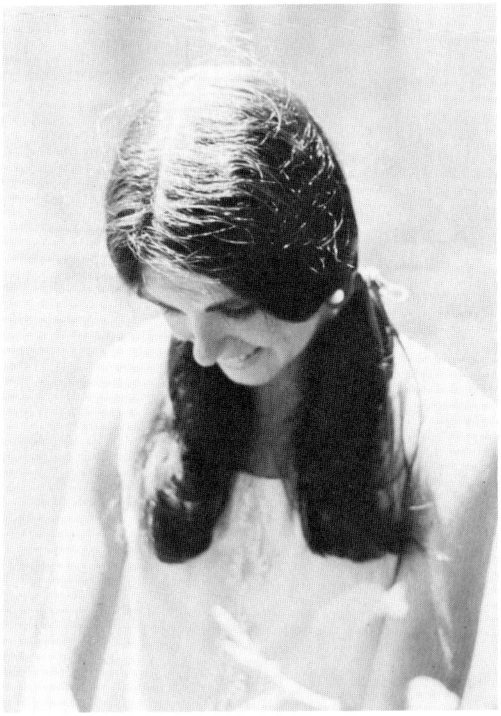

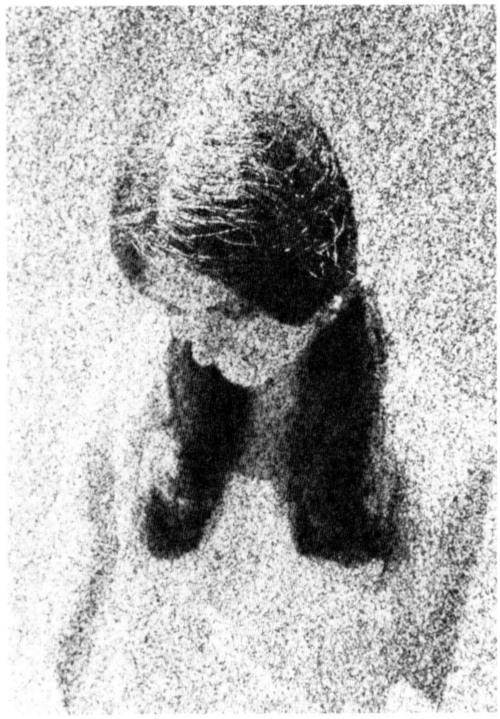

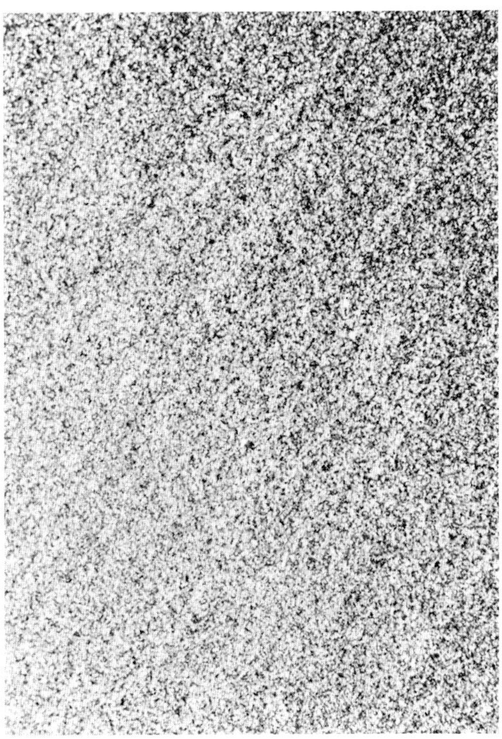

The negatives of the two prints on the left were sandwiched together to get the strong textural effect of the print above. The photograph on the lower left is wet beach sand.

screen will be opaque and overpower the image.)

Fabric, pieces of lens tissue, Kleenex, papers, and many other items can be used to add texture to an image. Some photographers create their own texture screens by drawing the patterns and designs they want to use. This method also allows them to make the pattern the size they feel will work best with a particular subject or print size.

A texture pattern has a different effect with different print sizes. It may feel right when used on an 8×10 print, and may be entirely wrong when it's used on a 16×20 print. Regardless of the type of texture effect or procedure you use, remember that texture must add to the feeling of the image, not dominate or conflict with it.

Paper Negatives

A procedure frequently overlooked in our obsession with sharpness is the paper negative. Yet the paper negative is one of the oldest, simplest, and least expensive methods for retouching and altering parts of an image. This technique also provides an easy method for making negative prints.

To make a paper negative, you simply contact a positive print with an unexposed piece of paper, and develop it. This produces a negative image which, in many cases, can be quite exciting. But the "paper" negative can also be retouched, and then contact printed again to make "final" positive prints.

The easiest way to make a paper negative is to soak the positive print in water for several minutes, and then place it emulsion down on the emulsion of a piece of unexposed printing paper. Make sure you're working on a flat surface, and then squeegee the two print papers together. Because they are wet, they will adhere together uniformly. Once the prints have been squeegeed together, make your exposure through the back of the positive print. You should only need a 100-watt overhead light, four feet (1.22 m) from the print, and a one- or two-second exposure. But test to determine the proper exposure under your circumstances.

When using the paper-negative technique, it's helpful to think of the positive and negative print generations as transparencies. Only by viewing the "negative" print illuminated from behind can you get an adequate feeling for how it will translate, and how to retouch it. Normal print values do not produce the best effects. With each generation, contrast is increased. Therefore, make the initial positive print and the subsequent paper negative low in contrast and fairly heavy in density, with both shadows and highlights maintaining good detail. A grade 1 paper is recommended for both the initial positive and negative print.

Since you will be printing through the paper, glossy, single-weight paper is recommended in order to minimize loss of sharpness, and the texture the paper can cause. A rough or slightly textured surface can be used for the final print, to help hide flaws as well as any signs of retouching.

Retouching Paper Negatives. Retouching should only be done while the prints are being viewed as transparencies, that is, by transmitted light. Use a light box, or tape the print to a window. Mask off the area around the print so your eyes aren't overwhelmed by the surrounding light. Then, use soft pencils to touch up white spots and add tone to the print. It is best to use a conventional, non-gloss, fiber-based printing paper as pencils don't work well on glossy and RC surfaces.

Lines and fine details that need good definition should be retouched on the emulsion side of the print, while larger areas that need gradual shading and a blending of tones should be done on the back side of the printing paper in order to make the retouching less obvious. When retouching, any marks or density added on the positive print will appear as added density in the final print. Any density added to the negative print will lighten the final print. By carefully retouching both the initial positive print and the negative print, the final image can be greatly improved or altered. One caution: be careful not to over-retouch. Sometimes no retouching at all is better than too much retouching.

High-Contrast Paper Negatives. With paper negatives, the contrast is increased each time you go from one generation to another. That's why it is suggested that you use a lower-than-normal grade of paper. However, by beginning with a

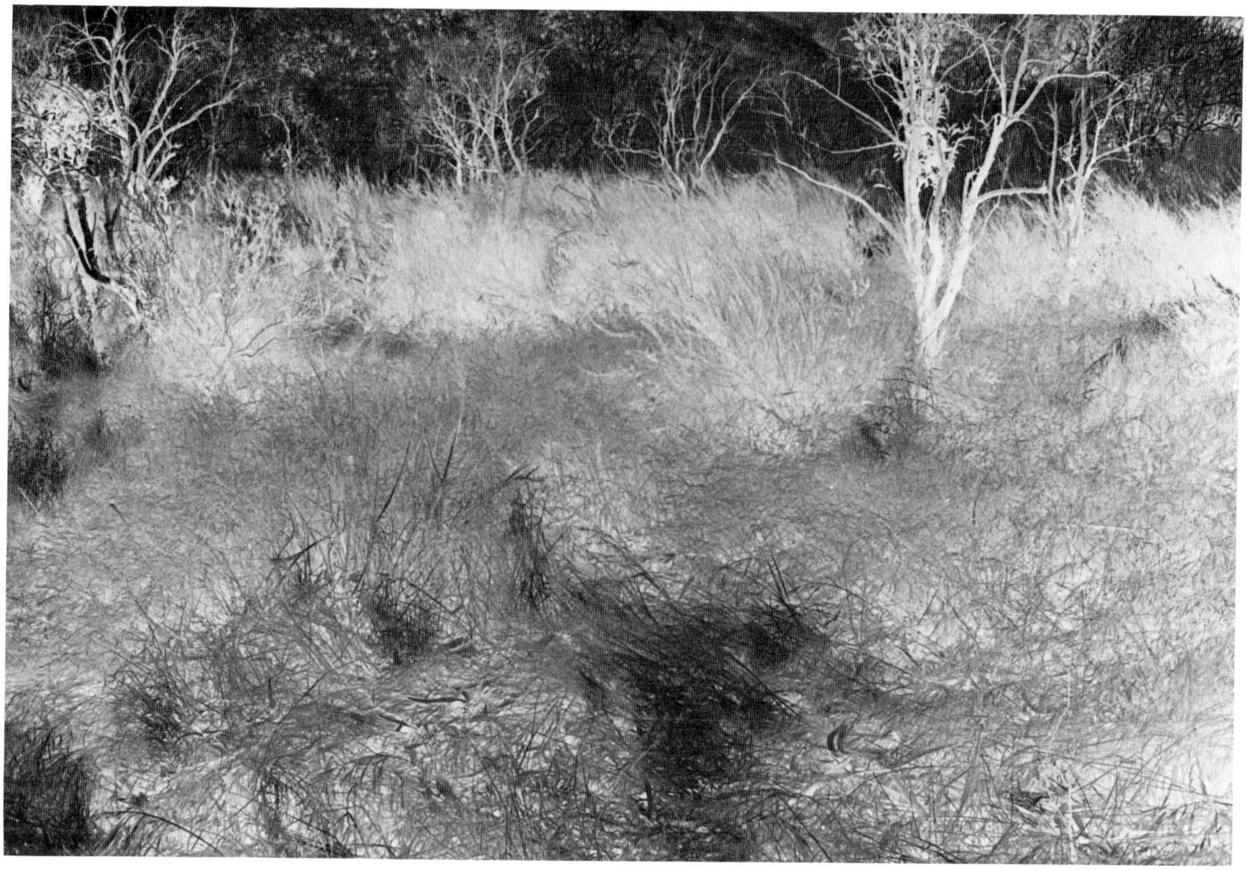

We are so used to thinking of a photograph in terms of a positive image that we frequently overlook the beauty of the negative image.

higher-than-normal grade of paper (such as 5), you can take advantage of the increase in contrast and end up with high-contrast print with no middle tones.

Use the same procedure as before, only this time use a high-contrast paper. Enlarge your negative on a number 4, 5, or 6 paper, then process it. After fixing, rinse it in running water for two minutes. Then take the print and place it, emulsion-to-emulsion, on top of an unexposed piece of paper of the same grade. Squeegee them together and expose through the back of the positive print. You'll get a high-contrast negative print.

After processing the negative print, repeat the washing and exposing procedure to make another positive print. This print will look like it was made from a litho negative, the final image will be pure black and white.

Many of the techniques in this chapter, such as print flashing and paper negatives, apply more to black-and-white than color materials. Yet these basic approaches pertain to both. The applications are varied, and depend on how you choose to use the medium. Photography is a tool, nothing more. But, when used with control, deliberation, and creative intent, it provides many rewards.

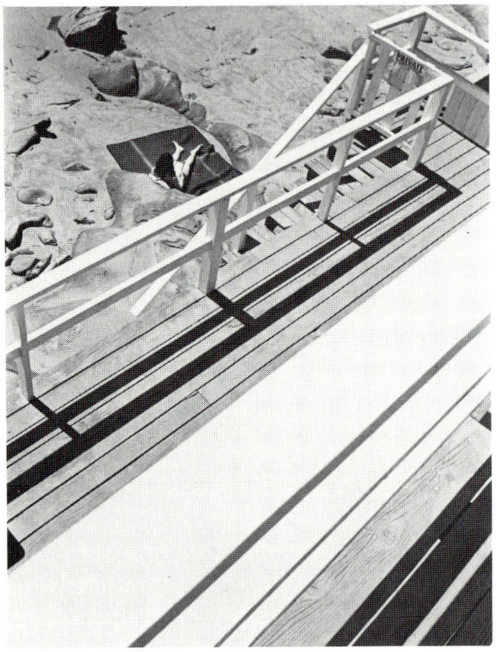

Paper negatives can be used to increase contrast without changing paper grade; to add texture to a print; or to do retouching on. This print was made from an original negative.

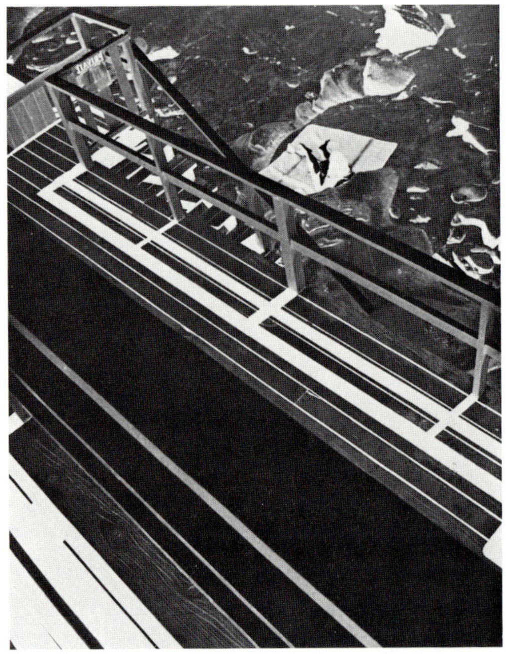

This paper negative is a contact print of the previous positive print. It can be used as an image in itself, or as a step to alter the original photograph.

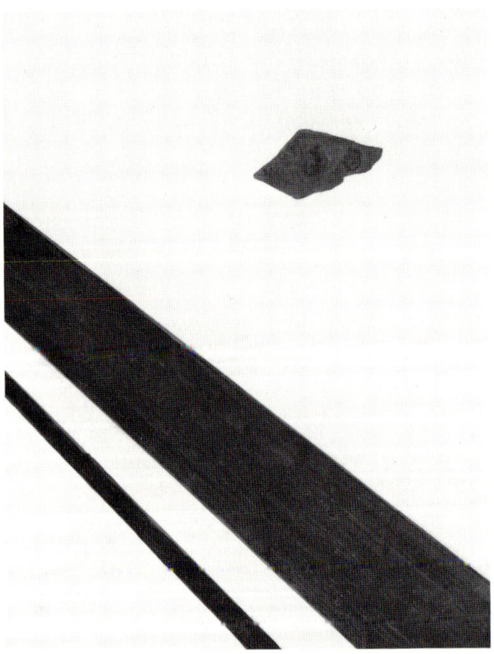

This illustration shows the retouching on the back of the original positive print above.

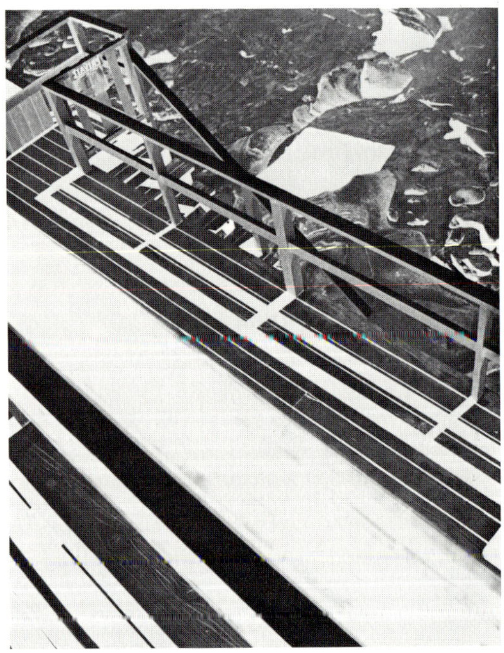

This paper negative was made from the retouched print on the left. Notice the difference between it and the unretouched paper negative shown above.

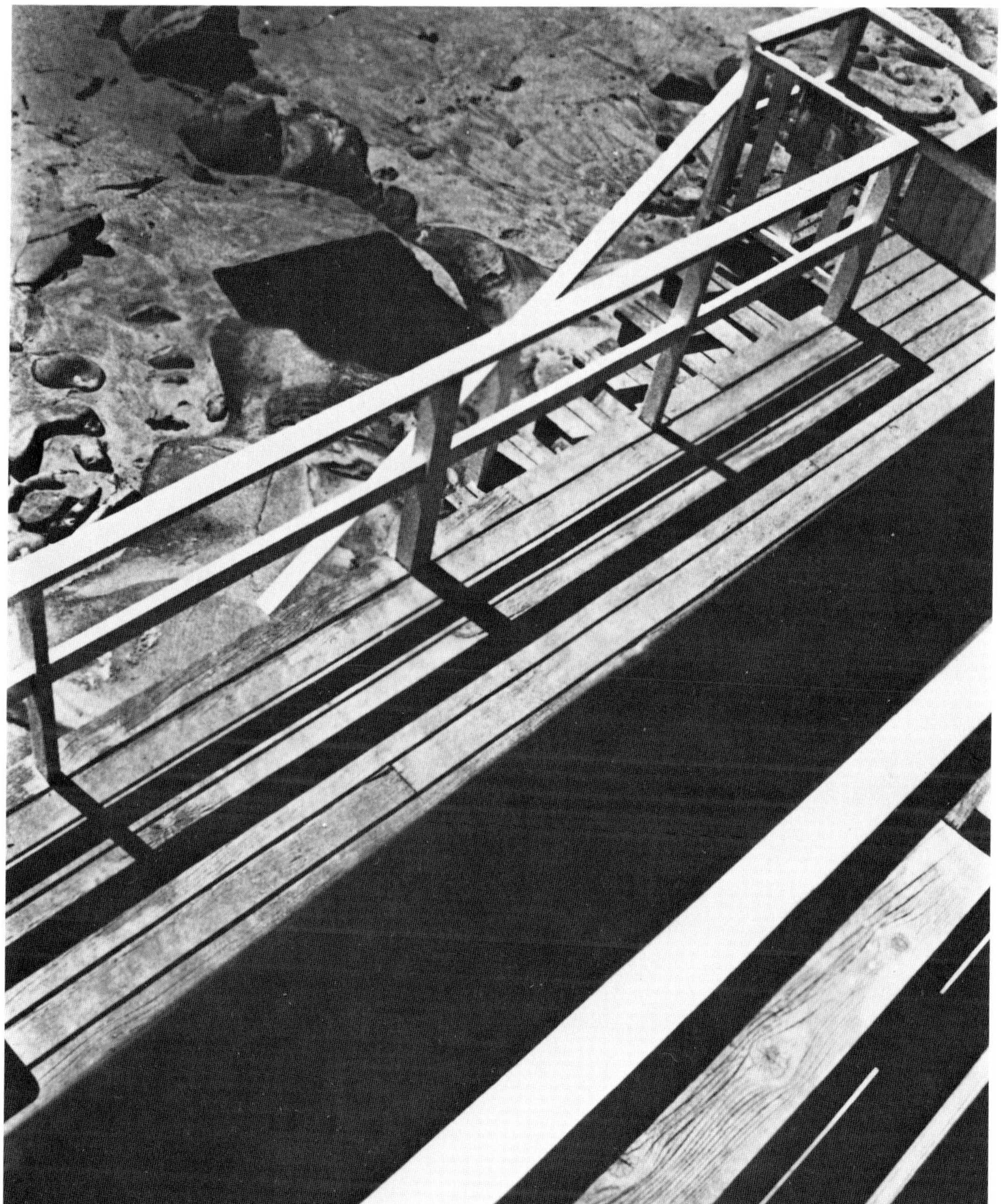

This print from the retouched paper negative on the bottom right of the previous page shows what can be done with paper negatives. Both positives and negatives can be retouched to add, delete, deepen, or lighten parts of a photograph.

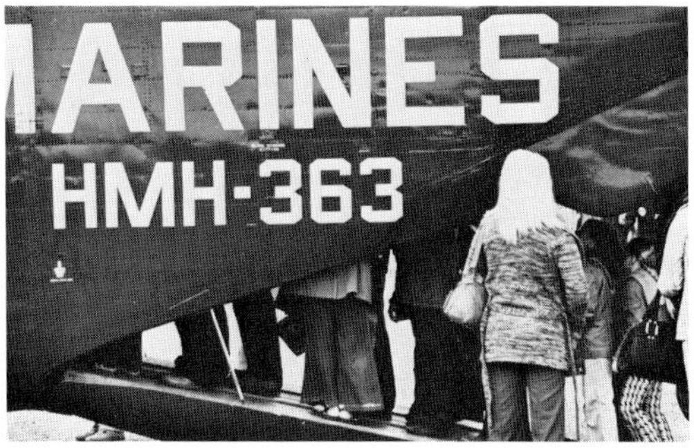

This series of print variations by Gejar began with this photograph, printed on a grade 4 Ilfospeed paper.

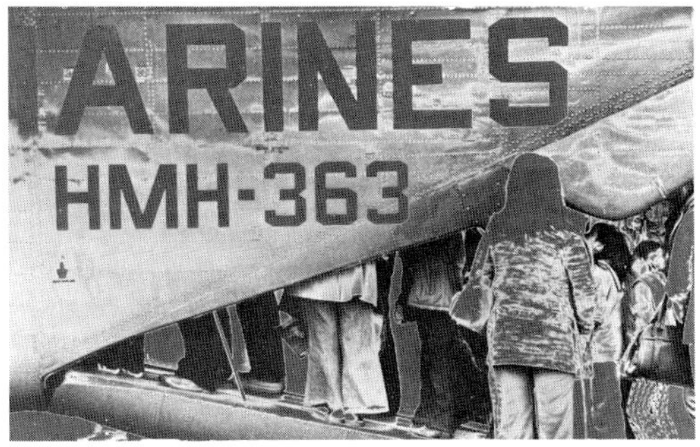

This is a print of the same image with the Sabattier effect. It was used as a paper negative to contact print the next image.

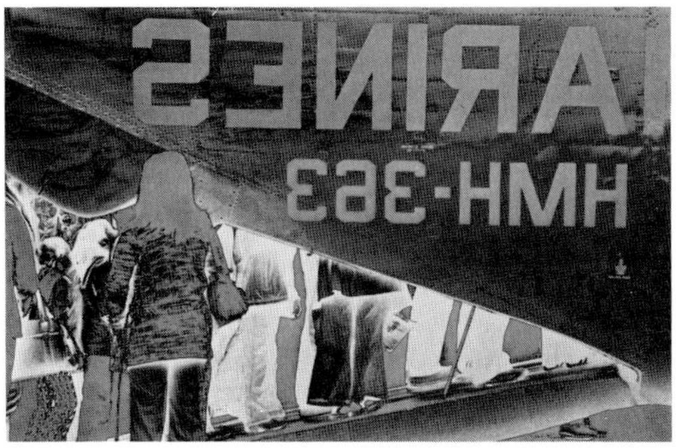

Notice the increased range of tones in this negative print. This second-generation image can be an end in itself, or used to abstract the photograph further.

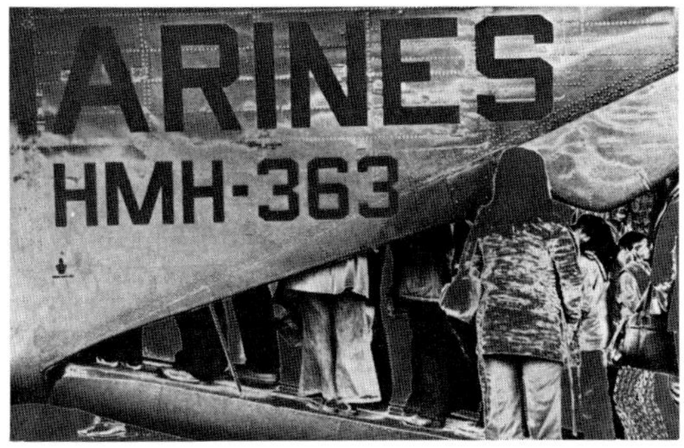

The third-generation print is a positive, and has much more contrast and life than the original Sabattier-effect image.

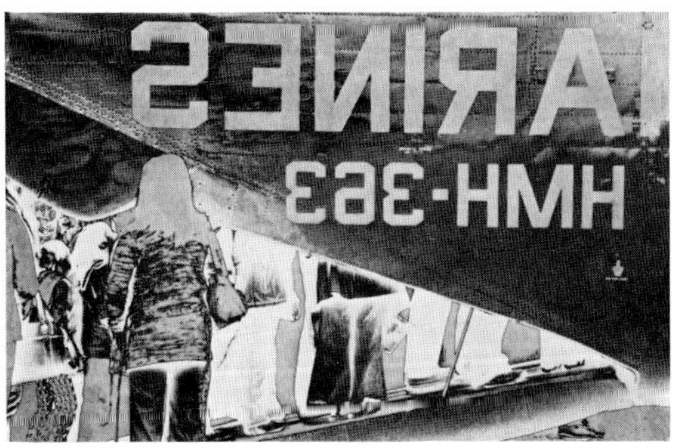

With each generation the contrast increases. This fourth-generation, negative-image print has much more contrast than the preceding images.

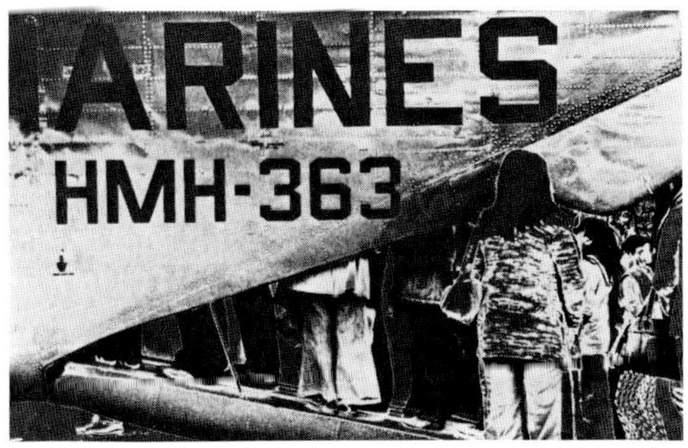

The final image in the series is a fifth-generation, high-contrast, positive print. The change from the original print is quite dramatic.

5

Making Oversize Prints

Traditionally photographs have been relatively small, but today the attitude seems to be the bigger, the better. Large prints, whether color or black-and-white, attract more attention than smaller ones. Photography normally begins with a process of reduction. The shutter is clicked and an image is frozen on film, a miniature record of reality. This is subsequently enlarged, and a print made that is still a miniaturization of the original situation. This difference in size allows the viewer to feel secure and uninvolved, because the photograph is only a representation. But a large print, which reproduces the subject on the same scale, or even larger, than the original subject, can have more impact because the size alone overwhelms us.

Making large black-and-white or color photographs, frequently referred to as mural prints, is not as hard as it may seem. These do become expensive, and it will be necessary to make a few modifications in your darkroom and processing procedures, but the excitement and satisfaction you'll gain from making an oversize print should be worth it.

Both color and black-and-white printing papers can be purchased in sizes up to 30×40 inches (76.2×101.6 cm). They can also be purchased in long rolls 4 feet (122 m) wide by 30 to 100 feet (9.1 to 30.4 m) long. Your negatives must be standardized because color paper comes just in one grade, and black-and-white mural paper is usually available only in grades 2 and 3.

Some black-and-white mural papers are easier to work with than others. Kodak's

Scale plays an important role in the way that we react to an image. A small print is more intimate, while a larger one has more impact.

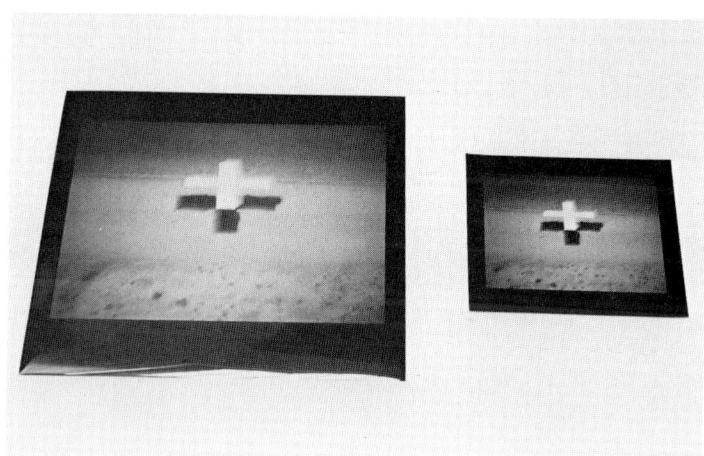

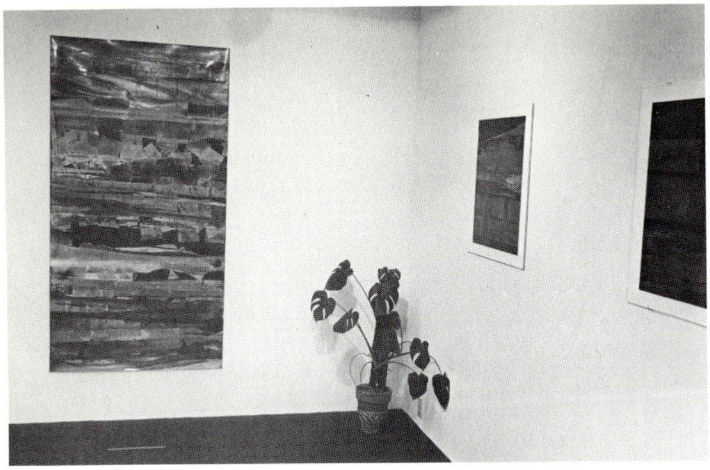

Notice the large print in this photograph. This 40 × 74½ inch image is part of an exhibition of work by Susan Rankaitis. The monoprint is on black-and-white paper manipulated by multiple development and bleaching to produce color effects and tonal variations.

mural paper resists abrasion and can be gently wrinkled and/or folded during processing without creating permanent surface flaws. Some other brands lack this advantage and are more difficult to work with.

Processing Large Prints

You can process large prints in several different ways. Large daylight-processing drums are the most economical and controllable method to process large color prints. These are identical to the small variety and have removable end caps. You'll find them in camera stores that carry home-darkroom equipment. The drum or tube can be agitated manually by rolling it on a counter top, or by a motor device designed for smaller tubes. Most manufacturers make processing tubes up to 20×24 inches (50.8×60.9 cm), but large tubes must be ordered directly from special manufacturers. Paper is limited to a 20-inch (50.8 cm) width, but the length can be as long as you like. A full frame 35 mm image enlarges nicely onto a piece of 20×30-inch (50.8×76.2 cm) paper. The tube used for that size should be 30 inches (76.2 cm) long and the end caps the same as those designed for 20×24-inch (50.8×60.9 cm) prints. To make color prints larger than 20 inches (50.8 cm) wide, you'll have to buy either a larger tube, more sophisticated equipment, or try processing them in larger trays.

Black-and-white prints can also be developed in large tubes, but due to the less complicated nature of black-and-white processing, large trays or troughs are adequate.

Basic large trays can be quickly made with sheets of plastic and wooden two-by-fours. Construct a framework with the two-by-fours, then lay the plastic over them. These trays should be large enough for the prints to lie flat in them. Make three separate trays, one for each chemical, and process the prints by submerging them in the chemicals. If the prints are too big for you to control by hand, use a mop to make sure that the print is thoroughly submerged in the chemistry. After processing, wash

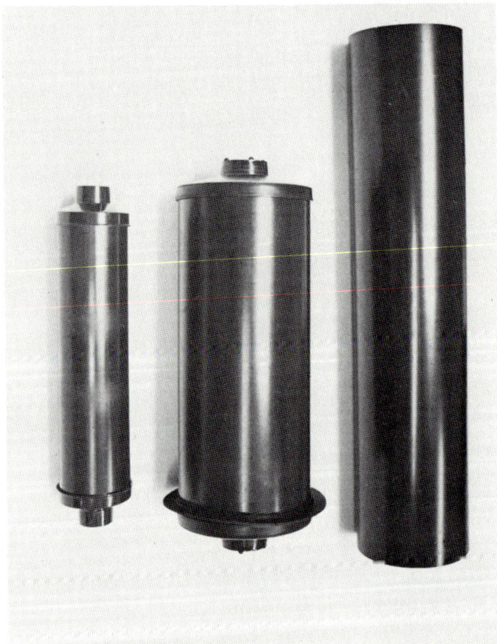

Commercially made daylight processing tubes are easy to use, and relatively inexpensive. They can be used for both black-and-white and color prints, and come in a variety of sizes for large and small prints.

the prints in another large tray (or in your bathtub) with running water.

Another way to process large black-and-white prints is to make large wooden troughs. The troughs should be 7 inches (17.7 cm) wide, 6 inches (15.2 cm) deep, and 4 feet (1.21 m) long. Make three troughs and have them fiberglassed or lined with plastic, so they hold the chemicals. This is a good system because it uses a smaller amount of chemistry than large trays, and the troughs require little space when in use, or when being stored.

To process prints in the troughs, first roll the paper up, then insert the outer end emulsion up into a trough filled with developer. After you have submerged the end of the printing paper in the trough, take that end and begin rolling the paper up inside the trough until all of the paper is immersed. Then, reverse the procedure and roll the paper the other direction, keeping it submerged. Use this procedure for each processing step. First roll the paper into a tube shape in one direction, then roll it back the other way. This provides adequate agitation and should give even processing. Once you've completed all three steps, use a hypo eliminator, then wash the print with running water in a similar tank, or in your bathtub. After the print is thoroughly washed, squeegee the excess water off and use clips (clothes pins) to hang the print for drying. Put weights on the bottom edge to keep the print from curling.

Enlarging Problems. One problem you may run into when making mural prints is that you can't get a big enough image on the baseboard of your enlarger. Many photographers solve this problem by designing their darkrooms so the baseboard can be removed allowing the image to be projected onto the floor.

Home-made processing tanks, such as this one, process large prints without a lot of chemistry or a lot of space. They can be made of wood, and made to hold liquid by using a plastic liner or coating of fiberglass. (Prints are rolled back and forth for processing.)

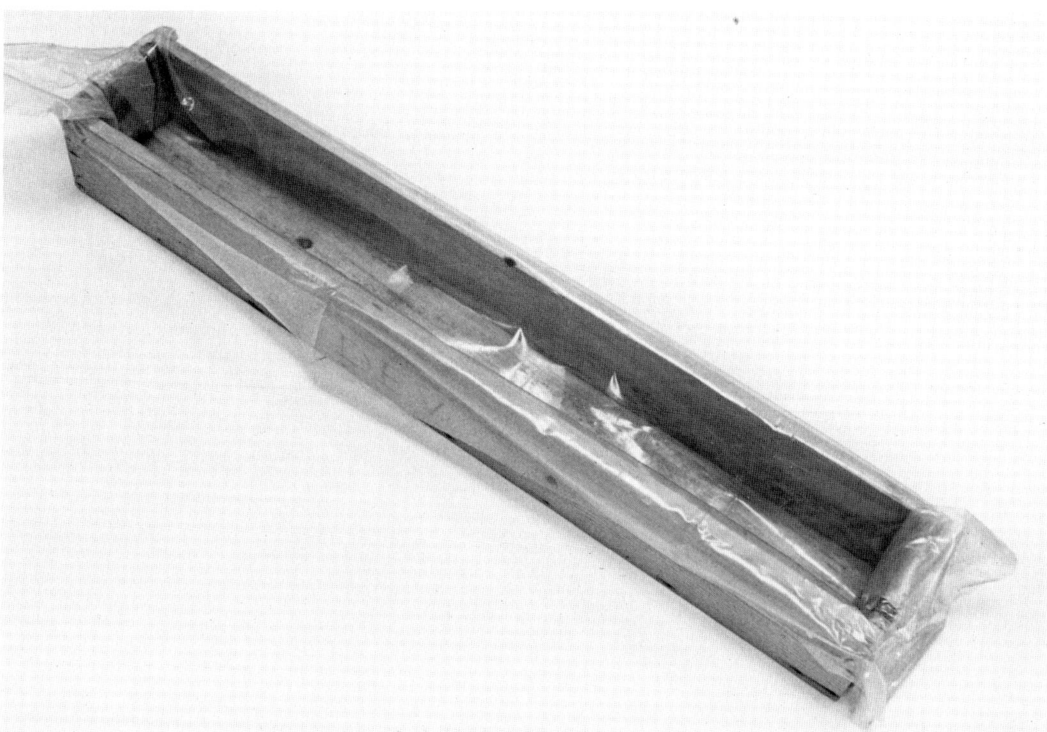

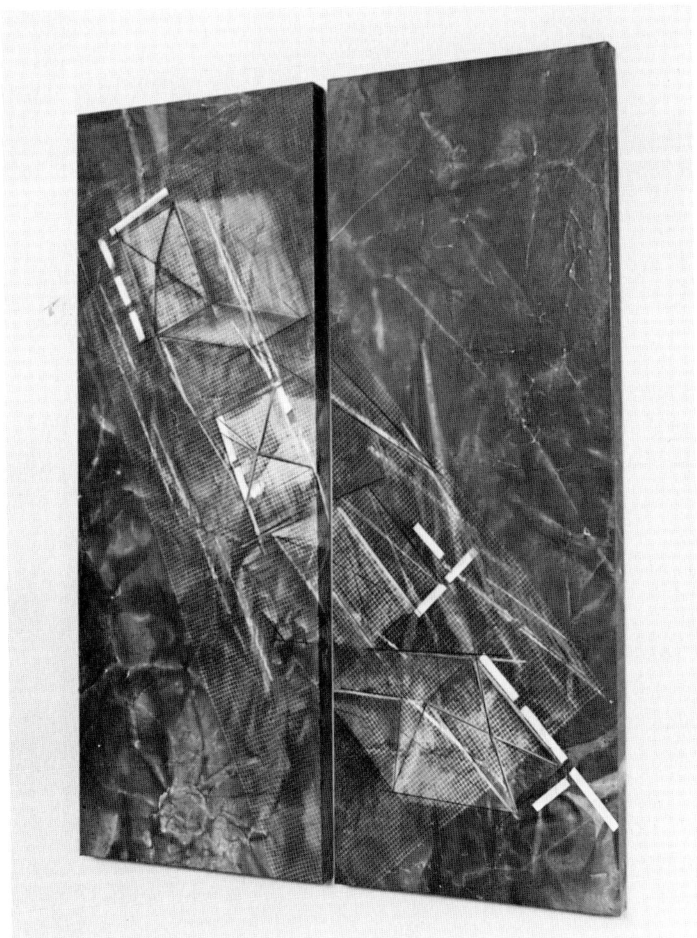

This two-panel image by Barbara Kasten, black-and-white photo paper on canvas, has a combined size of 37 × 48 inches.

Some enlargers, like a Besseler, have heads that tilt so the image can be projected onto a vertical plane. Then you can project the negative onto a wall, using it as your baseboard. The paper can be held in place with pushpins and/or two-sided tape.

If neither of these options works for you, try positioning a mirror at a 45-degree angle below the enlarger. Project the negative onto the mirror, which will in turn project the image onto a wall or other surface you can use as a baseboard. The mirror reverses the image, so be sure to put the negative in your enlarger with the emulsion side up.

Mounting Large Prints

Few photographers have a dry mounting press large enough to mount photo murals, so most use either a cold- or wet-mounting process. Cold-mounting processes are the easiest, the neatest, and can be done without an elaborate setup. Cold-mounting methods include spray adhesives, transfer-mounting tissues, and double-stick mounting tissues. There are a number of different products available, but be sure you use one designed for photography. Many adhesives contain chemicals harmful to photographs and should be avoided.

Large prints need to be mounted on a firm support. Most matte board isn't sturdy enough. Wet-mounted prints should be mounted on ½-inch or ¼-inch (12.7 or 6.3 mm) tempered masonite. Cold-mounted prints can be mounted on masonite, Plexiglas, or aluminum.

Cold Mounting. Resin-coated print materials must be cold-mounted. Wet mounting only works with conventional silver-based printing papers. If you use a spray mounting adhesive, thoroughly coat the back by spraying it from several directions. Then let it dry for about a minute, so the adhesive is still tacky but doesn't come off when touched lightly. Place the print on the mount board. First position one side, then lay the rest of the print in place. Don't press the print down until it is positioned properly. Once you're satisfied, cover the print with another piece of paper and use a roller to secure it in place. When using the roller, work from the center out to eliminate air pockets.

There are a variety of transfer and double-stick mounting tissues available. Procedures for using them vary but usually they are easy to work with and come with adequate instructions. Sometimes it's difficult to find the larger sizes, and you may have to special order tissue large enough to handle mural prints. If you can't get a large enough size to do the job, try using two small pieces rather than one large one. However, this should be avoided if possible, because two pieces tend to create a crease; but it can work if handled carefully.

Wet Mounting. Wet mounting is the procedure to use if you are working with fiber-based printing paper. Although a little more time consuming and harder to use, it is much more secure and permanent than any other procedure.

The necessary materials include a piece of ½- or ¼-inch (12.7 or 6.3 mm) tempered masonite the size of the print, glue, a brush for applying the glue, a squeegee, a print roller, wooden one-by-twos to make a framework so the back of the masonite won't bow, finishing nails, wood glue, a knife or scissors, kraft paper, a sponge, and a bucket of water. Choose a paper glue that won't cause the eventual deterioration of the print. Many photographers use a white glue like Elmer's or Wilhold, which should have minimal effect on the life of the print. However, there are some special glues proven to give long print life that are used for bookbinding and wherever permanence is necessary.

Methyl cellulose, rice paste, or wheat paste are glues that will not harm your photographs. You can purchase methyl-cellulose glue through Light Impressions Corporation, Box 3012, Rochester, New York 14614. It comes in powder form and dissolves in water to make a mounting paste. It has a long shelf life and a neutral pH, and is non-toxic, odorless, and verminproof; it dries clear and will not decompose.

Both rice paste and wheat paste are easy to make yourself. Rice flour is recommended over wheat flour because it's whiter.

Recipes for flour pastes vary and you may want to devise your own proportions. Because the pastes thicken when they cool, they may have to be thinned with water. A standard recipe for a rice-flour paste or wheat-flour paste is:

1 cup (2.5 dl) flour
1 cup (250 ml) cold water
4 or 5 cups (1 or 1.25 l) boiling water

Put the flour in a saucepan or double boiler, and gradually add the cold water. Stir well until all lumps are removed. The mixture should be runny like a thin cream. Then slowly add the boiling water and cook

This photogram by Sheila Pinkel is the size of a twin bed. It was made by laying an old bed spring on photo-mural paper. Before making the exposure, Sheila jumped onto the bed springs, and produced what could be called a life-size self portrait.

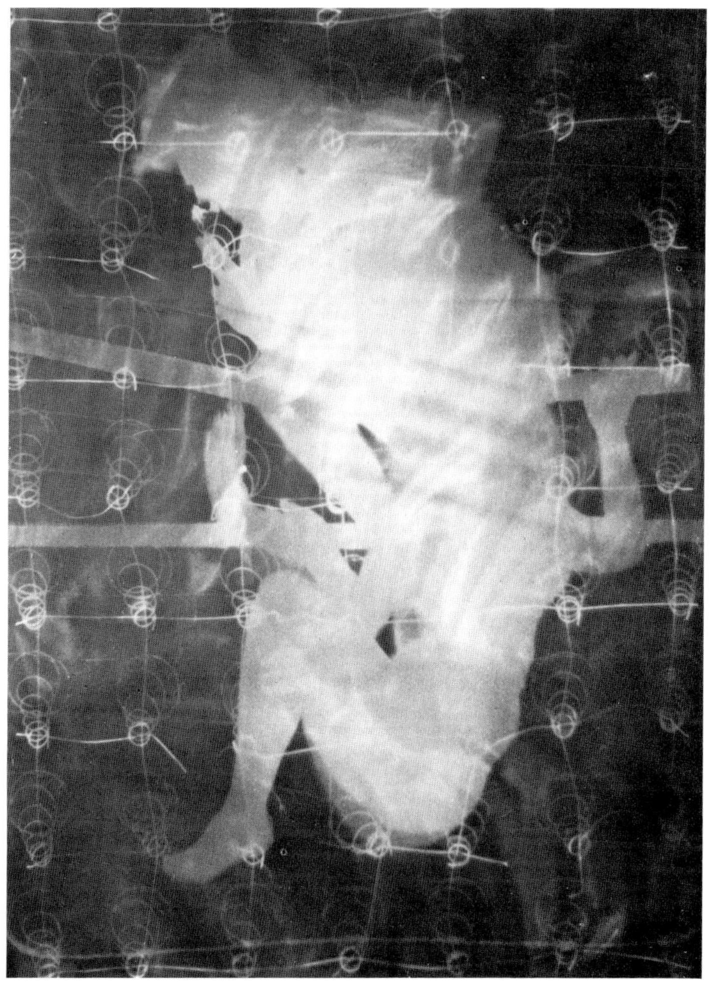

the mixture for three or four minutes with constant stirring. Let the mixture cool.

If the paste is to be kept for several days, a preservative should be added. Two teaspoons of powdered alum can be added during the mixing stages. Powdered clove, or several drops of oil of clove, can also be added to prevent mildew.

Before you mount the print, cut the masonite to size and sand the edges. For wet mounting, prints should be made with two to three inches of extra border on all sides. These borders are then folded over the edges of the masonite and glued down, resulting in a bleed or borderless mount.

Once the masonite is ready, cut a piece of kraft paper to mount on the back of the board. This provides resistance to warping. Apply the paste liberally to the back of the masonite and wet the kraft paper. Then lay the paper in place on the back of the masonite. Starting in the center, squeegee the excess glue out to the edges.

The next step is to prepare the mural print for mounting. If still wet from processing, it can be mounted immediately. If not, soak the print in water before mounting. Once the print is wet, squeegee off the excess water and lay the print on the masonite. Position it so there is at least a two-inch (5 cm) overlap on all sides. Cut the paper diagonally at each corner, so the borders won't overlap when folded onto the back of the masonite.

Once the corners are trimmed, apply the paste to the surface of the masonite. Avoid using too much, but coat it thoroughly. Then reposition the print on the masonite and squeegee it from the center out. Next, apply paste to the overhanging borders of the print, and fold them onto the back of the masonite. Once the print and the kraft-paper backing are securely in place, wipe off the excess paste and suspend the mounted print on sawhorses (or an equivalent surface) so it dries on both sides.

When the print is dry, attach the wooden one-by-twos to the back. These will prevent the masonite from warping, set the print off from the wall, and provide a convenient means to hang it. Attach the one-by-twos with wood glue and secure them in place with finishing nails. Position these strips about three inches (7.6 cm) in on all four sides and they will provide plenty of support.

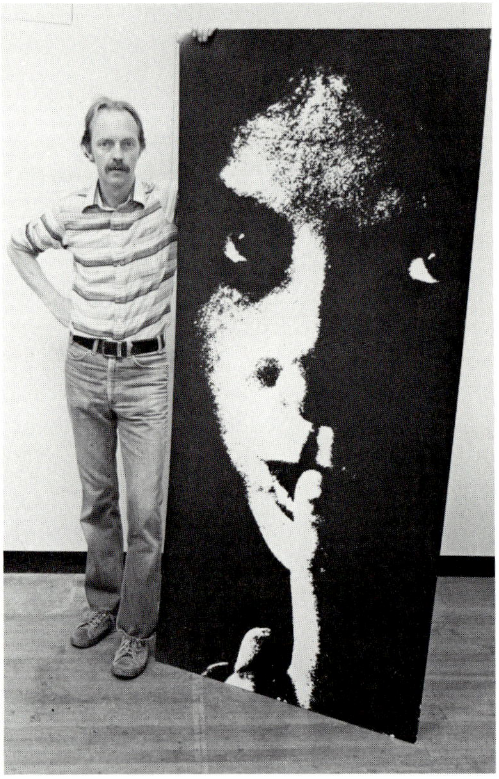

This 3½ × 7 foot photograph was made in a small darkroom. The enlarger was tilted sideways. The print was processed by hand in large print-troughs, and then wet-mounted onto a masonite backing.

If you're restricted in the image size you can make by darkroom or paper limitations, consider making several panels to be presented together. Another option is to make your own emulsion, and apply it to cloth or some other material which allows you to work on a larger scale. Whether your image is camera-made or a photogram, scale should be considered. With today's simplified techniques, size should not be a limitation.

6

Darkroom Magic

One of the advantages of doing your own processing and printing is the opportunity to explore many different avenues. It can open the door to another world of your own creation. In this chapter, you'll find a variety of methods to alter and enhance your images.

The Sabattier Effect

The Sabattier effect has been obscured by a kind of mysticism, because it's one of those magic darkroom tricks that is unpredictable, but great when it turns out. Many photographers have experimented with the Sabattier effect, but often with little control and less predictability. However, the technique can be controlled and used creatively to add new dimensions to your images.

As explained in chapter 1, the terms "solarization" and "Sabattier effect" are frequently used interchangeably, but there is a distinct difference between the two. Technically, solarization refers to the reversal of an image on film that occurs with extreme overexposure, while the Sabattier effect (which is named after Armand Sabattier, a French doctor and scientist who discovered the process more than a century ago) is the reversal of an image that occurs when film or photographic paper is re-exposed to light during the developing process. Photographs re-exposed in this manner have a negative/positive effect. The image starts developing as a positive, and partially reverses to a negative after the re-exposure to light. A distinct characteristic of the Sabattier effect is a narrow band, called a Mackie (or bromide) line, that forms between the highlight and shadow areas of an image.

The Sabattier effect can be created with both black-and-white and color films and papers. Most photographers prefer to use the Sabattier effect on prints, because the opportunities for variety and experimentation are easier and quicker to attain. Working with film involves more time and expense, particularly if you aren't satisfied with your first attempt and have to start over again. The main advantage of film is that, once a satisfying result is achieved, the negative or slide can be used to make many identical prints. This is much more difficult when working with paper. However, the basic procedure is the same for both printing paper and film.

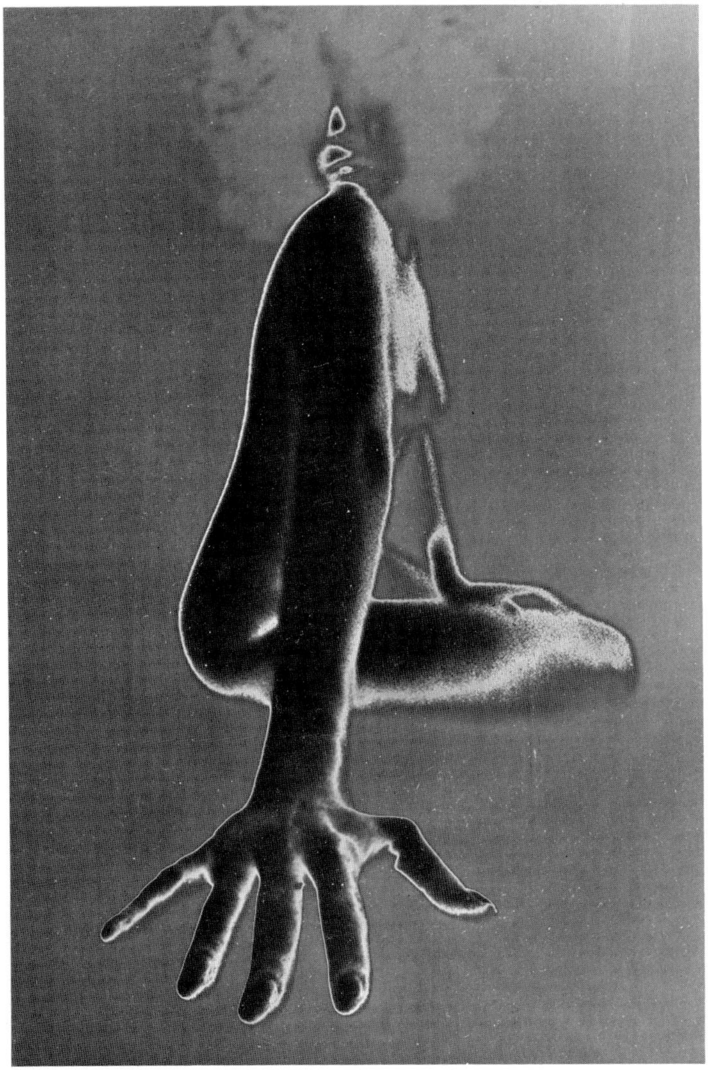

Mark Chamberlain used the Sabattier effect, commonly called solarization, to create this image.

The Sabattier Effect on Black-and-White Prints

The process for the Sabattier effect is simple and basically the same regardless of what photographic material you use. First, expose a print (or film) so that it has more contrast than usual, then develop it either completely or part-way. During development, re-expose it to a dim light. Then fix and wash it normally. Although the procedure is simple, unless you understand the following variables and how to control them, your results will be sporadic and unpredictable.

1. The initial exposure of the print (or film) determines if the resulting image will be predominately positive or negative. A longer exposure gives a more positive image; a shorter exposure produces a more negative image.

2. The amount of development before re-exposure is another variable. A fully developed image will have less reversal than an image receiving only partial development. Try re-exposing your image after it has received one-half of its normal development time. Compare the results with a print that has received more development. The print with less development will have more tone reversal, and a stronger negative image, than the more developed print.

3. Variations in the amount of re-exposure determine the density of the negative parts of the image. A strong re-exposure produces deep blacks in areas that would normally be white; less re-exposure causes a lighter tone.

4. The amount of re-development after re-exposure is another variable. As a rule, the re-development time for a print should be at least 60 seconds. The mistake most people make is giving too much re-exposure. This starts the print re-developing too fast, so we're inclined to pull the print out of the developer immediately, before it gets too dark. Since control is the key to any photographic process, by decreasing the amount of re-exposure and allowing the print adequate time to re-develop, you will alleviate problems, such as mottling which is caused by overexposure and inadequate development. A longer re-development time also produces more dramatic Mackie lines.

5. Contrast also affects your results when producing the Sabattier effect. Since the Sabattier effect tends to lessen contrast, a grade 5 or 6 black-and-white paper generally produces the best results with normal negatives. Avoid variable-contrast papers (such as Kodak's Polycontrast) when using

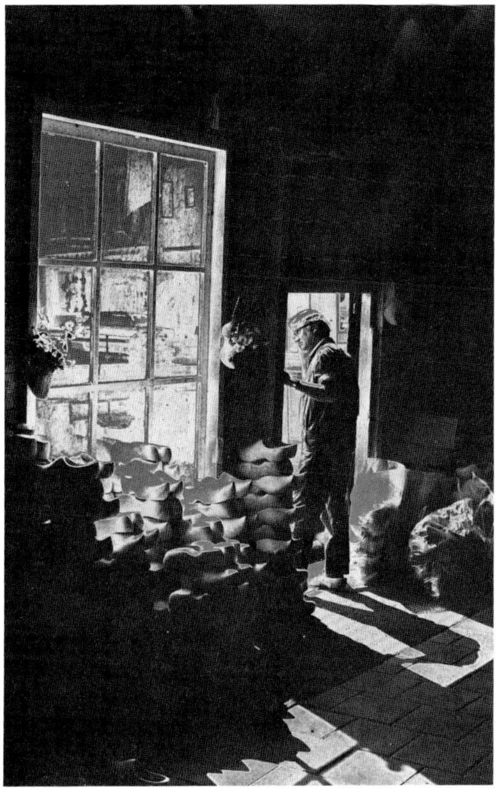

Variations in initial exposure, and re-exposure, cause different results with the Sabattier effect. This print received a long initial exposure, and a short re-exposure.

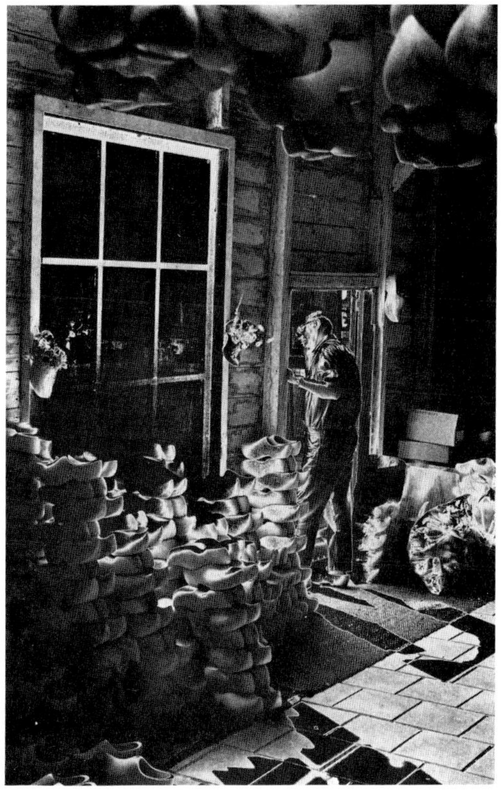

A short initial exposure, and a long re-exposure, was used for this print. The difference is quite dramatic.

the Sabattier effect. Graded papers work better.

Chemicals. You can use your regular developer at its normal dilution, or you may want to try a special developer like Solarol, which is designed for this technique. Either product will produce good results. Normally, a slightly exhausted developer (which has built-up waste deposits) produces more dramatic results than fresh developer. Solarol, which comes with excellent instructions, is easy to use and enables you to control the process in a more predictable and repeatable manner. Solarol, distributed by Kalt Corporation, can be ordered through your camera store.

Many photographers use a water bath following the developer and before the stop bath and fixer. The print can be re-exposed in the water bath, allowing it to re-develop more slowly than if it was re-exposed in the

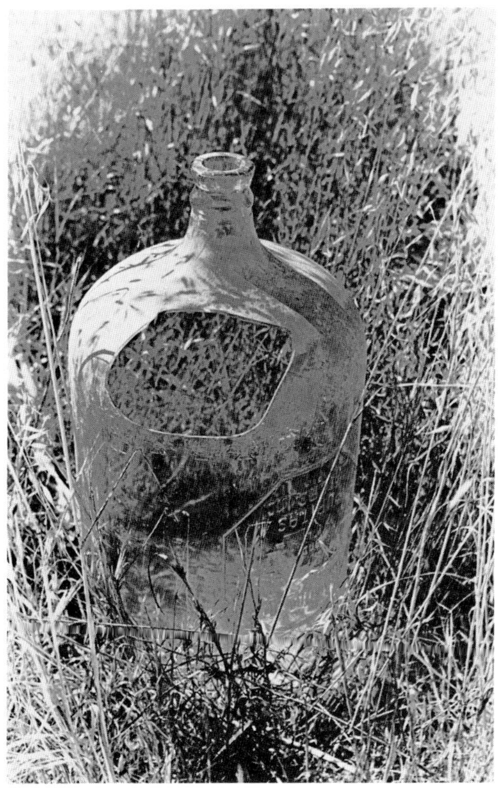

When a print is re-exposed to a very small amount of light, only a partial reversal occurs. This image was printed on high-contrast grade 6 paper. After partial development it was re-exposed with a small penlight.

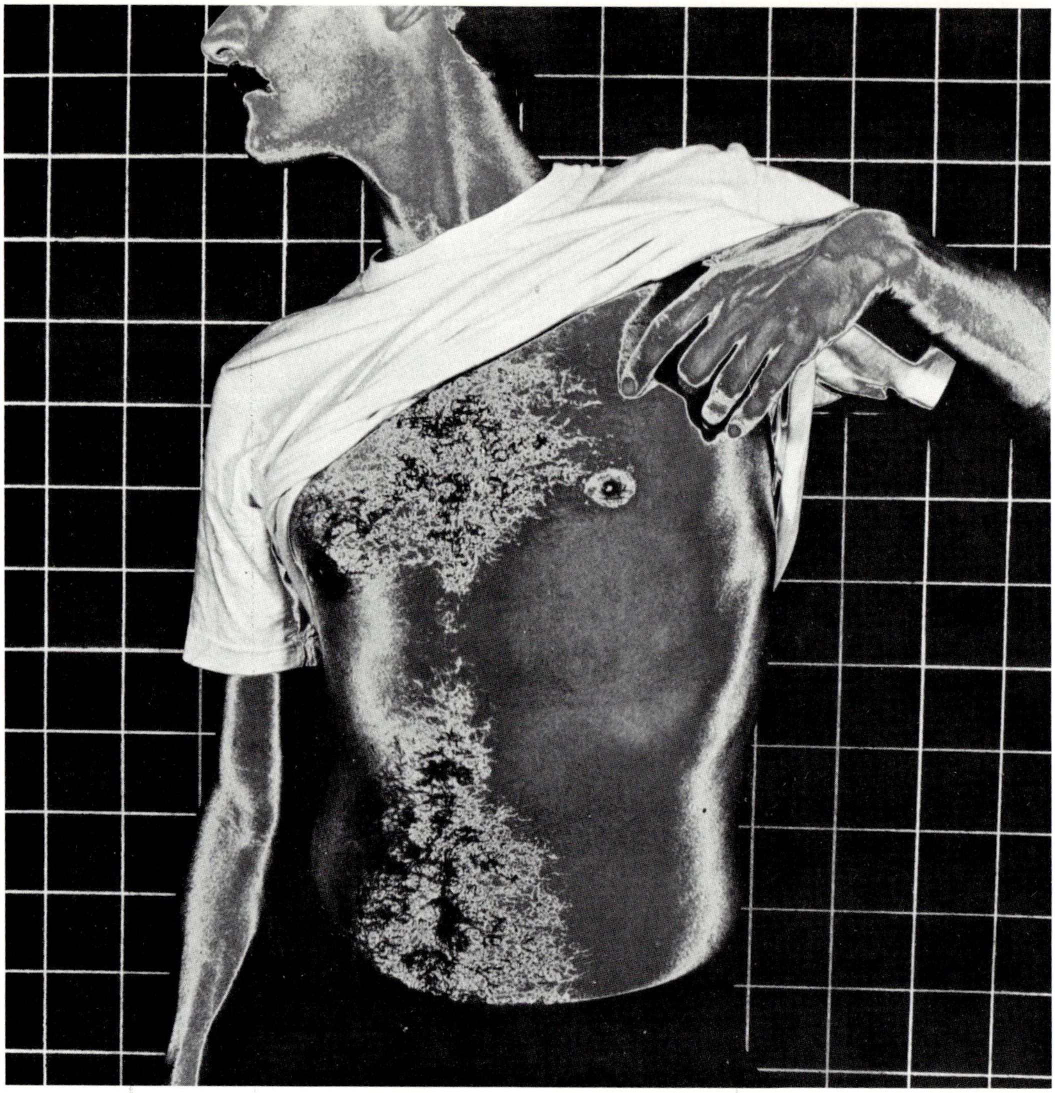

This print is from a series titled Breast Plates, *by Jeff Gates. He uses the Sabattier effect as a visual veil, to separate the photograph from reality.*

developer. After re-exposure, move the print back to the developer for the duration of the development time. Although a water bath is not always necessary, it gives you a little extra control.

Exposures. To produce the Sabattier effect on a print, you have to make two separate exposures. The initial exposure is made when you enlarge your negative onto the printing paper. The second exposure, called re-exposure, is made during (or after) development with almost any light source. The initial exposure controls the amount and density of the positive part of the image. The re-exposure determines the density of the reversed, or negative, part of the image. Re-exposure is normally done once development is one-third to one-half complete. Beginners generally just switch the overhead room light on and off for the re-exposure, but this provides very little control. A better approach is to place an ordinary 15-watt light bulb about three feet (0.9 m) above your developing tray and hook it up to a timer. This way you can control the amount of re-exposure you give the print. (With Solarol, it is suggested that you use a 40-watt bulb). Re-exposure can be varied by changing the amount of time, or by altering the distance of the light source

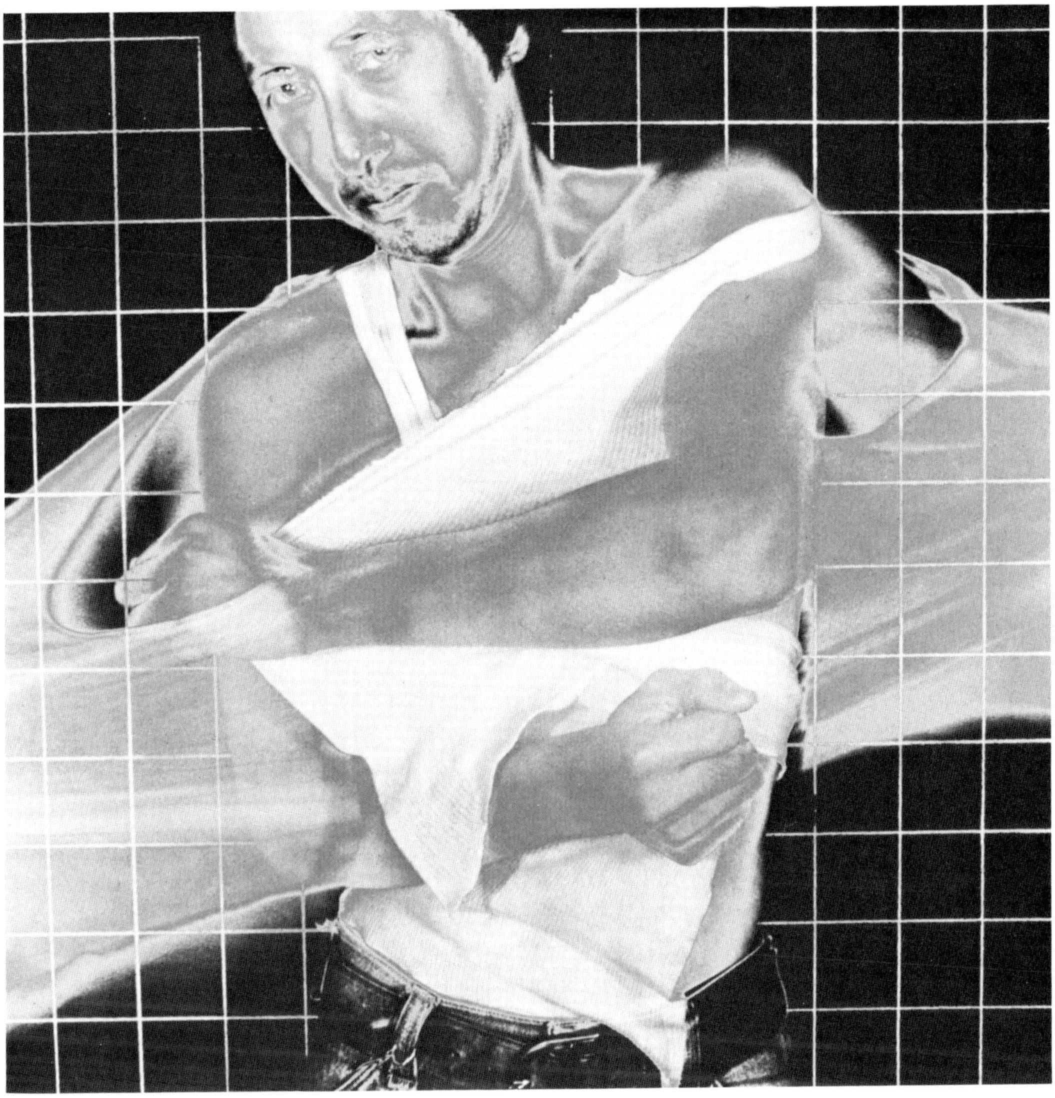

In this photograph from the same series the reversal effect is less apparent, because less re-exposure was given.

from the paper. You could also use a dimmer switch to change light intensities. The amount of re-exposure can vary from a quick flash to continuous illumination, depending on the effect you want. A short, intense re-exposure generally produces better contrast than a longer, weaker one, but longer exposure gives you better control. A normal re-exposure time is one or two seconds.

Normally, you re-expose prints while they are still in the developer; but, as mentioned, some photographers prefer to re-expose prints that are in a water bath. Others prefer to take the print out of the developer, rinse it with water, and squeegee the paper before re-exposing it. This provides extra control, but does not necessarily produce better results. After re-exposure, put the print back in the developer and let it finish developing.

Mackie Lines. When the print is re-exposed, the image's shadow areas have already developed significantly. The rest of the image still needs additional time in the developer and has light-sensitive areas ready to react to more light. Re-exposure causes these areas that haven't been fully developed to re-develop rapidly. This creates an excess of waste bromide ions that collect around the areas of density due to chemical reactions. These concentrations of the bromide ions impede development and cause the outlining that identifies the Sabattier effect. These outlines, called Mackie or bromide lines, appear between the highlight and shadow areas of the image. To enhance Mackie lines, use a higher-contrast paper, and if you re-expose the print *while still in the developer*, cease agitation 30 seconds before re-exposure so extra waste materials have time to build up.

To save time and materials, try making a Sabattier-effect double-test strip. This one was made by Gejar. It's a good idea to write the exposures for the various sections around the outside of the print.

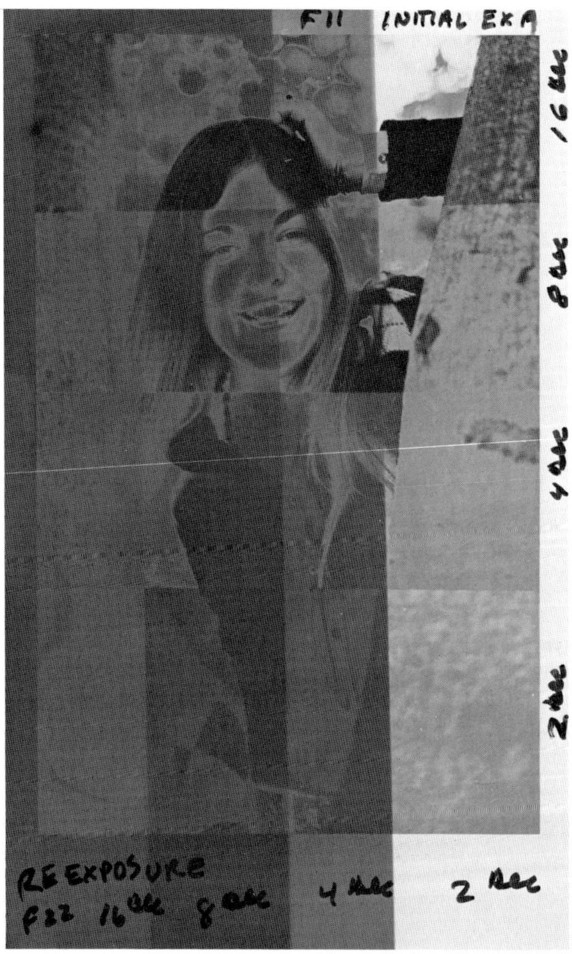

Test strips. Although you will probably develop standard procedures that simplify the Sabattier effect, a double-test-strip technique can make some of your initial decisions much easier.

First, make a test strip to determine your initial exposure: Use a whole sheet of paper and expose the entire sheet for two seconds. Then cover a narrow portion of it and make another two-second exposure. Continue the procedure, doubling the exposure each time as you progressively cover more and more of the paper. Your series of exposures will be: 2-2-4-8-16-32-64 seconds each. When the test sheet is developed, the final total exposures will be 2-4-8-16-32-64-128 seconds. Choose one of these totals to make the final print.

This is the original image by Gejar, prior to application of the Sabattier effect. It was printed on grade 4 paper, for higher contrast.

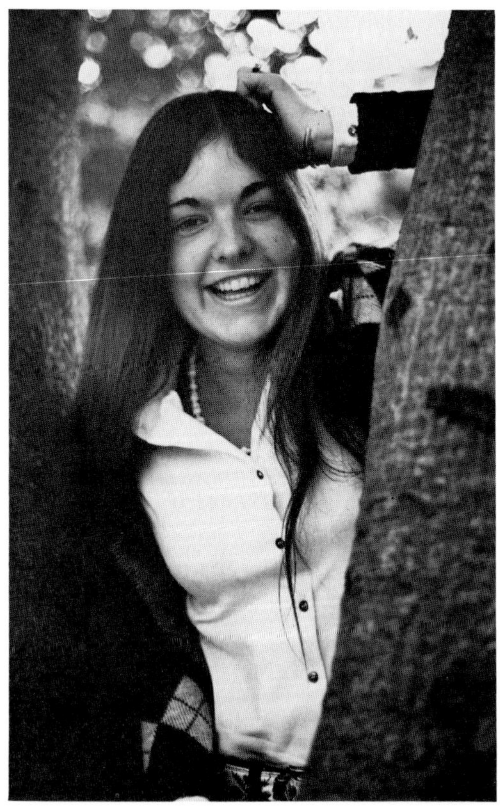

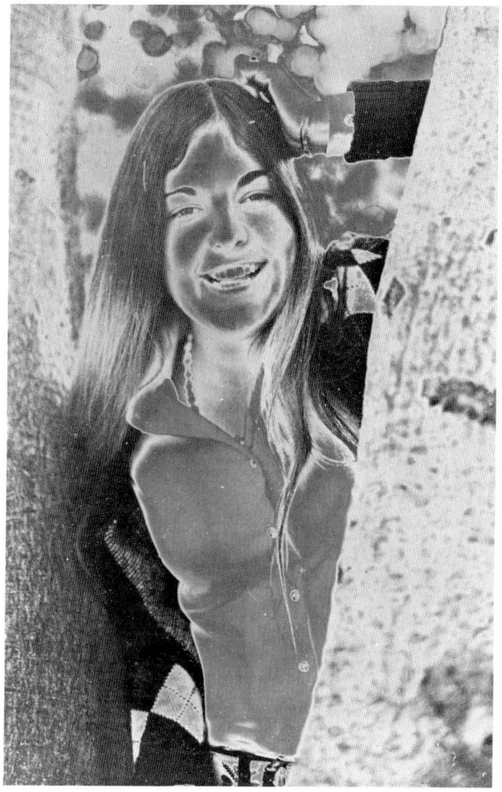

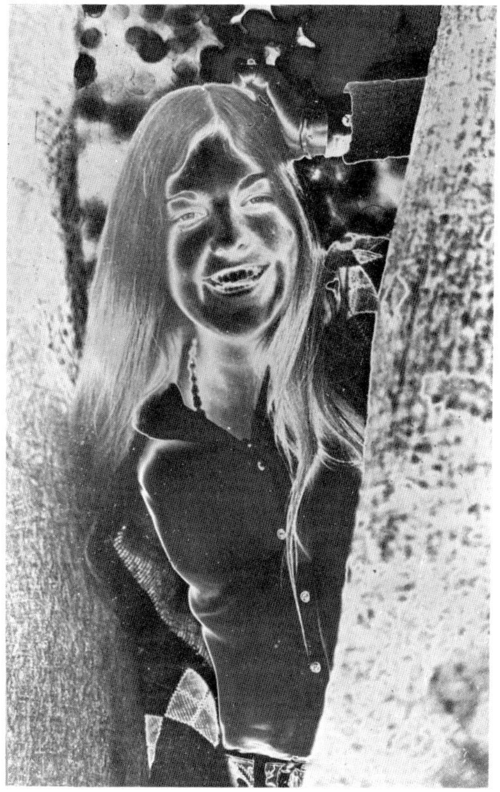

Both of these prints received an initial exposure of eight seconds at f/11. The image on the left was re-exposed to white light for four seconds at f/22. The image on the right was re-exposed at the same f-stop for twice the time, causing a greater reversal effect.

Once the test strip is exposed, process it for one-half your normal developing time. Then rinse the print in water and squeegee the surface. Now you're ready to make the re-exposure test on the same sheet of paper. Place the print under your re-exposure light and make another series of test exposures by progressively covering the paper with cardboard at right angles to the previous tests. The exposures should be 2-2-4-8 seconds each, adding up to a series of exposures totaling 2-4-8-16 seconds each. Then re-develop the print for the remainder of the developing time, and finish the processing as you normally would.

Your test print will have a wide variety of effects. The difference between a slight and a complete reversal should be readily apparent when the exposure times for both the initial exposure and the re-exposure are determined.

The Sabattier Effect on Color Prints

To achieve the Sabattier effect on color prints, use the same basic procedures given for black-and-white prints, as the same variables and principles apply. The Sabattier effect can be produced with both negative and positive color processes. Unfortunately, a positive process, such as Cibachrome or Kodak's Ektachrome 2203, will not produce the dramatic results a negative process will. With negative processes, the re-exposure to light adds density to the image, producing rich, vibrant colors. With a positive process re-exposure decreases the image density, allows for less control, and produces muted colors.

Since the advent of daylight processing tubes for color prints most people avoid tray processing. But, because you can't adequately re-expose a print while it is in a processing tube, the print must be removed from the tube for re-exposure. However, once the wet print is removed from the processing tube, it's impractical to try and put it back and tray processing thus becomes a necessity.

Many of the color processes available today can be used at room temperatures, provided you compensate by increasing the processing time. Tray processing is easier if the chemicals are at room temperature. However, if you want to maintain a higher temperature, put the trays in a hot-water bath. All of the initial processing steps must be done with a number 10 or number 13 dark-amber safelight filter, or in complete darkness.

Producing the Sabattier Effect on Color Prints. First expose the color print under the enlarger as you normally would, then develop it. Initial development should be about one-half the normal time. Develop the print in either a processing tube or a tray. If using a tray, remove the print from the developer after adequate development and place it in a shallow tray of water. If using a tube, give the print a 30-second rinse with water immediately after pouring out the developer. Then, with only the light from your color safelight, remove the print from the processing tube and place it in a tray of water. Let the print settle to the bottom of the tray before re-exposing it to light. The light source can be anything from a 10-watt to a 75-watt light bulb, and should be located about three feet (0.9 m) above the tray.

With a 10-watt bulb, re-expose the print for one second, keeping it as still as possible during re-exposure. The shadow areas of the print have already completely developed, but the highlights and middle values will still be affected by the additional light.

After the re-exposure, remove the print from the water, and without draining gently submerge it in a tray of developer. *Without agitation*, let the print redevelop for one minute. During redevelopment, the highlights and middle values will change rapidly and Mackie lines will form.

When redevelopment is complete, place the print in another water bath for one minute. This water bath is optional, but it reduces the chances of streaking and prolongs the life of the bleach. Next, transfer the print to a tray of bleach-fix, and bleach the print with agitation for the recommended time. Once the bleaching is finished, you can turn on the lights and examine your results before the final wash.

If a negative-positive process print is too dark, it means it was given too much re-exposure. With a positive-to-positive process print it means that not enough re-exposure was used. A mottled or uneven appearance means your processing procedure needs refining. Dry the print before evaluating the color. (Most color prints have an unnatural color cast before they dry. Kodak Ektacolor 74 prints have a blue veiling, while Cibachromes have a reddish cast.)

Determining Colors. The colors produced by the Sabattier effect depend on a number of variables. When enlarging the print initially you tend to emphasize the reality of the photograph. Later, through the application of the Sabattier effect, additional color is added while the image is partially reversed, creating a dichotomy between reality and illusion.

To vary the color balance of the image prior to the Sabattier re-exposure, try altering the filtration of the initial exposure. This varies the color of the middle values and shadow areas. Then, during re-exposure, the color of the highlights will be changed.

With negative-print materials, re-exposure to white light will produce a blue-gray tone. Re-exposure with another color of light produces that color's complement. Thus re-exposure with a red light will result in a cyan cast to the highlights of the print. To control color, try using colored gels over your light source. Remember, when working with color-negative materials, whatever the filter color is, its complement will result in the print.

With positive-print materials, the color filter you use is the color you get in the print. That's because you're using a direct-positive process. Also, the more exposure you give, the lighter the print will get. To avoid washed-out prints, it's best to use a print that was underexposed initially, so that re-exposure won't lighten it too much.

Partial Sabattier Effects

Once you've grown accustomed to working with the Sabattier effect, you may want to use the effect only in specific parts of a print. Simply mask off the part of the print you don't want affected during re-exposure.

The simplest way to do this is to block the light with your hand or a piece of cardboard. You can also re-expose the print by using a penlight flashlight with a snoot attached. (To make a snoot, wrap black construction paper around the end of the penlight.) Using this tool, you can control the light and re-expose select parts of the print.

A more involved procedure is to make a mask. This mask is placed on top of the print and blocks the light from affecting areas of the print you wish to remain normal. This mask can be made with film or print paper, but paper is easier.

To make a mask:

1. Make a normal print from the negative. Once processed, determine what parts of the image you wish to mask.

Tony De Fazio took the photograph on the left for a furniture ad, but the straight print lacked the drama he wanted. The final print below is a result of a collaboration between De Fazio and Mark Chamberlain. A penlight was used to subtly apply the Sabattier effect to part of the print and darken the sky. The moon was created by placing a circular object on the paper during the re-exposure.

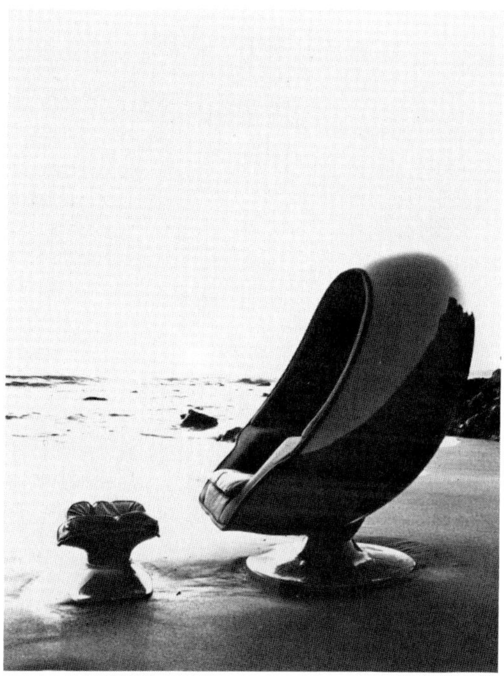

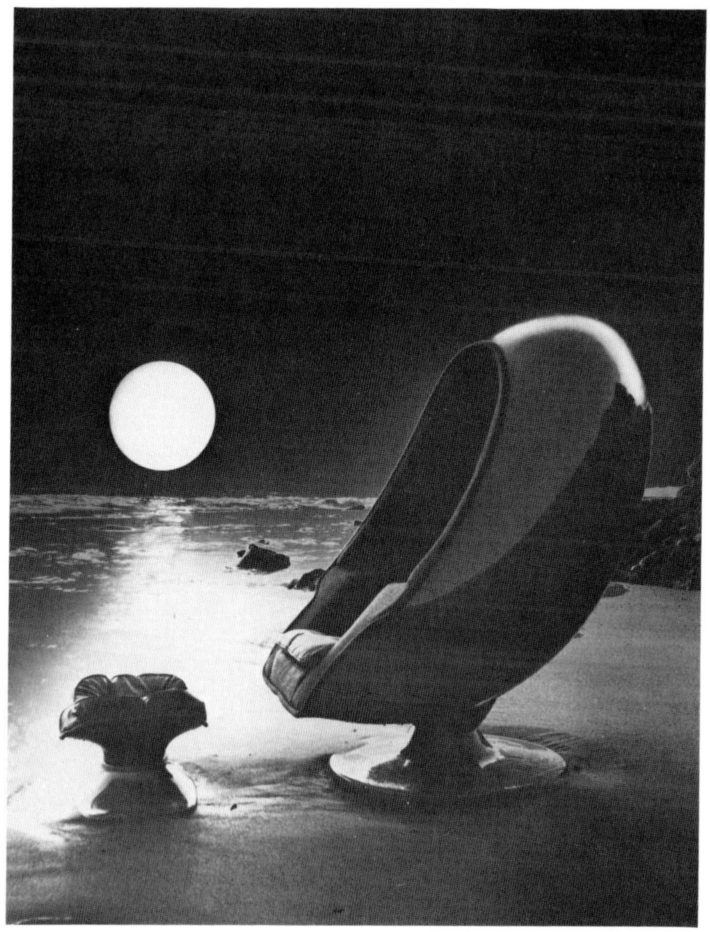

2. Make another identical print. After it has been developed, rinse the print with water and squeegee the surface.

3. Using a penlight equipped with a snoot, carefully burn in the parts of the print which will serve as a mask. With a little practice, you will learn to blacken the mask areas with a minimal effect on the surrounding parts of the picture.

4. Redevelop the print until the re-exposed portion turns black and proceed with normal processing.

To use the mask:

1. Expose another identical print and process it in the developer.

2. Once developed, rinse the print in water and lay it on a flat surface emulsion side up.

3. Then put the mask print, emulsion up, on top of the second print. Squeegee them together. Since the second print is still wet, the two will stick together.

4. Turn on the overhead light and re-expose the second print directly through the mask print. The mask print prevents light from re-exposing the areas of the print you wanted masked, while allowing the rest of the image to achieve the Sabattier effect.

5. Redevelop the print, and continue the final steps of processing.

The Sabattier Effect on Films

You can also use the Sabattier process on both color and black-and-white films. The technique and variables are basically the same as for prints. After processing, you can use the film to produce as many identical prints as you want. This alone is a great advantage, since it is hard to reproduce the same effect twice in a print unless it is copied.

Chuck Nicholson makes use of the Sabattier effect to alter the visual effect of his photographs within photographs. This image on the left is titled Franz Kline, *and the one on the right is* Facade. *Small prints are arranged and rephotographed. That image is then printed and delicately re-exposed. The borders of the print are scored with a knife or razor and the paper backing torn away. The print is then mounted on a piece of exposed (black) and processed photographic paper.*

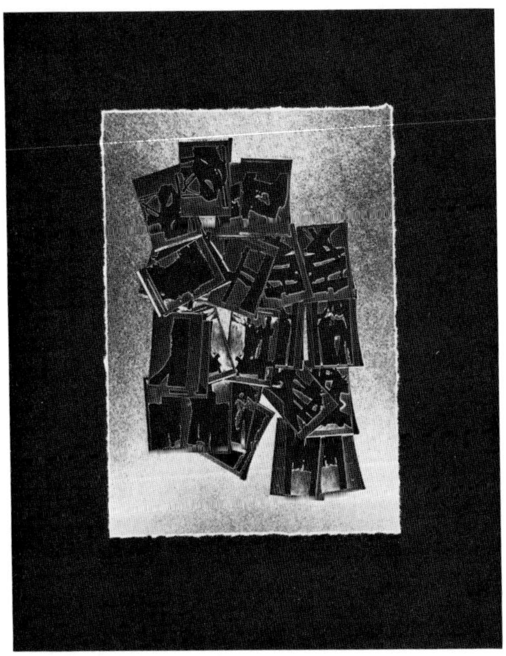

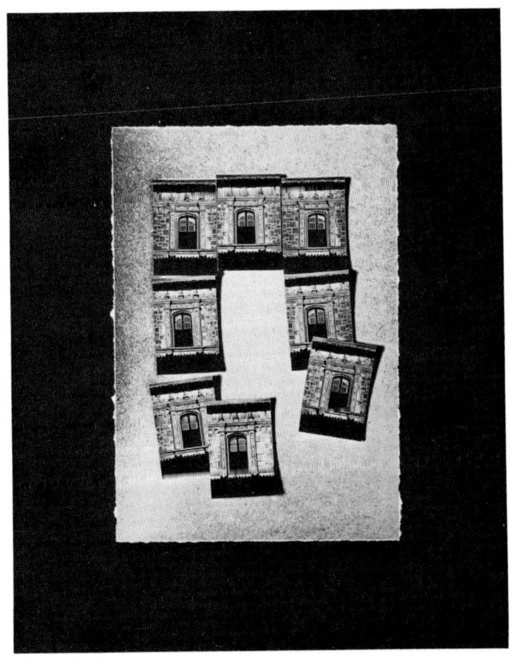

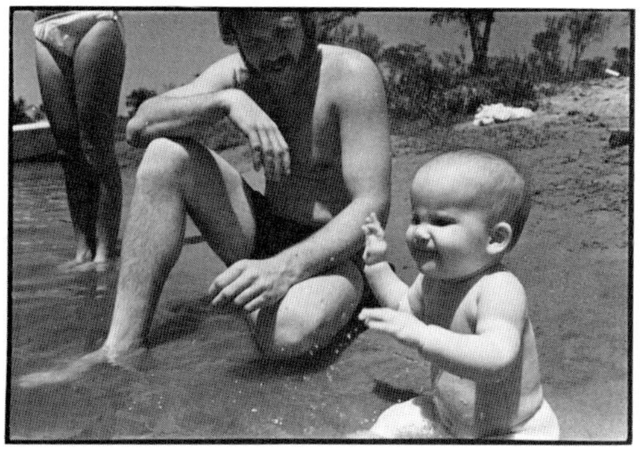

To apply the Sabattier effect to part of a print the re-exposure light must be carefully controlled. One way to control the light is to make a mask to protect the part of the print you want to remain normal.

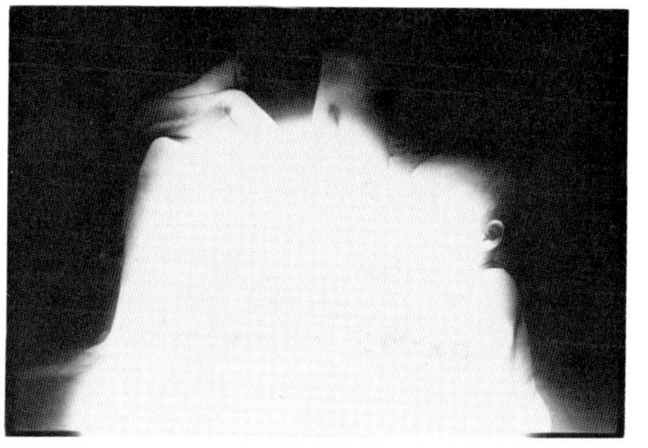

'This mask was made by dodging the center area of the print and burning-in the rest to black.

The final print was first exposed normally. Halfway through development the print was removed from the developer, and the mask placed on top of the print. They were squeegeed together and exposed to light. Then the print was developed for the remaining time. The mask protected part of the print, while the rest was affected.

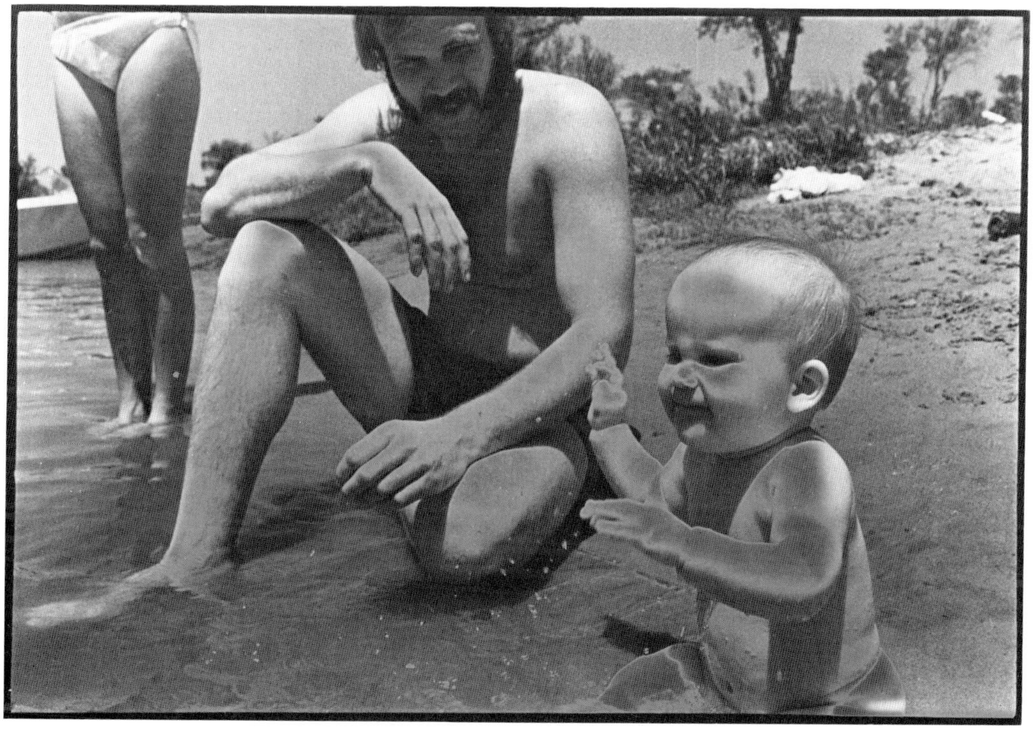

One word of caution. If possible, use duplicate negatives and transparencies, not original film. Then if the results of the Sabattier effect aren't what you wish, all you have lost is a duplicate that can be replaced by making another copy from the original. You may have to go to a custom lab to get the duplicates exposed if you're not set up to do it yourself. If you do decide to use a custom lab, make it clear you only want the film exposed, and that you will process it.

Duo-Tone Sabattier Effects

The duo-tone Sabattier effect, commonly called duo-tone solarization, is a technique many photographic artists use with black-and-white prints to add color and alter their reality. Like any Sabattier-related process, the technique can be partially controlled but maintains an element of magic that adds to its fascination and makes each print slightly different. Due to a combination of chemical reactions, vibrant colors can be added to black-and-white prints. Gold, brown, orange, and green are the most common tints produced by this process, but occasionally subtle pinks and blues can be produced.

Have you ever looked in your darkroom trash can and found a throwaway print that's turned brownish orange? This happens quite frequently in school darkrooms where a lot of people are working. Reject prints aren't allowed to fix long enough before the light is turned on and they are thrown away. While in the trash can, a print reacts to the light and the combination of chemicals it comes in contact with cause it to change color. This is basically what happens with the duo-tone process. A print is processed in normal developer, then raced through an acetic acid stop bath, into a weak fixer for a moment, and is then exposed to light. The developer is still working because the stop bath and fixer didn't get a chance to do their job properly. Consequently, the developer, acid stop bath, and fixer are all intermixed on the surface of the print, and when the print is exposed to light, an unusual chemical reaction takes place and produces the coloring.

Sounds simple, and it is. You will need four trays and the following chemicals: full-strength, undiluted print developer; acetic-acid stop bath; diluted fixer or sodium thiosulfate; and full-strength fixer. For the re-exposure, use a 150-watt floodlight, or a GE DXB photoflood bulb.

Here's the process:

1. Expose your negative onto high-contrast paper. Kodabromide grade 5 double-weight is excellent for this, but you can use almost any high-contrast photographic paper. Each type of paper and developer reacts differently and produces varying colors. Kodabromide grade 5 produces pinks, greens, and browns when developed in Dektol, while forest-green and rose hues result with Ethol developer.
2. After the exposure, place the print in the full-strength developer. Variations in the strength of the developer and the amount of developing time produce different results. Normally, the paper should be developed for as long as it takes for the image to appear.
3. Transfer the print, without draining, into the stop bath for one second. Too much time in the stop bath will stop the developer's action, so remove the print quickly. The stop bath should be a 28-percent acetic-acid solution mixed one part solution to 32 parts water.
4. Without draining, immerse the print for one second in a bath of one part fixer and six parts water. (A sodium-thiosulfate solution can also be used in place of the diluted fixer.)
5. Lay the print on a flat surface and expose it to the floodlight for 15 to 30 seconds. If you are using a 150-watt light it should be 1 to 3 feet (30 to 91 cm) from the print, while the GE DXB photoflood should be 6 feet away. The print can be squeegeed, or the chemicals can be left on the

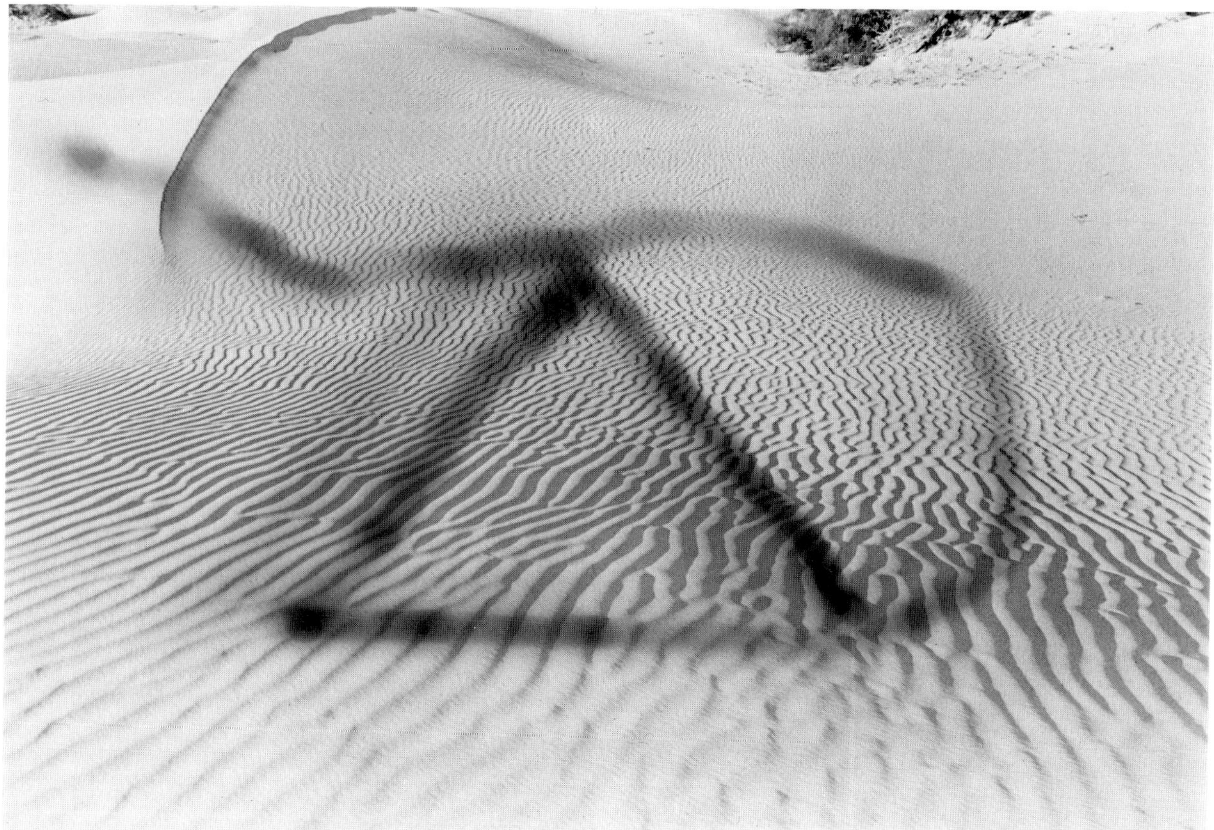

This photograph, from the Pyramid Series *by P.W. Derby, was made by drawing with light.*

surface and the print tilted to create a running, flowing effect. The light acts as a catalyst and exposes the partially stopped and fixed print while the developer continues to react. This chemical reaction produces the color.

6. Fix, wash, and dry the print normally.

Variations can be produced by using different papers, and by altering the strength of the developer, the development time, the type of developer, and the amount of re-exposure. Success and control come with practice and experimentation. The basic process is simple, but being able to apply it takes some effort. However, if you're willing to spend a few hours in the darkroom, I guarantee you will be fascinated by this process.

Drawing with Light

Photographers use light in many ways, but seldom do they use it to draw with as they would a pencil or paintbrush. But a small light source, such as a penlight flashlight, can be used to draw directly onto photographic paper.

This technique is an alternative method of burning-in. Parts of a print you want to go pure black can be quickly and selectively burned-in by using an additional light source. With color materials, colors can be added or altered at will by taping color filters over the light. This can also be used to selectively get the Sabattier effect on areas of a print, while leaving the rest of it normal. You can also write words and titles, or just draw objects and abstract designs on the print.

You'll need a small, weak light source that you can control as you draw. A penlight flashlight is the most accessible light source, but it may well be too bright and spread the light in too wide a pattern. To dim the light, try putting several layers of masking tape over it. Experiment to find out how much you need to better control the light. Next, make a snoot to cut down the spread of the light. If you plan to do a fine drawing or write words, the snoot must have a very small opening that really concentrates the light.

A snoot can be made by taping black paper so it extends several inches beyond the end of the penlight. This forces the light to travel in a straight line. You can vary the size of the snoot opening so either a broad or very thin beam of light projects on the photographic paper. With practice, you should be able to draw whatever you desire, perhaps not with the same finesse that a pencil or paintbrush provides; but the results will be definitely unique and photographic.

Selective Burning

Have you ever burned-in a print and then realized that you forgot to make the initial exposure? If you developed the print before realizing your mistake, you might have

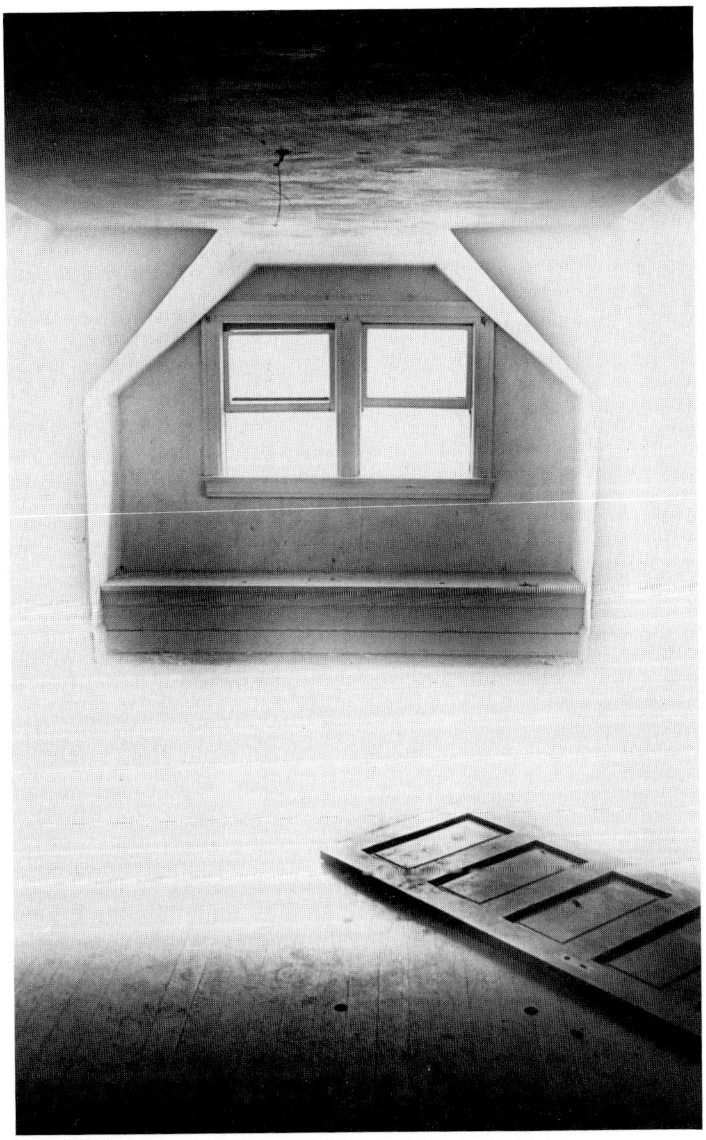

Selective burning is a technique that can be employed to abstract an image, or isolate objects within the confines of the print paper. The print on the left was made by exposing select areas of the image through a small hole in a piece of cardboard. The unmanipulated photograph is shown below.

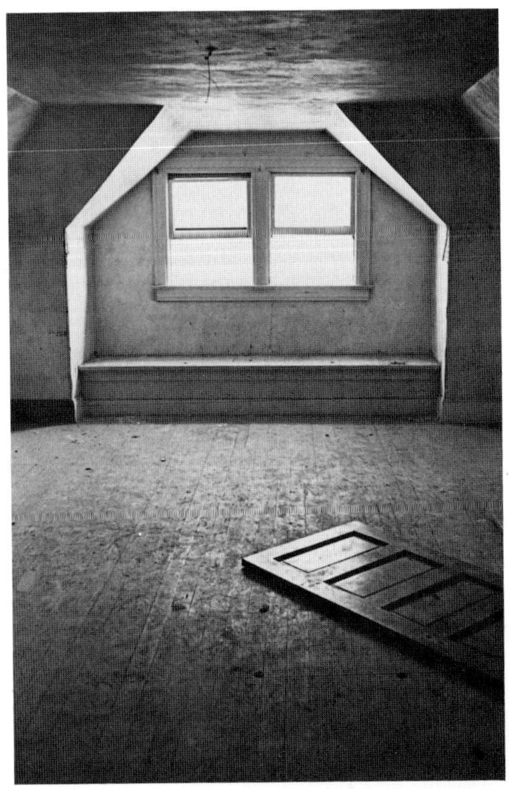

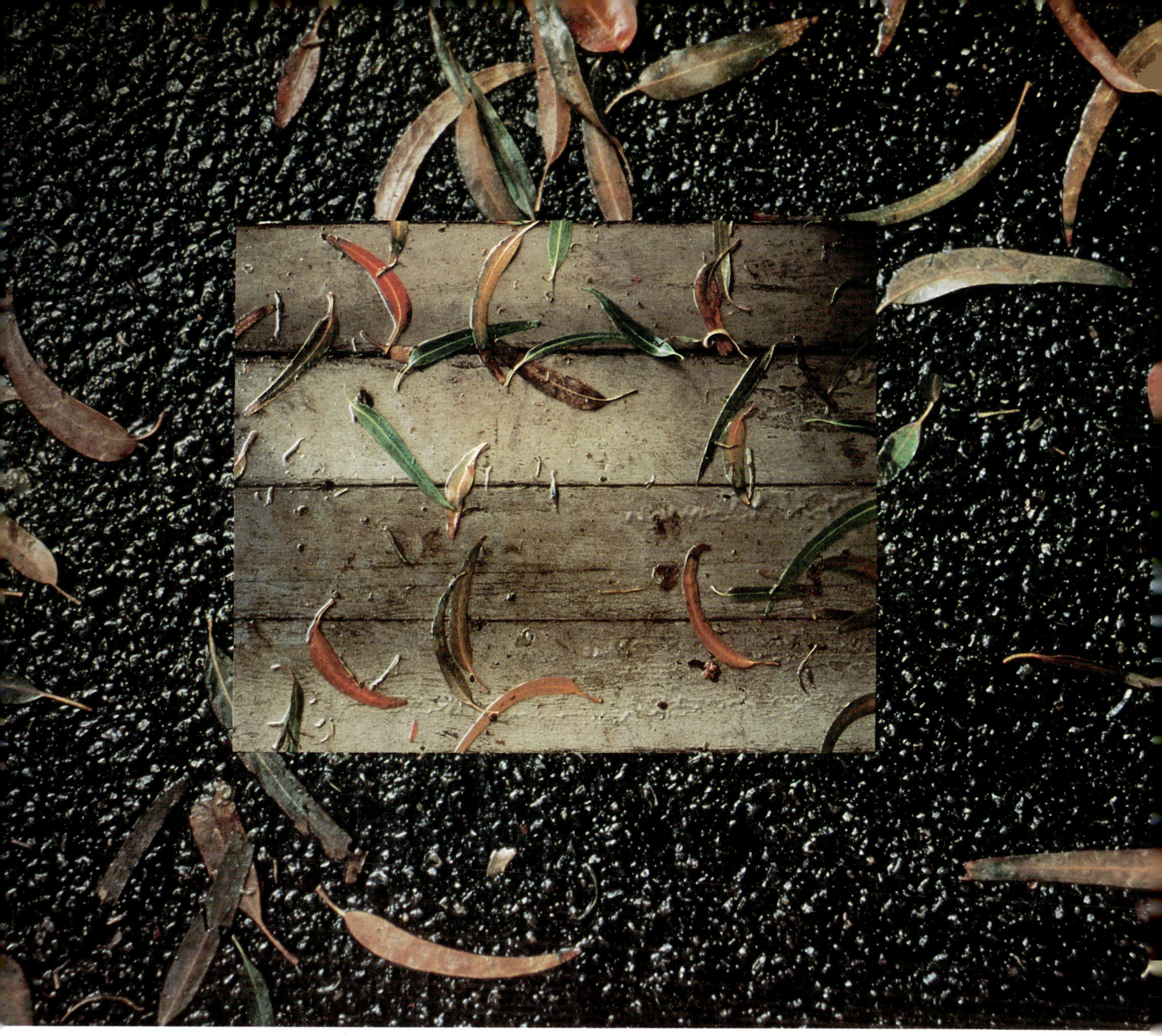

The photograph above by the author, entitled Details—Leaf Series #1437, *is actually from two transparencies printed separately onto one sheet of color-printing paper. A cardboard mask shielded the area used for the second transparency while the first was being printed, and vice versa.*

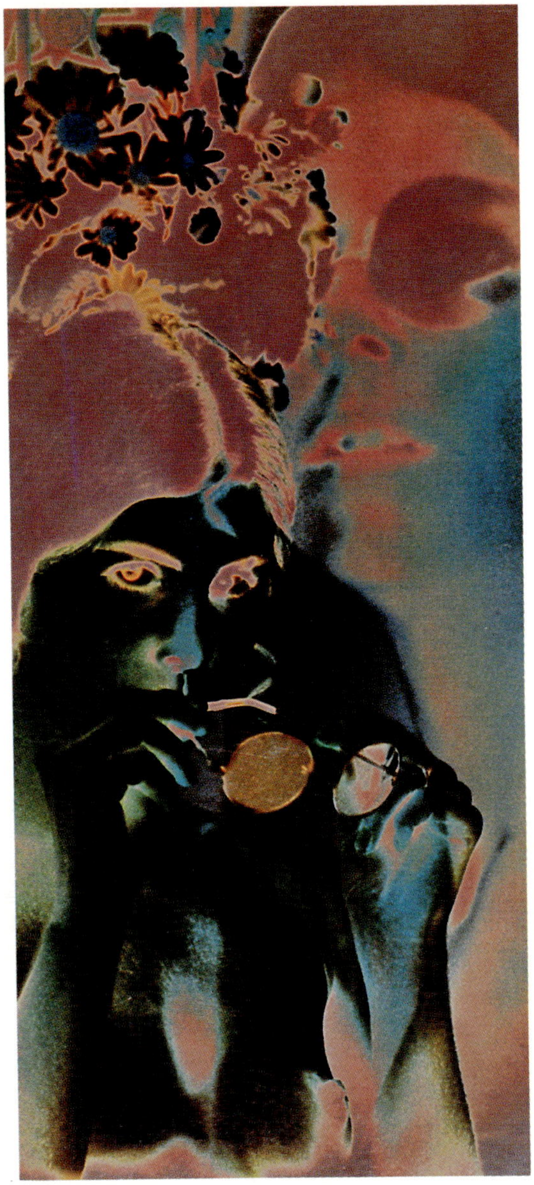

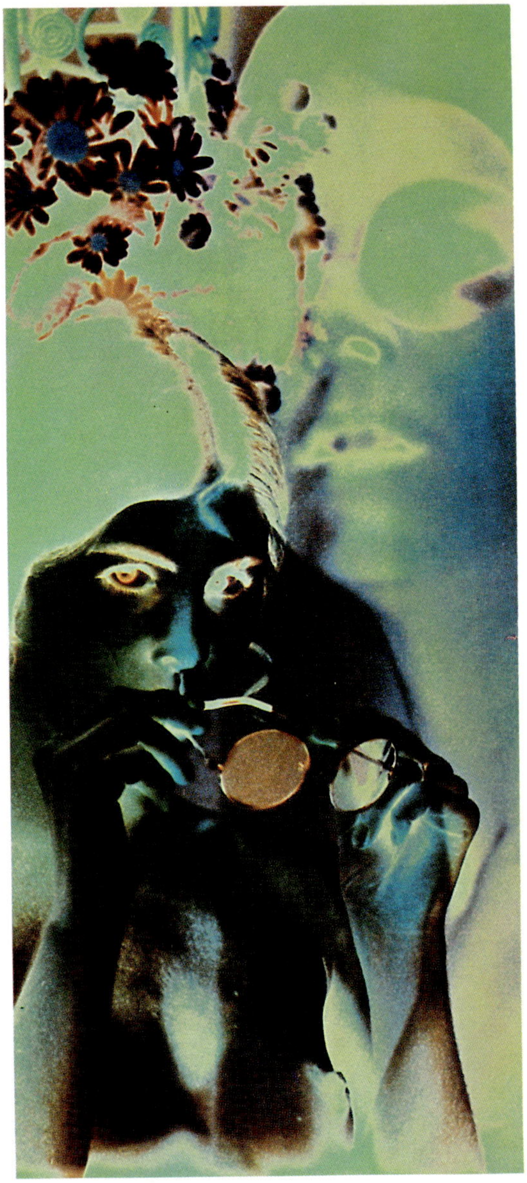

These negative images were produced by sandwiching slides and printing them together onto color-negative paper. The exposed printing paper was then re-exposed to light during development to add the Sabattier effect. The reddish color of the image on the left was the result of re-exposure to green and blue light, while the green cast of the image on the right was produced by re-exposure to red and blue light.

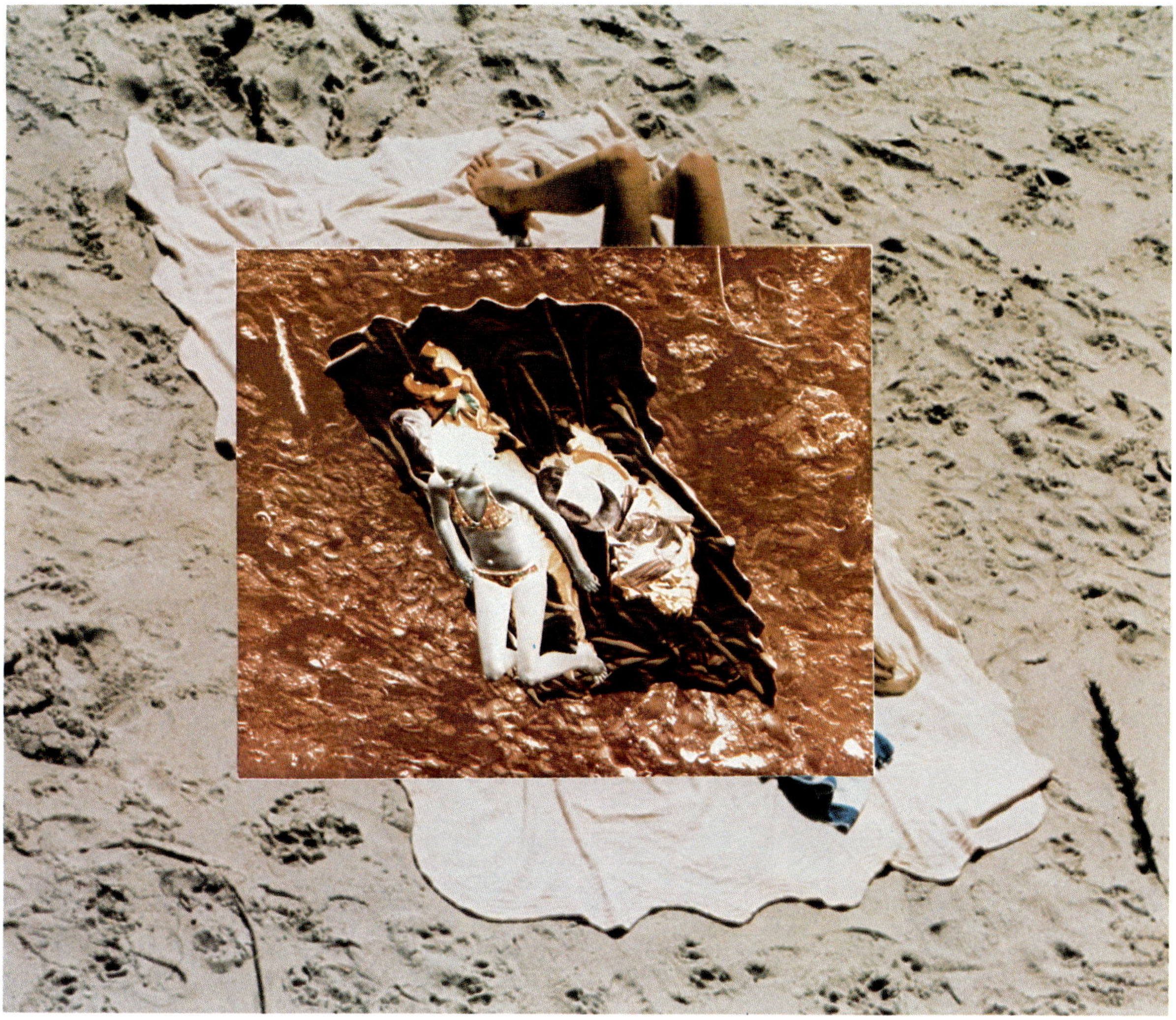

The image above is a double print of the same original photograph in negative and positive versions. The area used for the central, negative image was protected from exposure by a cardboard mask as the larger, positive image was printed. Another mask protected the positive image while the negative one was exposed.

The color photogram on the right was made with the rusted bottom of a tin can and part of a small plant. The red color was produced by separate exposures of the paper through green and blue filters. The blue color, and the outline, were the result of the Sabattier effect.

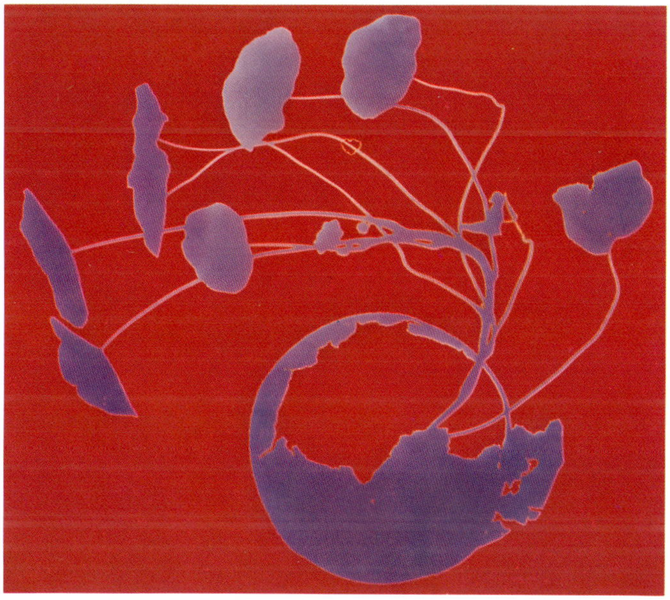

The photograph below looks like a straight photograph, but is made from two separate transparencies both shot from an unusual angle and then printed on the same piece of paper.

The image on top of the facing page is an example of hand coloring directly on a color slide prior to printing it. Here, a black felt tip pen was used to eliminate the background and isolate the objects.

The image on the bottom of the facing page, Triad, *is actually three separate images printed onto the same sheet of paper. The pelvis X-ray was contact printed, and the deformed carrot and artificial trees are enlarged 35 mm transparencies. A drawing was used as a guide to the positioning and enlargement of the images.*

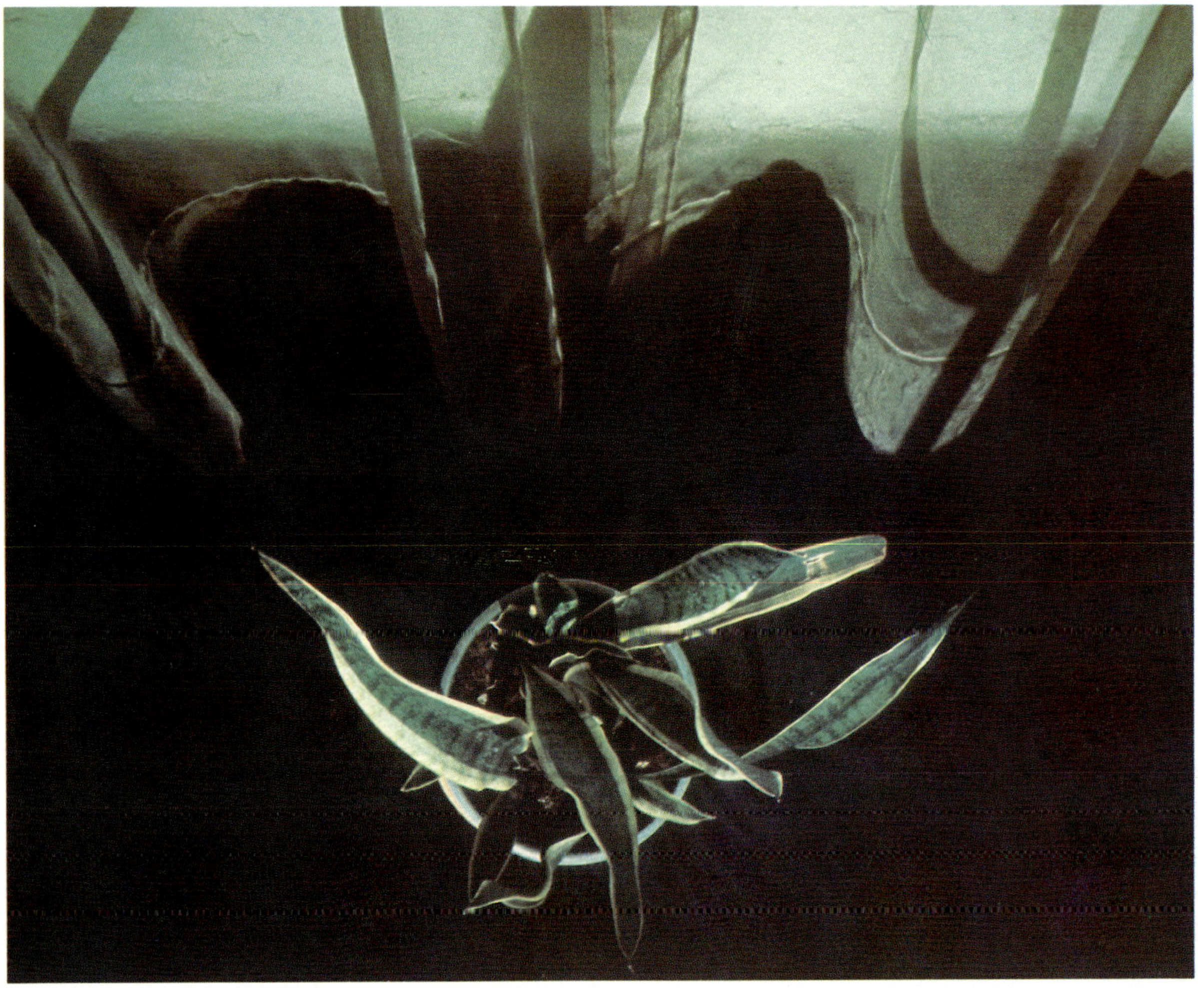

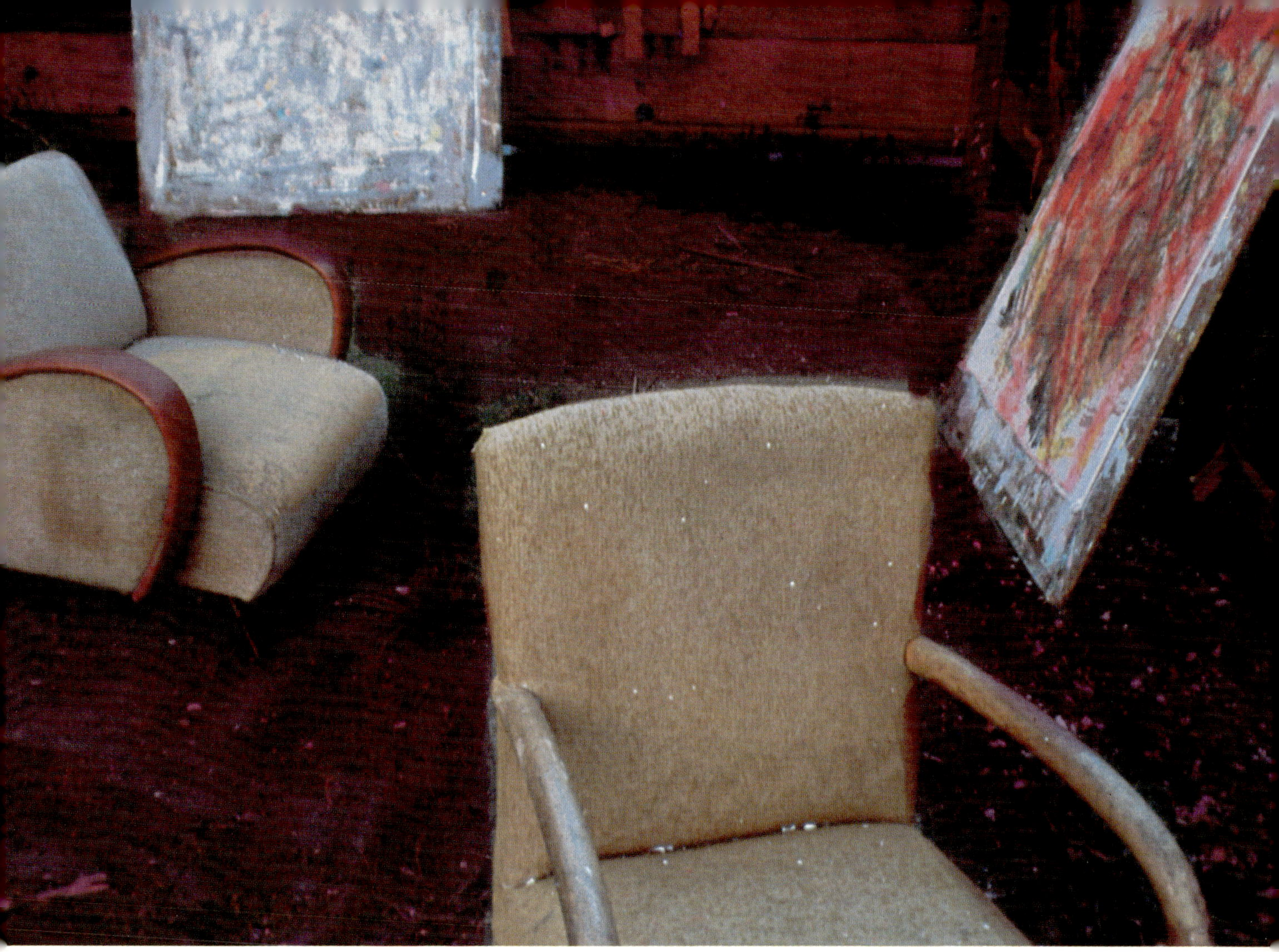

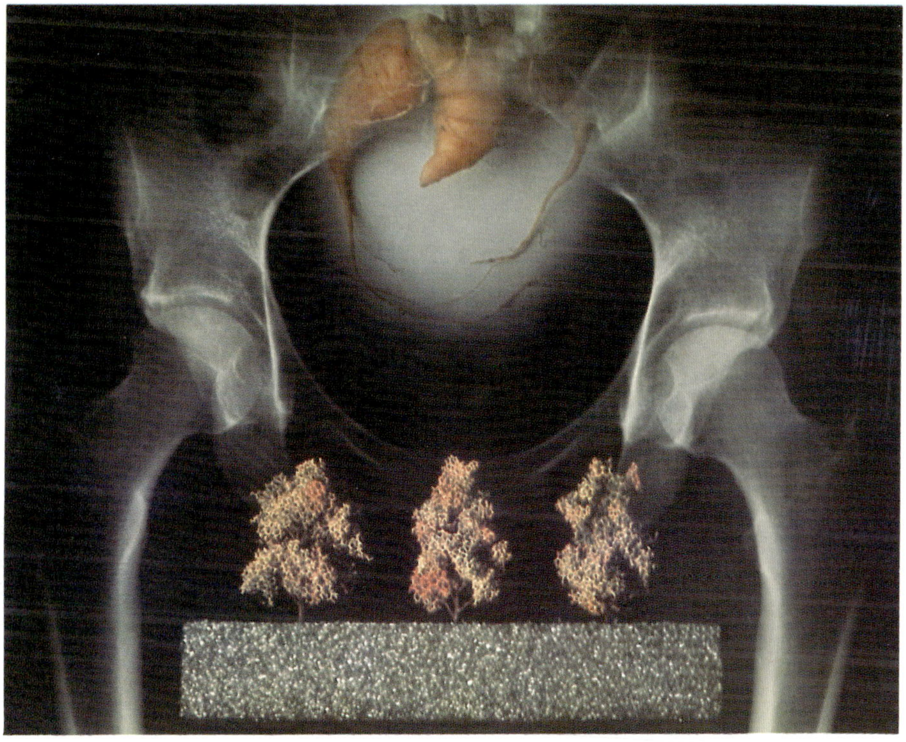

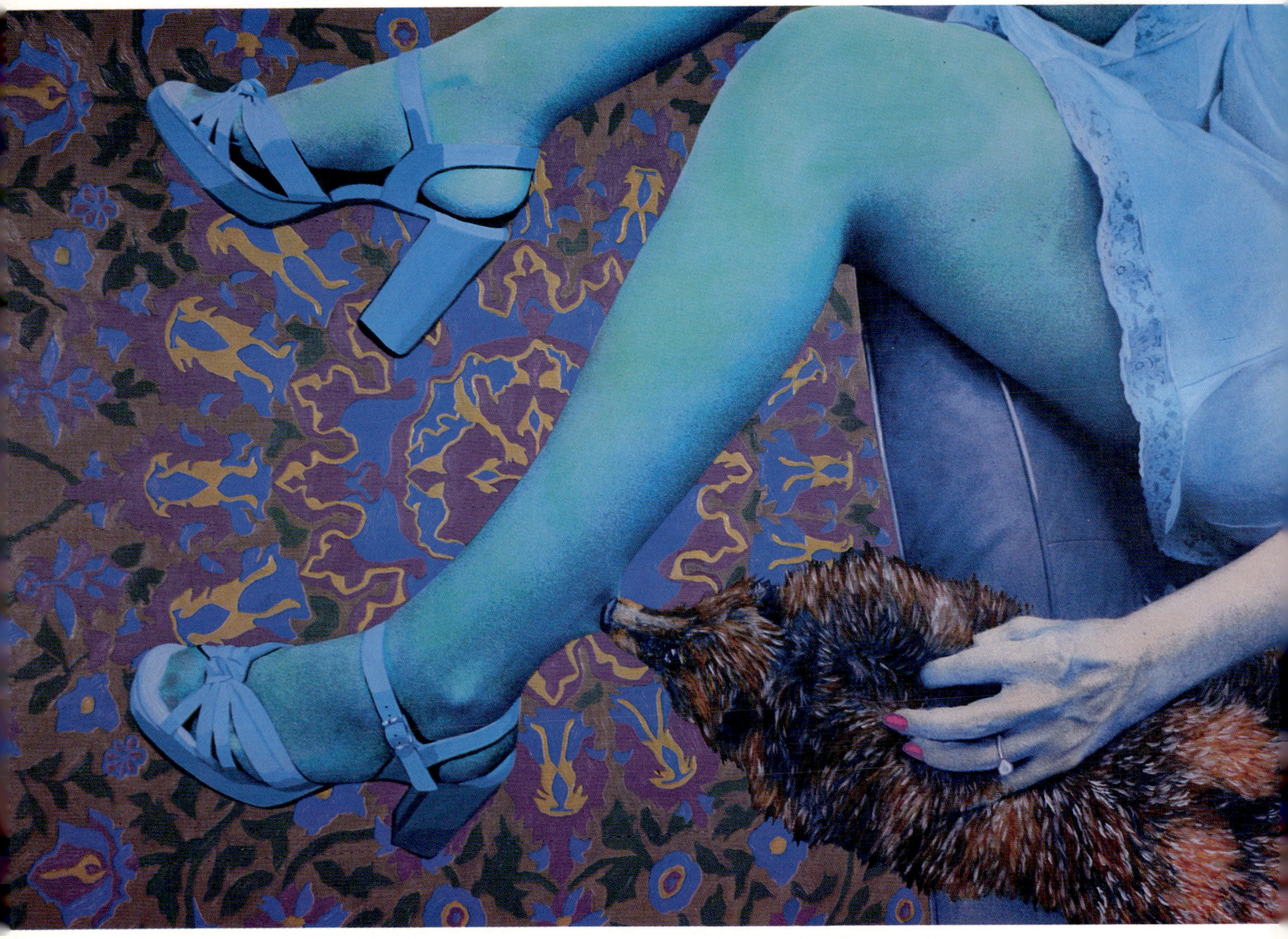

Karen Traux spends days coloring her photographs by hand. The image above, from the Painted Women *series, began as a black-and-white print. It was toned in blue toner and then painted with both transparent and opaque oil paint.*

The photograph on the facing page by the author was originally shot on infrared transparency film. The slide was then printed onto negative color-print paper which was re-exposed to white light during development, causing yellow outlines and a brownish color.

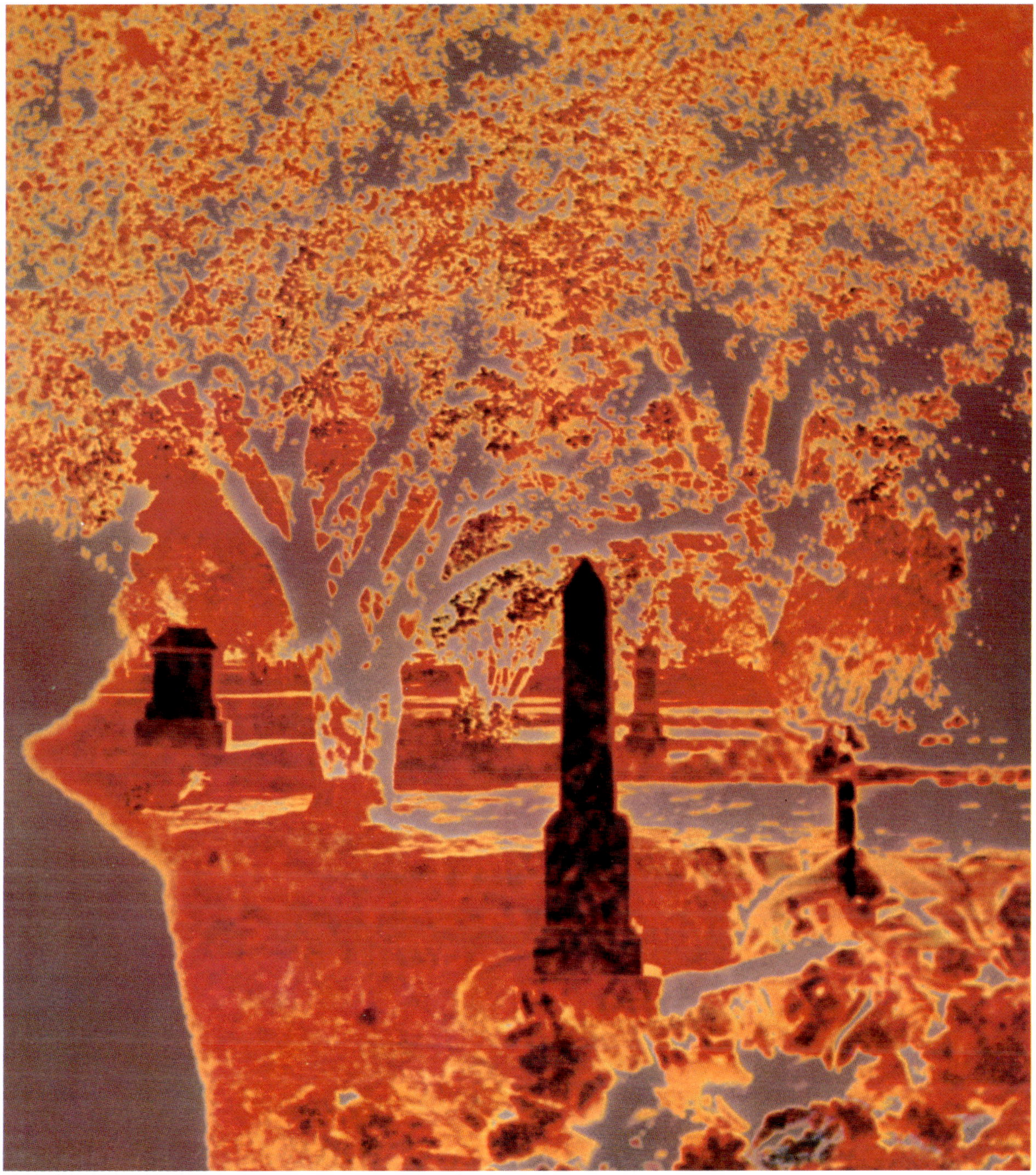

The color posterization by Robert Routh below, shows some of the interesting tonal effects, color variations and image alterations possible through posterization.

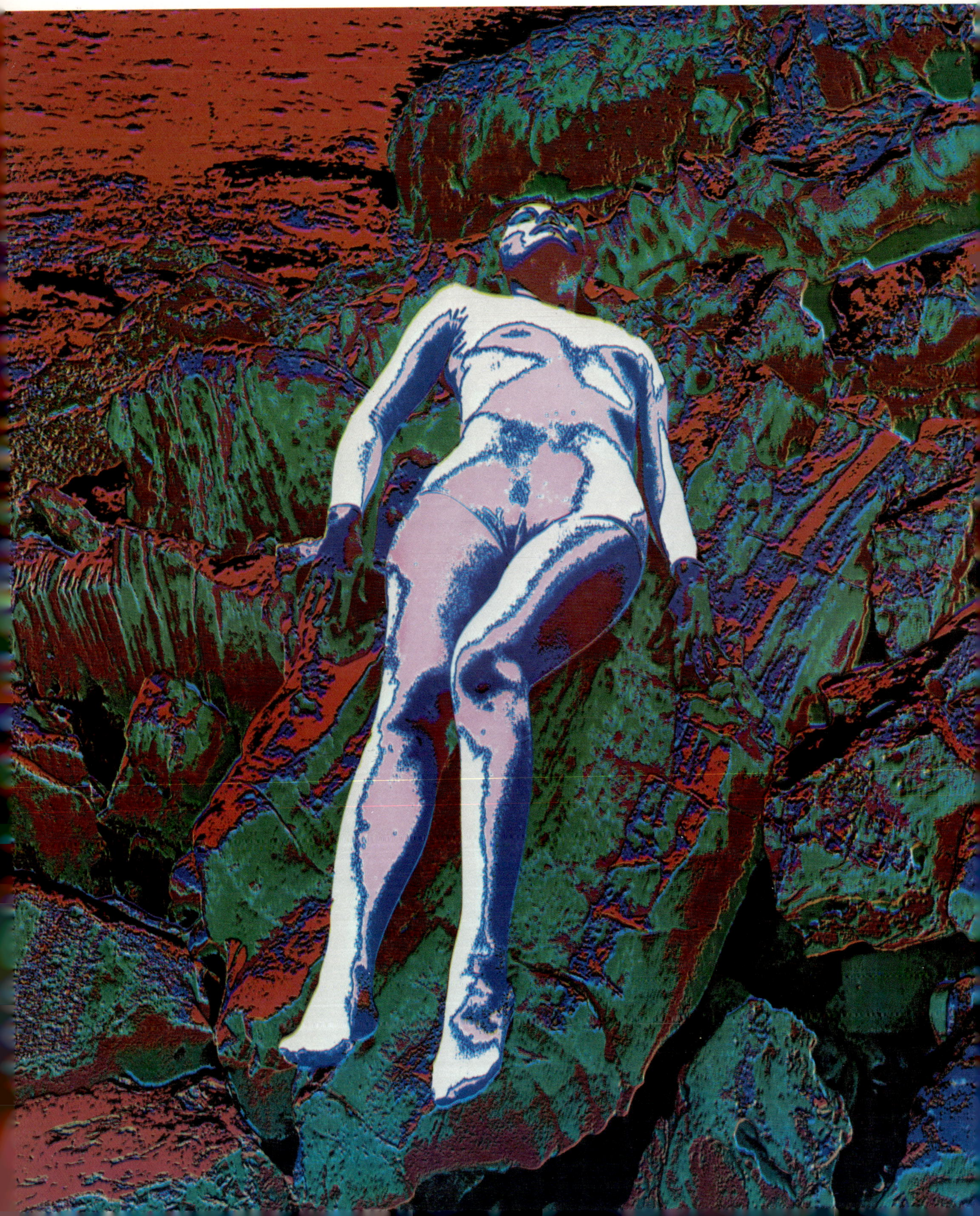

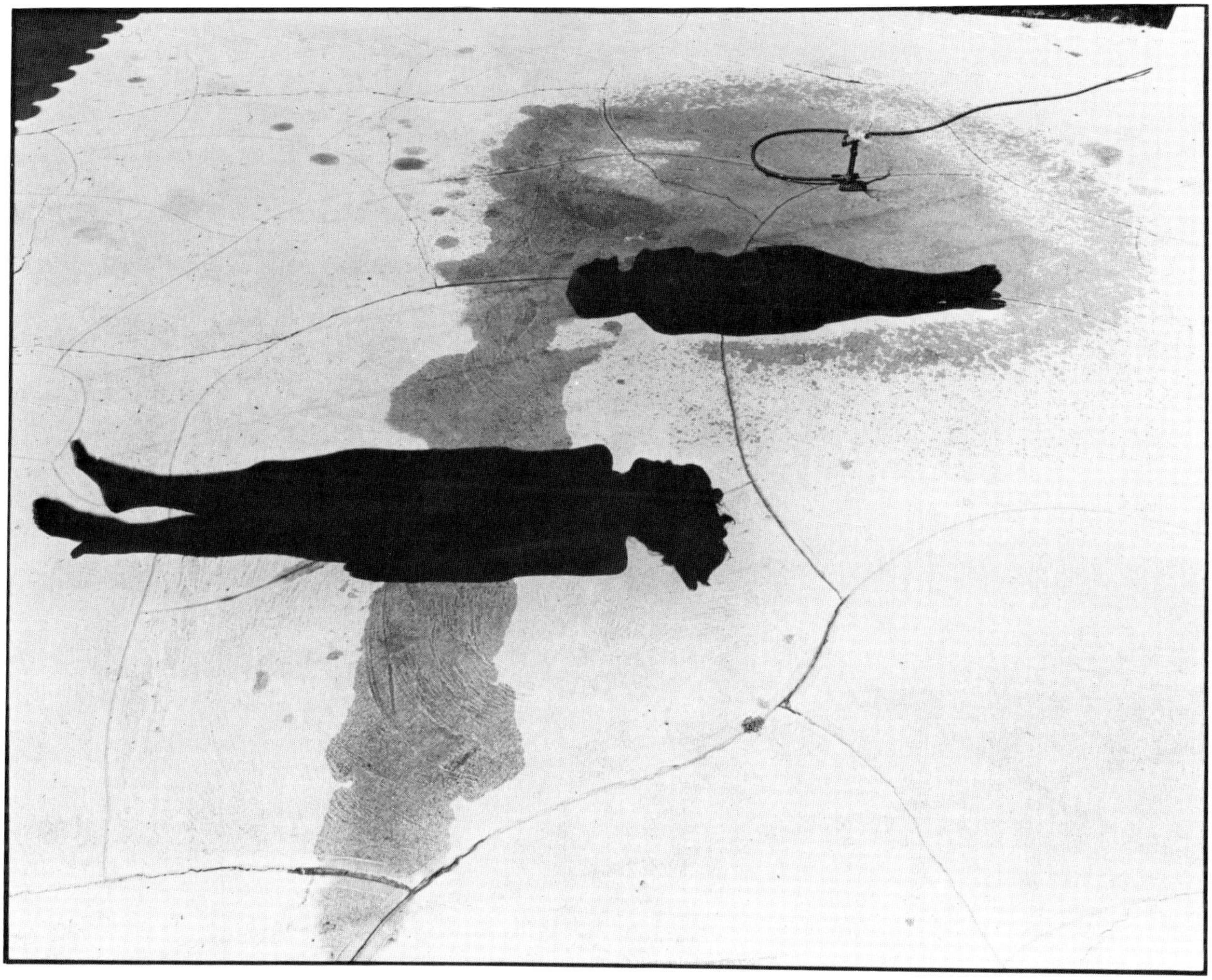

This image is from the Black Sun Pictures *by JoAnn Callis. It was made by cutting cardboard masks and burning-in the figures to the desired darkness. The mask was placed on a sheet of glass several inches above the print, and moved slightly during the exposure to obtain the blurred edges.*

been pleasantly surprised at your results. Instead of a normal image, only the burned-in portions of the image would be visible.

Accidental results are usually not worth keeping, but planned and controlled results can be fascinating. The following technique allows you to selectively burn-in parts of an image. Objects may be outlined or completely omitted at your will. It is another approach to drawing with light, only in this case you have an image as a guide. The technique is simple and can be used with either black-and-white or color:

1. Make a small centered hole in a piece of cardboard that's black on one side and white on the other.

2. Put your negative in the enlarger and project it onto your easel. Set it up as if you were going to make a normal print. Make a test strip to determine the proper exposure.

3. Make a print using the selective-burning technique with the black side of the

cardboard facing down and the white side up. This prevents light from reflecting off the underside of the cardboard and also lets you see the image as it is projected onto the white side of the cardboard. Since you will see the image on the cardboard, it should be easy for you to determine what parts of the image you want to burn-in. Then use the hole in the cardboard to expose the areas you want. With a little practice you should be able to create unique and exciting images with a totally different effect than anything produced in the conventional way.

Chemical Alterations of Images

Chemicals can also be used to alter images by selectively applying and mixing them during the processing of your prints.

This is another of JoAnn Callis's Black Sun Pictures. *When using a mask to burn-in selective areas of a print make sure the bottom side of the mask is black, otherwise it may reflect light back onto the print, affecting areas you wish to remain untouched.*

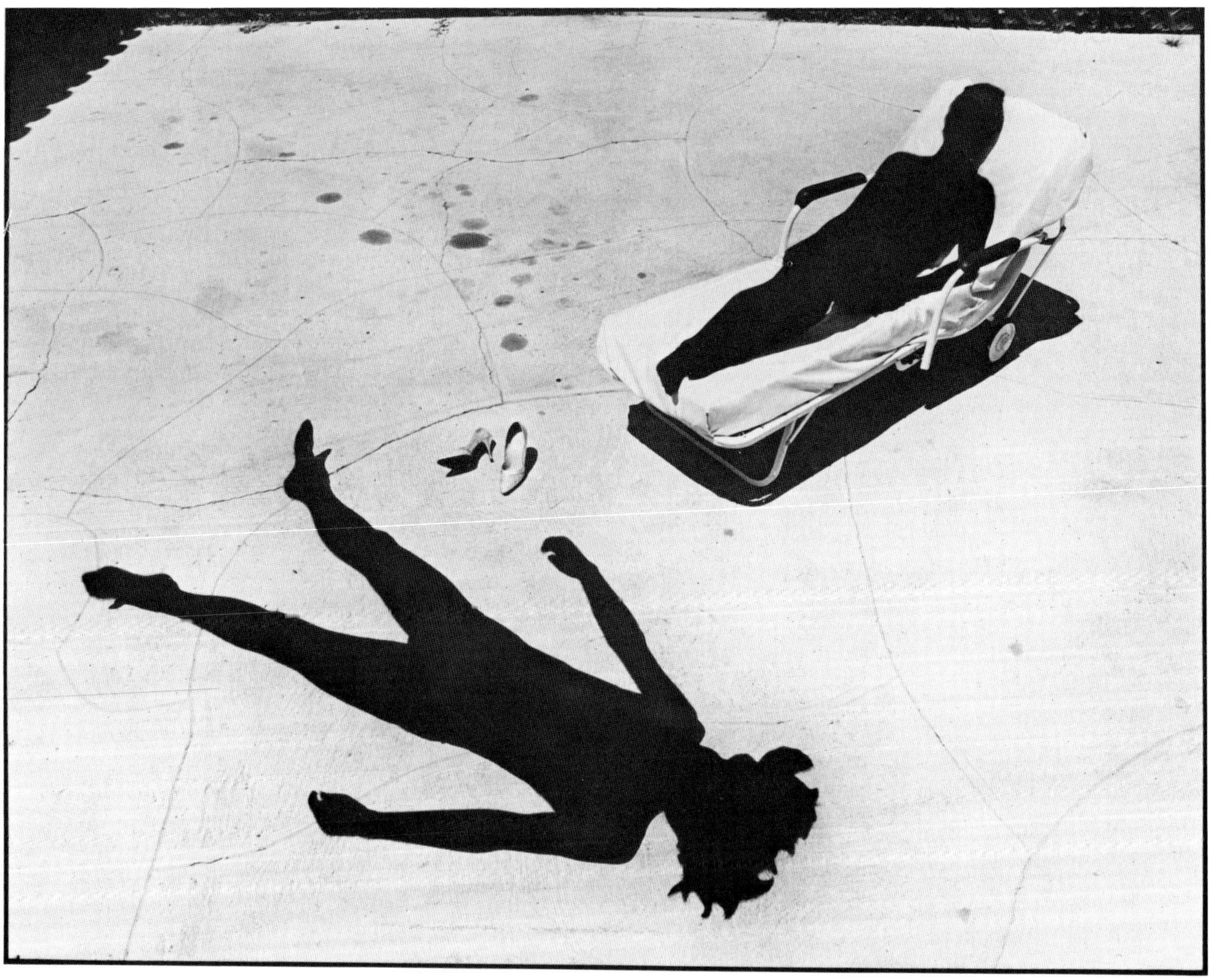

Like many of the other techniques discussed, this can be done with both black-and-white and color materials.

Selectively applying the developer is one such way to alter your images. Instead of totally immersing the print in the developer, try applying the developer to the surface of the print with a brush or cloth. This develops some parts of the image more than others and produces additional textural effects from the method of application. Brush strokes, splattered, dripping, or running developer can add to the graphic impact of the photograph.

You can also add a little hypo to the surface of the print and allow it to mix with the developer. This causes a discoloration with black-and-white prints similar to the effect of duo-tone solarization. With color materials, add a small amount of bleach-fix to selected parts of the print while the developer is still working. This causes an altera-

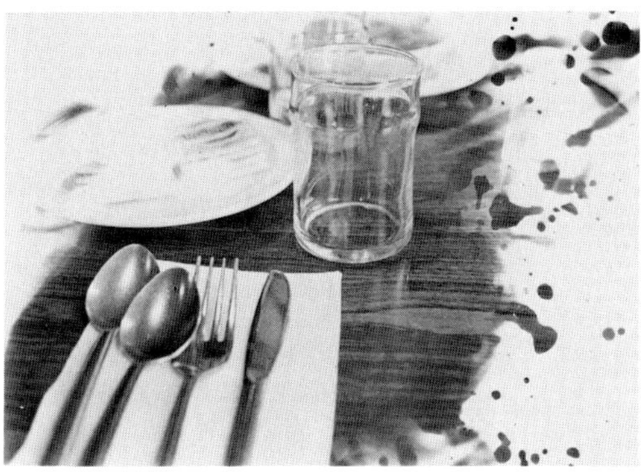

Chemically altering prints during processing has tremendous image-making potential. These two prints were made by selectively applying the developer, rather than immersing the prints in the chemical.

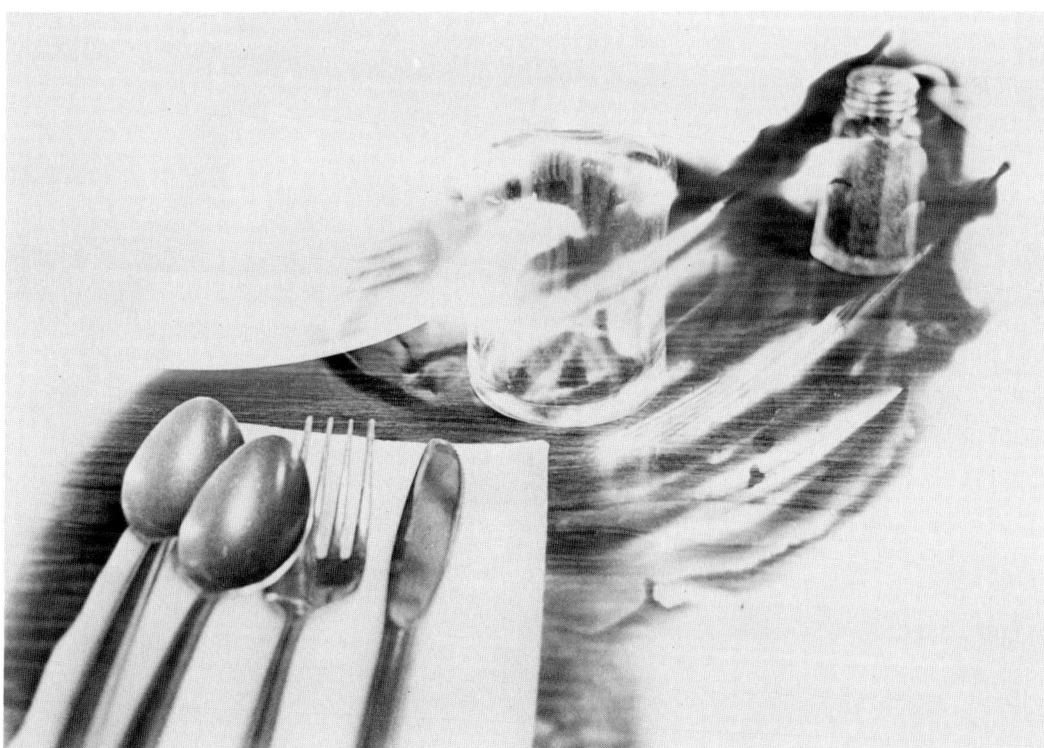

tion in color as well as image development.

Selective Chemical Alterations. If you want to alter only part of a print while keeping the rest of it normal, try masking with rubber cement or Maskoid. Both of these products can be purchased at photo or art-supply stores. Use a brush to apply them to the part of the print you want to remain normal. If the print is wet, squeegee it before applying the masking material. Give it several minutes to dry and then chemically alter the rest of the print. Even if you totally immerse the print into a chemical solution, the rubberized coating will not let the masked portion of the print be affected. When you're ready to remove the masking material, simply rub it off, even if the print is still wet. It's very easy to work with.

The masking technique can also produce some very unusual effects with direct-positive color processes such as Cibachrome. The first developing stage of most direct-positive processes produces a negative black-and-white image. At this point, rinse the print with water, and then squeegee the surface liquid off. Using the proper safelight illumination, apply the masking material to a portion of the print's surface. Then, with the masking material on the print, continue processing through the bleaching stage. After the bleach, rinse the print with water and remove the masking material from the surface of the print. Then continue the processing normally. Part of the resulting photograph will be a negative black-and-white image; the rest will be a normal positive color image.

Techniques like selective alteration, drawing with light, and the Sabattier effect have tremendous potential. Not only are they fun to work with, but these techniques allow you to extend your photographs beyond the reality of the straight camera-produced image.

Remember that a technique for technique's sake is not enough. It is how you use it that is important. A particular technique should add to the content and impact of your photographs, otherwise it is mere novelty.

7

Multiple Images

The single image frequently limits the statement you can make. Combining images can let you delve into innovative, unusual areas. Artists such as Jerry Uelsmann, Bart Parker, and Robert Heineken have used multiple images to express concerns in a way that would otherwise be impossible photographically.

There are many approaches to creating multiple-image photographs. The simplest way is to make several exposures on one frame of film in your camera. Unfortunately, many cameras are designed so making multiple exposures is awkward, if not impossible. Also, once you place more than one image on a piece of film, it's impossible to change your mind. However, multiple printing in the darkroom gives you the freedom to make revisions, variations, and refinements until you are satisfied.

Whether non-silver, color, or black-and-white, the materials play an important role in the process. To use materials to your advantage, you must know and feel comfortable with them. A multiple image photograph is like a family unit. It's made up of many parts that must work together to be effective. It can be much more time-consuming and demanding than the single image, but it also lets you use the photographic medium in a way that can lead to rich and rewarding discoveries.

Sandwiching Images

Sandwiching is a simple method to combine two photographs into one image. By putting two transparencies or negatives in contact together you make a single image that can be printed, viewed, or projected. Next to multiple exposing your film in the camera, it's the easiest way to produce a multiple-image photograph.

If you anticipate using an image for a sandwich, alter your exposure when you're shooting so you don't get excessive combined density in the sandwiched film. With negatives, *underexpose* each negative by half a stop; with transparencies, *overexpose* each image by half a stop. When properly exposed negatives or transparencies are combined, the density will be in a range that's easy to print or project.

Many photographers use the sandwich technique with slides because they can instantly see their results. A black-and-white negative sandwich must be printed before you can determine whether the effect is

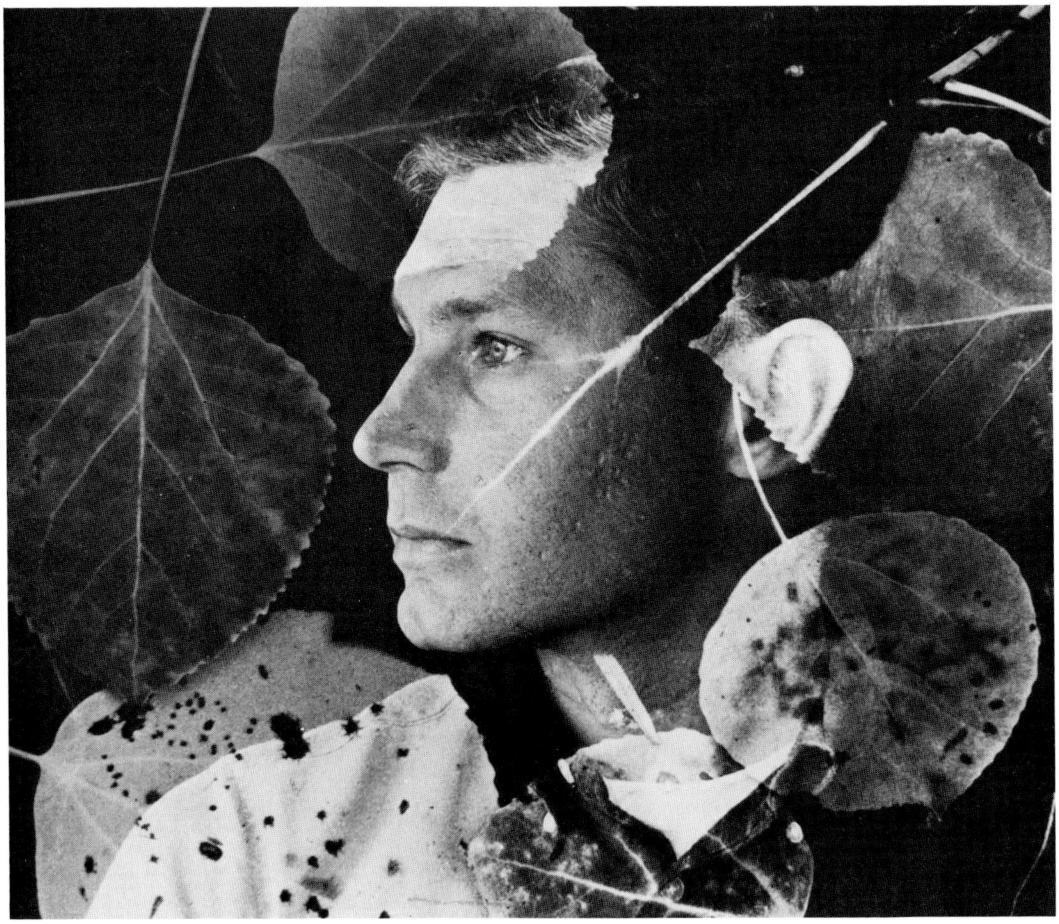

Bill Collins made this image by sandwiching two black-and-white negatives.

what you want. It's hard to judge by just looking at sandwiched negatives. Color negatives should not be used for sandwiching. When a color print is made from two sandwiched color negatives, filtration problems occur and a heavy cyan tint results. This is because of the orange mask inherent to all color-negative films. However, color negatives can be printed separately on one sheet of paper to produce a multiple image.

Another disadvantage of sandwiching is that you can't alter the size relationship of the two images. They must work together as they are. Multiple printing enables you to alter the size and cropping of the images as needed.

Multiple Printing

Multiple printing combines two or more photographic images onto one print. It enables you to emphasize one image more than another and to create visual relationships impossible in a single image or sandwiched photograph.

Techniques vary considerably from one photographer to the next, but they are essentially the same for both black-and-white and color. Regardless of which process you use, each image must be individually tested for the proper print exposure at the correct enlarger height. Color images also have to be individually tested for the filtration needed to produce a good color balance. With black-and-white materials, a variable contrast paper permits you to print negatives of varying contrasts on the same piece of paper and manipulate them for a blended appearance.

Approaches to Multiple Printing. There are two basic approaches to multiple printing. In the first, you make the separation or overlap of images obvious. The other method is to blend images together, making it hard to distinguish whether they are made from a single photograph or a combination of separate photographs. The approach you choose depends on the type of image you're working with, and the statement you wish to make.

Masking is the key to multiple printing. No matter how many images you plan to combine, you have to mask off one portion of the print while you expose another. The simplest way to mask a part of the print is to block the light from the enlarger with your hand or a dodging tool. The difficult part is masking so that the images blend together smoothly.

Another approach to masking is to use a cardboard cutout or a film mask made to suit the needs of a specific print. This is more time-consuming and more technically involved, but in many cases is the only solution. Each multiple-image print has its own demands, and the approach is dictated by what seems best for that particular visual combination.

Preplanning Images. Photographers who consistently work with multiple images tend to tailor their shooting to that end. Not every negative works for a multiple print. Therefore, preplanning while shooting makes the job in the darkroom a lot easier. You'll find that backgrounds become an extremely important consideration. If you plan to combine an object, like a hamburger, with another image (as Jerry Uelsmann has done), you must consider its background. To make the object float isolated in the sky of another image, the hamburger should be shot on a white background, preferably a lightbox so the background is completely blank. In other instances you will need to

Myself-Sitting Down, *by Steve Polite, consists of four separate negatives, which were multiple-printed to make a single image. The photograph was preplanned and carefully set up to create a sense of motion.*

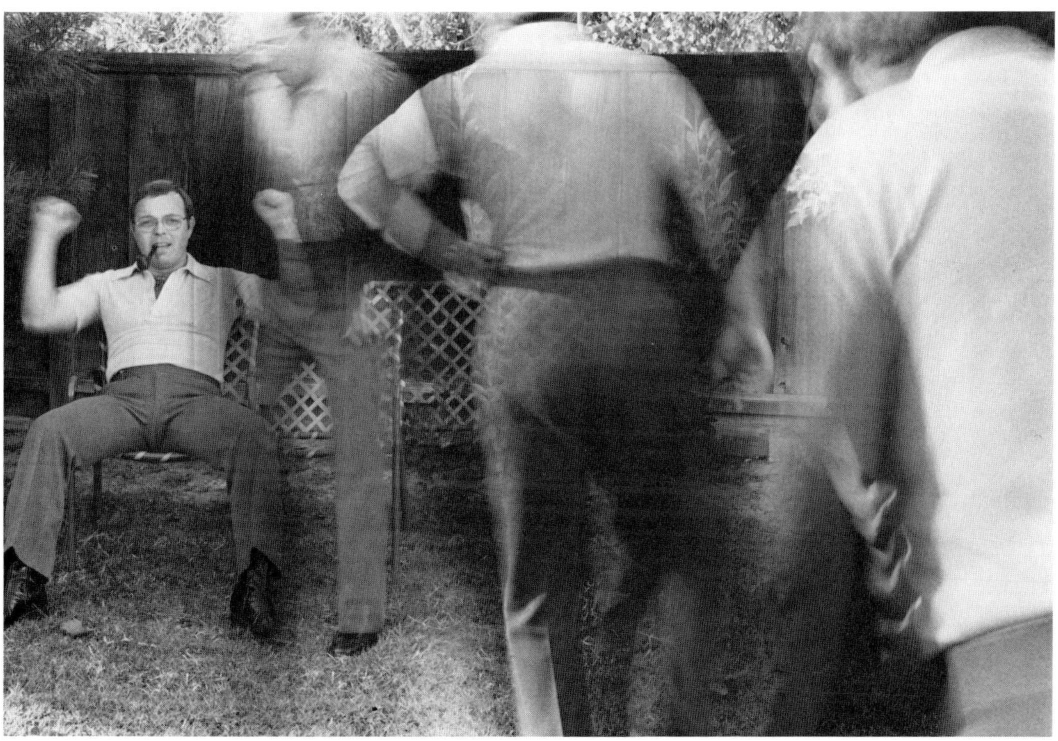

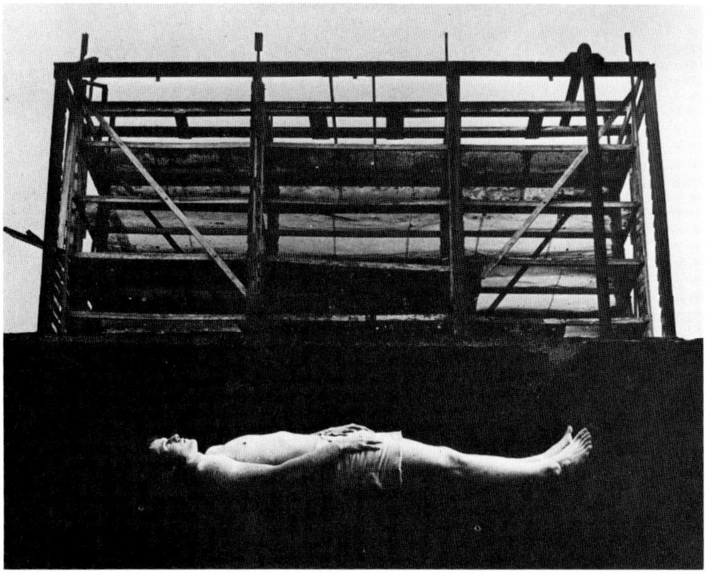

This multiple print by Bill Collins illustrates the importance of a proper background. When the top portion of the photograph was exposed, the bottom portion was dodged so that the figure could be printed. The dark background made it easy to blend the two images.

isolate the object against a black background. With black-and-white or color negatives, a white background is usually best. Then, when the negative is printed, only the object will record on the printing paper. With transparencies, a black background should be used if you plan to print with a direct-positive material, like Kodak's Ektachrome 2203 or Cibachrome. If you plan to make an internegative from the transparency and print on negative-print materials, you should shoot the object on a white background. The process you choose should be determined by the type of image you want to make. In printing with negatives, it's easier to *float* objects shot on a white background. When you're working with transparencies and direct-positive print processes, it's easier to *float* objects on a black background.

When shooting landscapes, try to have neutral foregrounds or backgrounds. This makes it easy to drop out the unimportant neutral part of the picture and blend it with another image. The type of background, light or dark, depends on what you plan to do, and whether you are working with positive or negative film. The important thing is to consider these variables during the shooting and plan ahead; otherwise, you may find your efforts in the darkroom more frustrating than they need to be.

Blending Images. Blending is the combination of several images into one final print that appears to have been made as a single image. Frequently you can use simple masking techniques like your hands, a piece of cardboard, or your normal dodging and burning tools. However, in some instances, it may be necessary to make a special device suited to the needs of a particular image.

Photographs, like the eye in the toilet-bowl (see page 000) or the freeway-scene in the mouth (see page 000) can be made with normal dodging and burning tools. To make a similar multiple print of two images, the first step is to determine the proper enlargement for each negative. The toilet image was placed in the enlarger first, and projected onto the easel to establish the proper cropping and positioning in the planned composition. Then, a discarded sheet of enlarging paper was put into the easel, and a rough sketch of the projected image was made as a reference for positioning the second image. Next, a test strip was made to determine the proper *f*-stop and exposure time for the first image. (For a color image, the proper filtration would also have to be determined through testing)

After testing the first image, the negative of the eye was put in the enlarger. With the sketch as a guide, the eye was enlarged and positioned to work with the first image. It was then added to the sketch (for future reference) and tested for the proper exposure.

When making the final print, the toilet image was exposed first. The sketch was used as a guide to position the easel, and the aperture and exposure time were set according to results of the first test strip. A dodging tool made from a thin wire with an oval-shaped piece of black cardboard attached to one end blocked the light from exposing the center of the toilet. The dodging tool should be held several inches above the paper and kept in constant motion, allowing the edges to bleed out softly. (It may take several trial runs before you feel comfortable with the procedure.)

After the toilet image was exposed, the printing paper was taken out of the easel. An arrow, to indicate the top of the print, was drawn in pencil on the back of the paper, to make it easy to replace properly in the easel. Once marked, the paper was stored in a light-safe container. The negatives were switched, and the sketch was used to position the eye correctly.

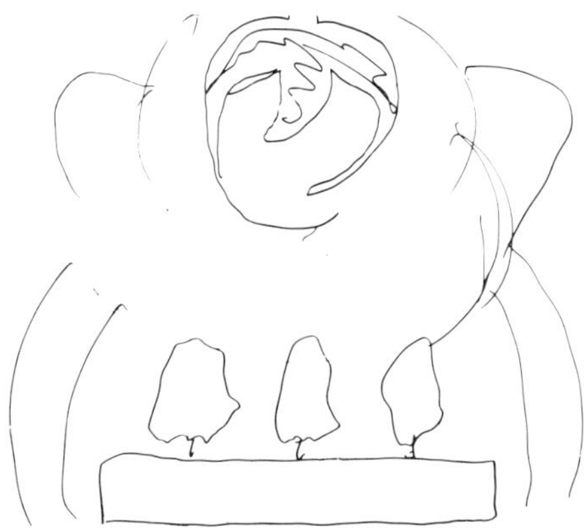

This photograph by the author, entitled Triad, *is a combination of two 35 mm transparencies enlarged and printed separately. The pelvis X-ray was contact printed. The black background of the artificial trees made them easy to print on Cibachrome. The deformed carrot had a white background which was dodged to coincide with the shape of the carrot and the pelvis. The drawing on the left was used as a guide for the print. It was made by projecting the transparencies onto a sheet of paper. Before printing, and between exposures, each image was lined up by projecting it on the drawing. The original of this photograph is reproduced in the color section.*

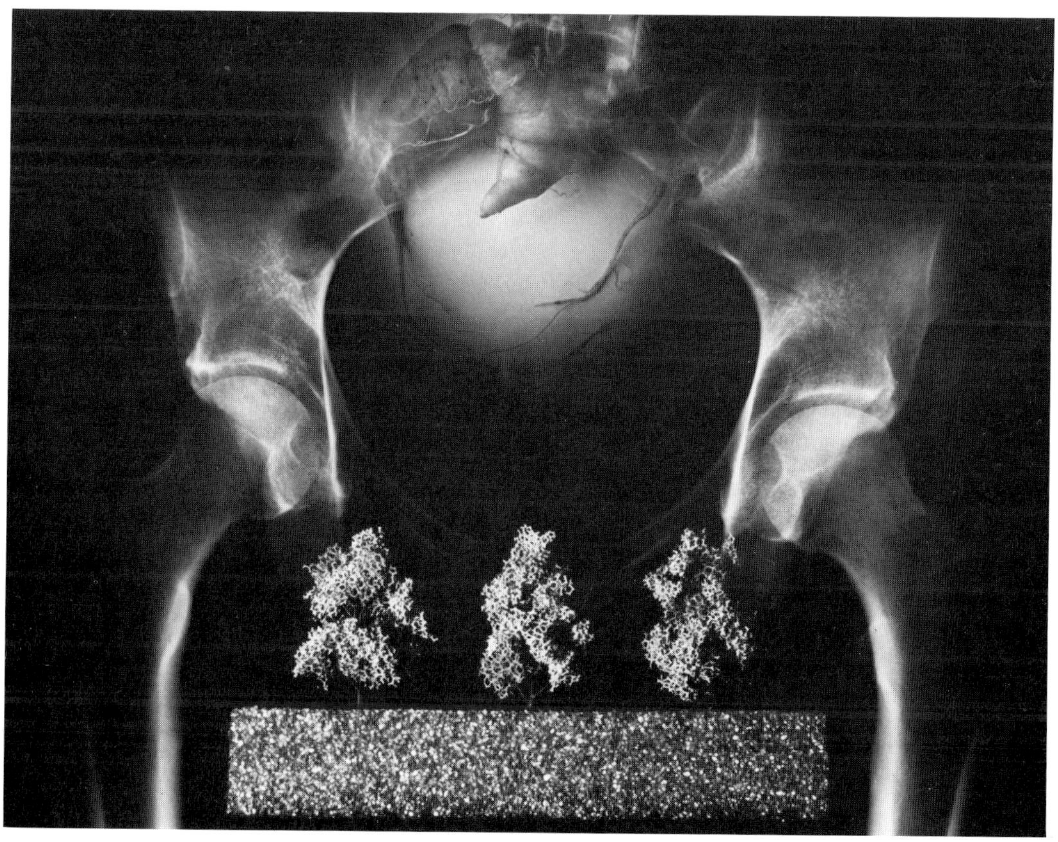

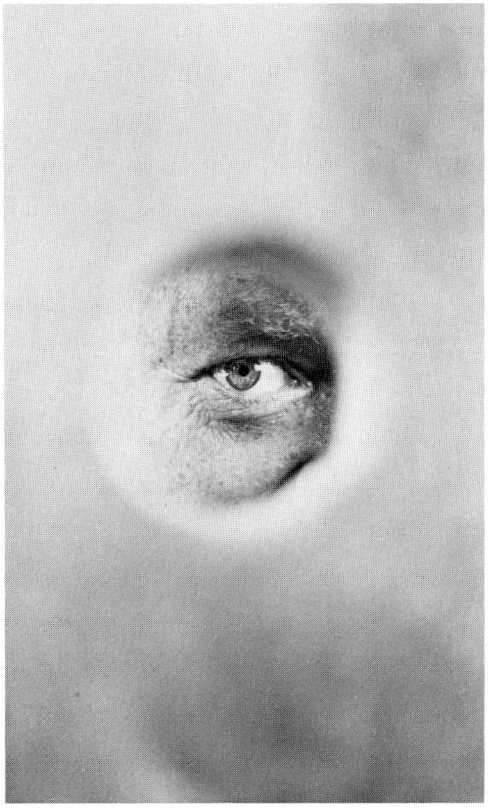

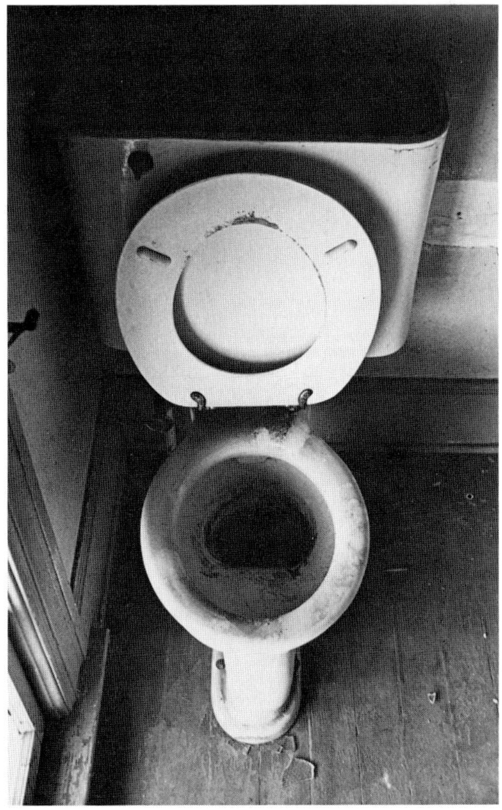

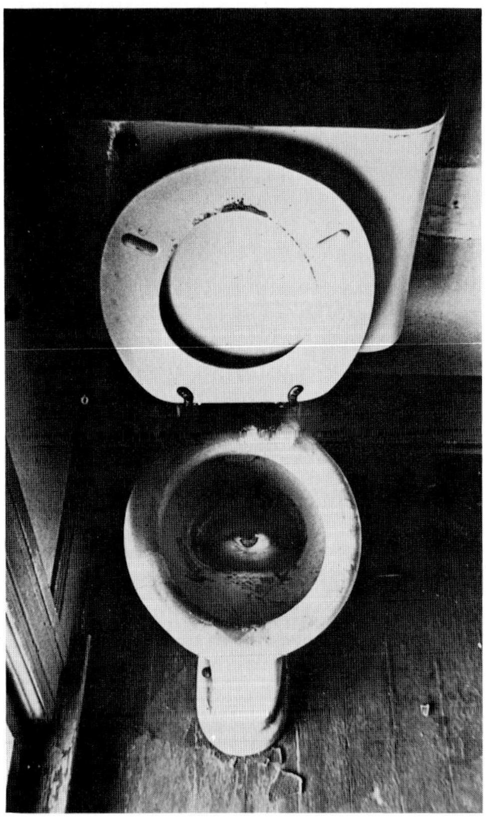

The two images above were combined into the print on the left by blocking the light from one area while the other was being printed. The toilet image was printed first; while the center of the toilet bowl was dodged to keep it from getting dark. The eye was printed through a circular hole in a piece of cardboard. Since the center of the toilet had been dodged, the only difficulty was lining the two images up and blending them together.

When the eye was positioned, the sketch was removed from the easel and replaced with the previously exposed piece of printing paper. The arrow on the back of the paper was used to align it properly in the easel. A piece of cardboard (black on one side and white on the other) with a small hole in the center was used as a mask for printing the eye in the center of the toilet. The cardboard was held (black side down) several inches above the printing paper, and kept in constant motion during the exposure. This caused a soft edge that blended into the other image.

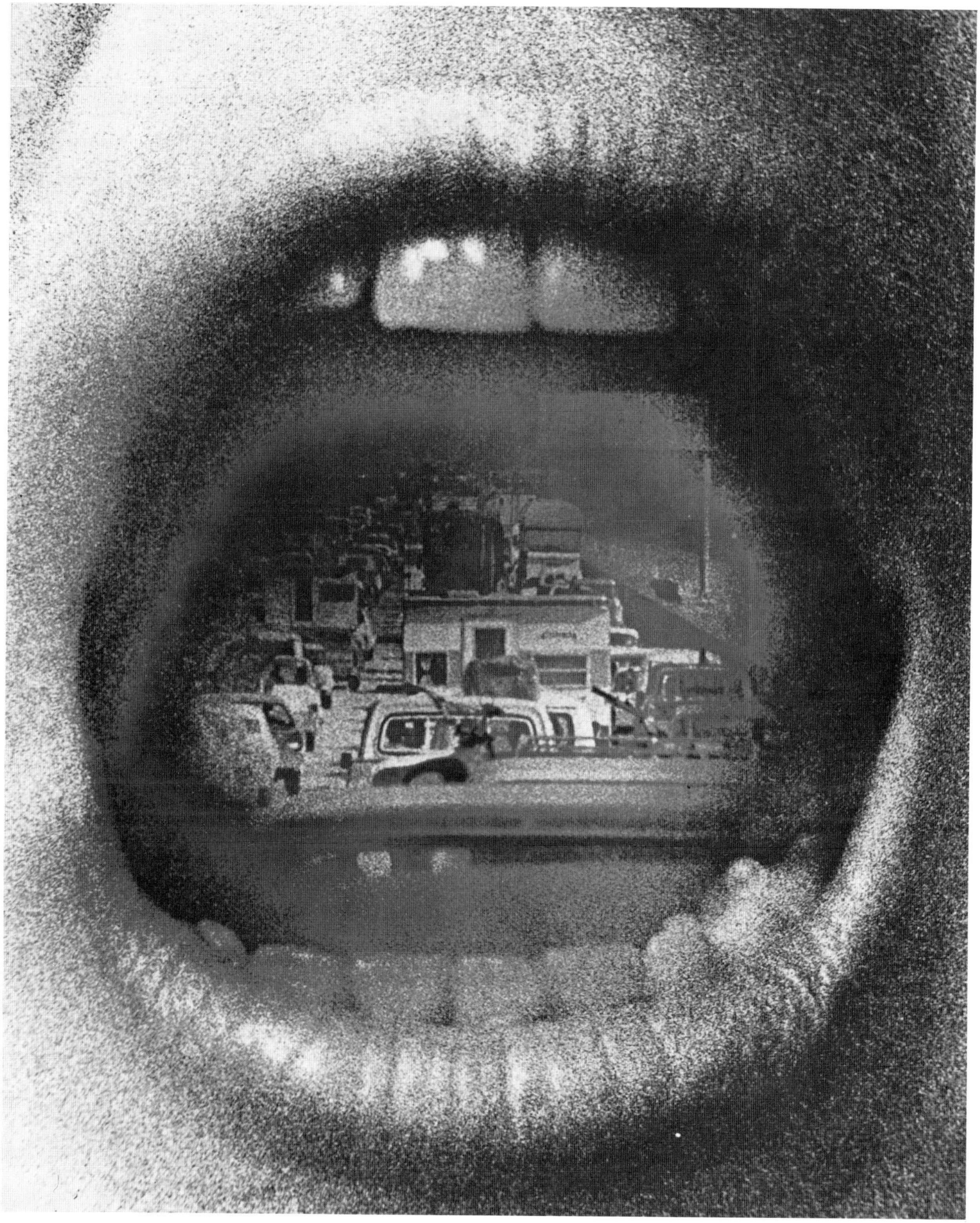

The blending between the mouth and the freeway scene wasn't as good as it should have been. Rather than remake the print, a penlight was used (while the print was still in the developer) to darken the area that wasn't blending exactly.

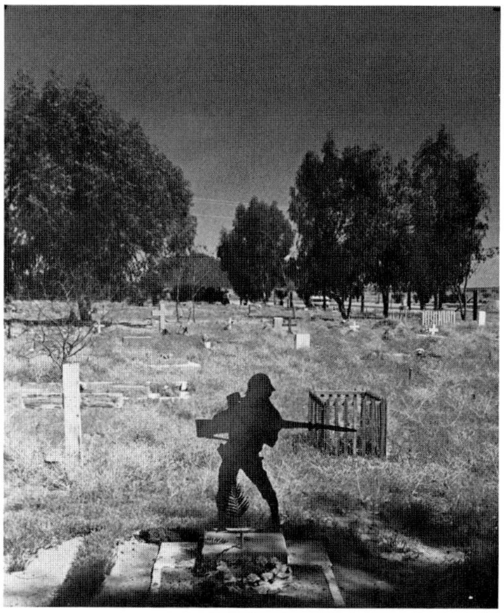

This is the original print of one of the two photographs used to make the multiple print on the following page.

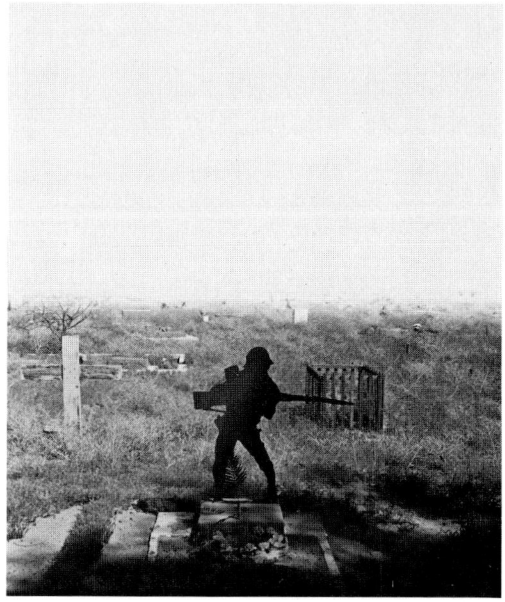

The top portion of this photograph was dodged, so that the other photograph could be printed in the unexposed area.

The success of your final image depends on how well the two images blend together technically, visually, and in content. Normally, several attempts are necessary before the procedure is adequately controlled and the content of the final image is successful.

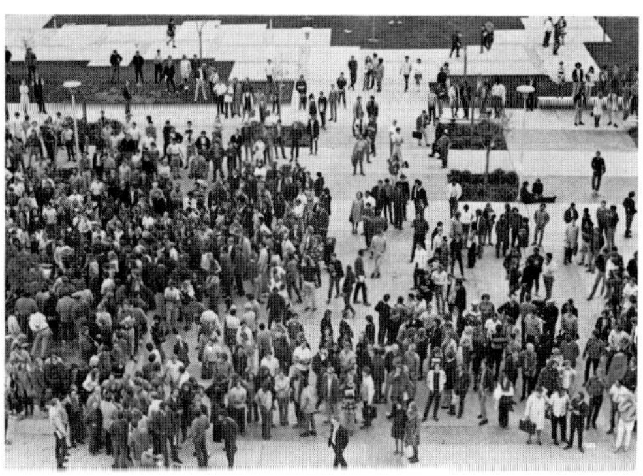

This is a straight print of the second image used in the print on the facing page.

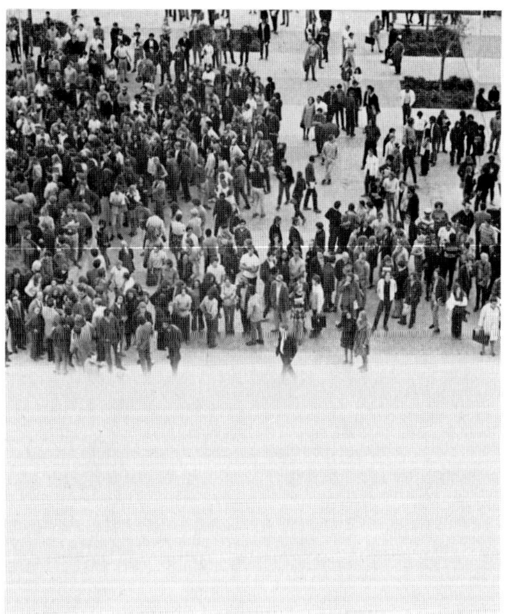

A trial print was made, and the bottom dodged in anticipation of a slight overlap between the two images.

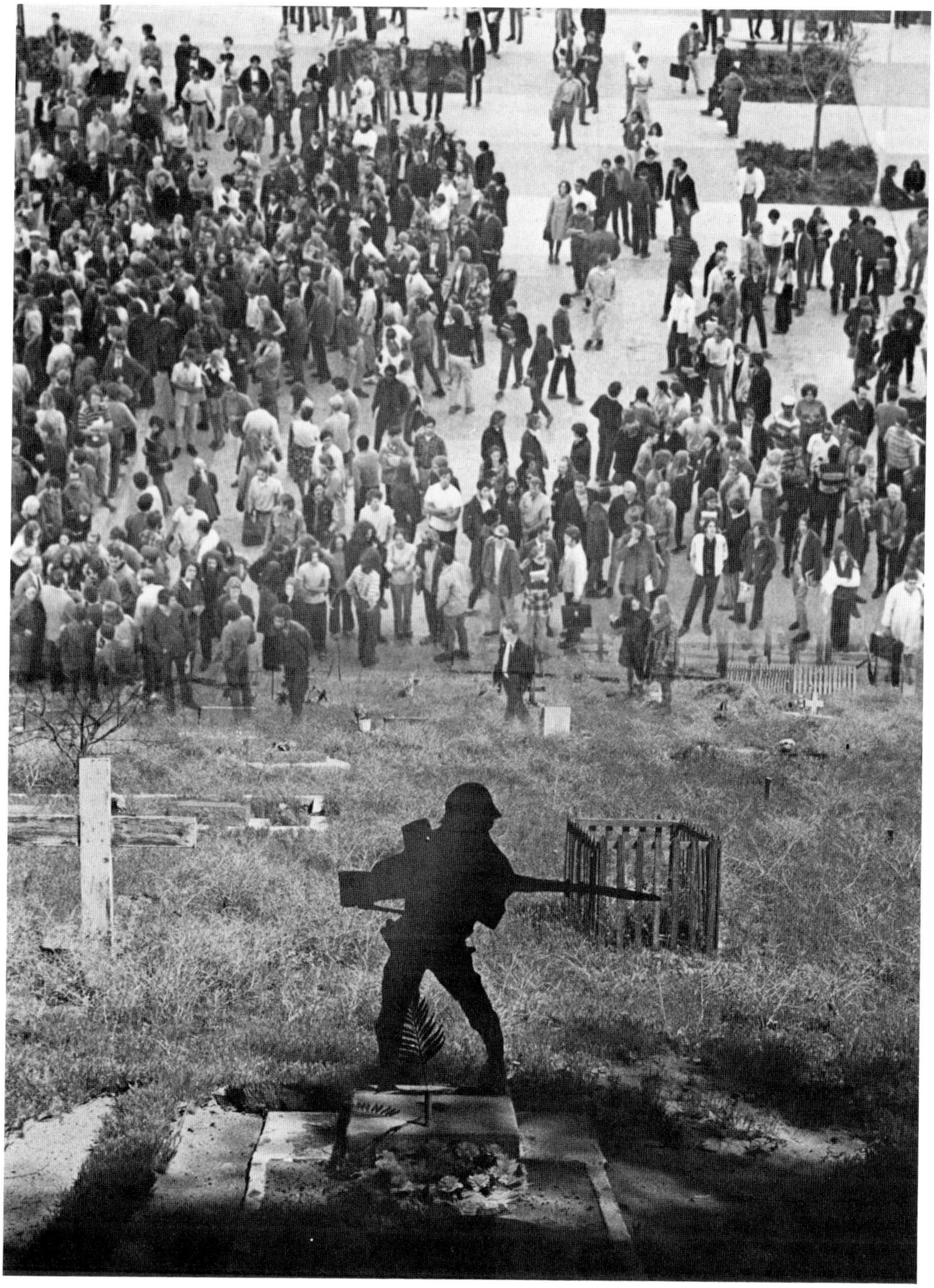

The final print shows an even blend between the two images, and results in an image completely different in feeling from the images used to create it.

A cardboard cutout mask made this double print on the right possible. The same technique was employed for the image below, only the contrast was reduced, and the masking was more subtle to allow for some overlap of the two images.

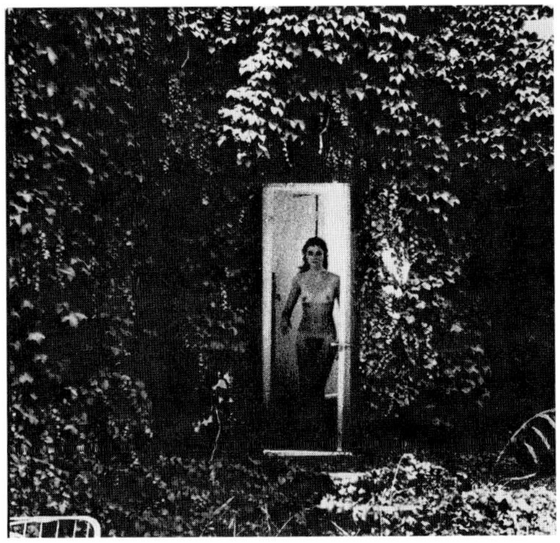

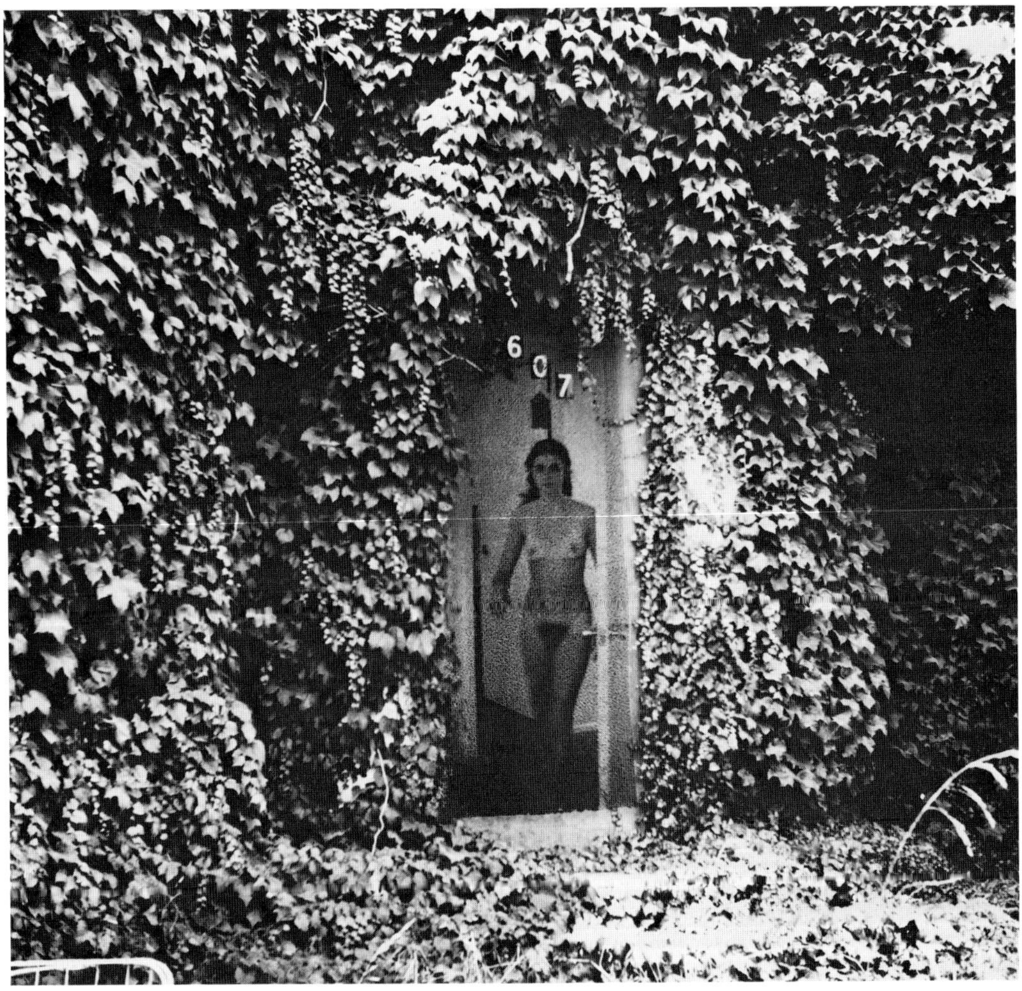

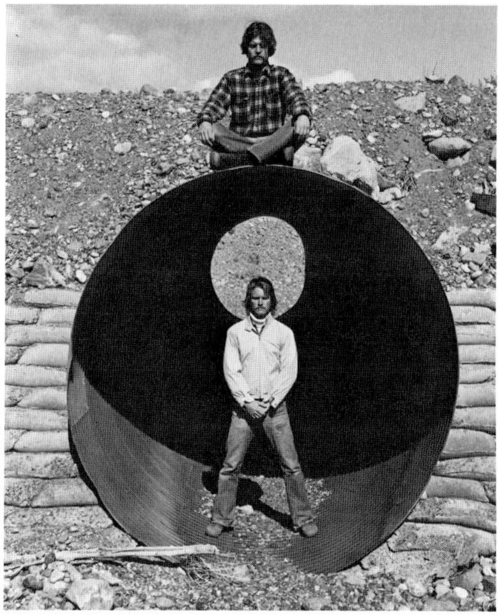

Bill Collins used paper-negatives and selective burning as masking tools to alter this photograph into a more surreal positive-negative image.

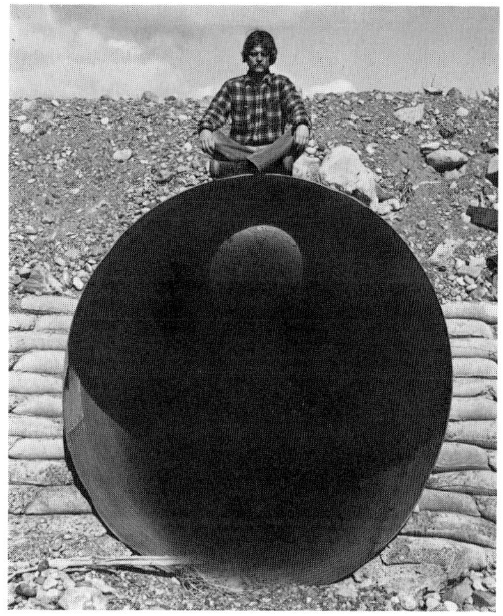

The center portion of this print was burned-in to black so the figure would disappear. The print was then used as a paper negative to produce a negative print.

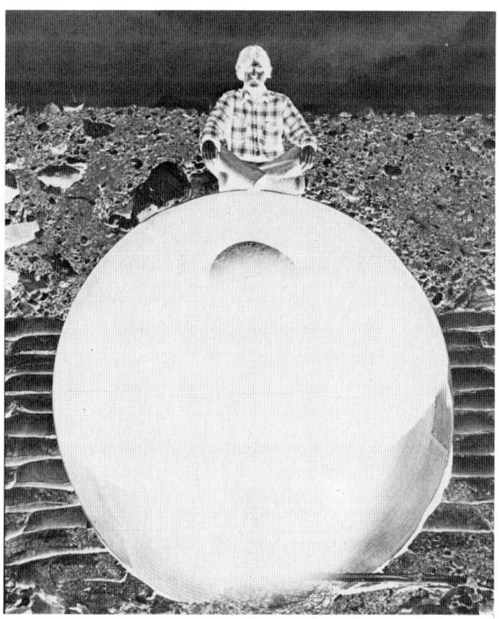

This image was the result of the paper negative. The area blackened in the print used as a paper negative came out white in the reversed print.

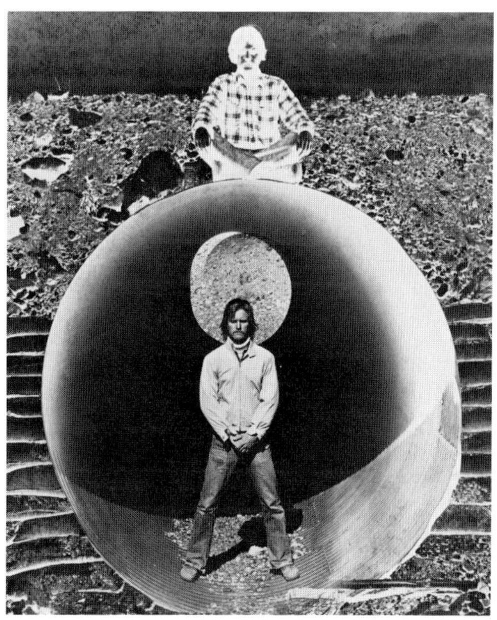

The final photograph had the figure printed into the white area of the reversed print, resulting in an intriguing positive-negative photograph.

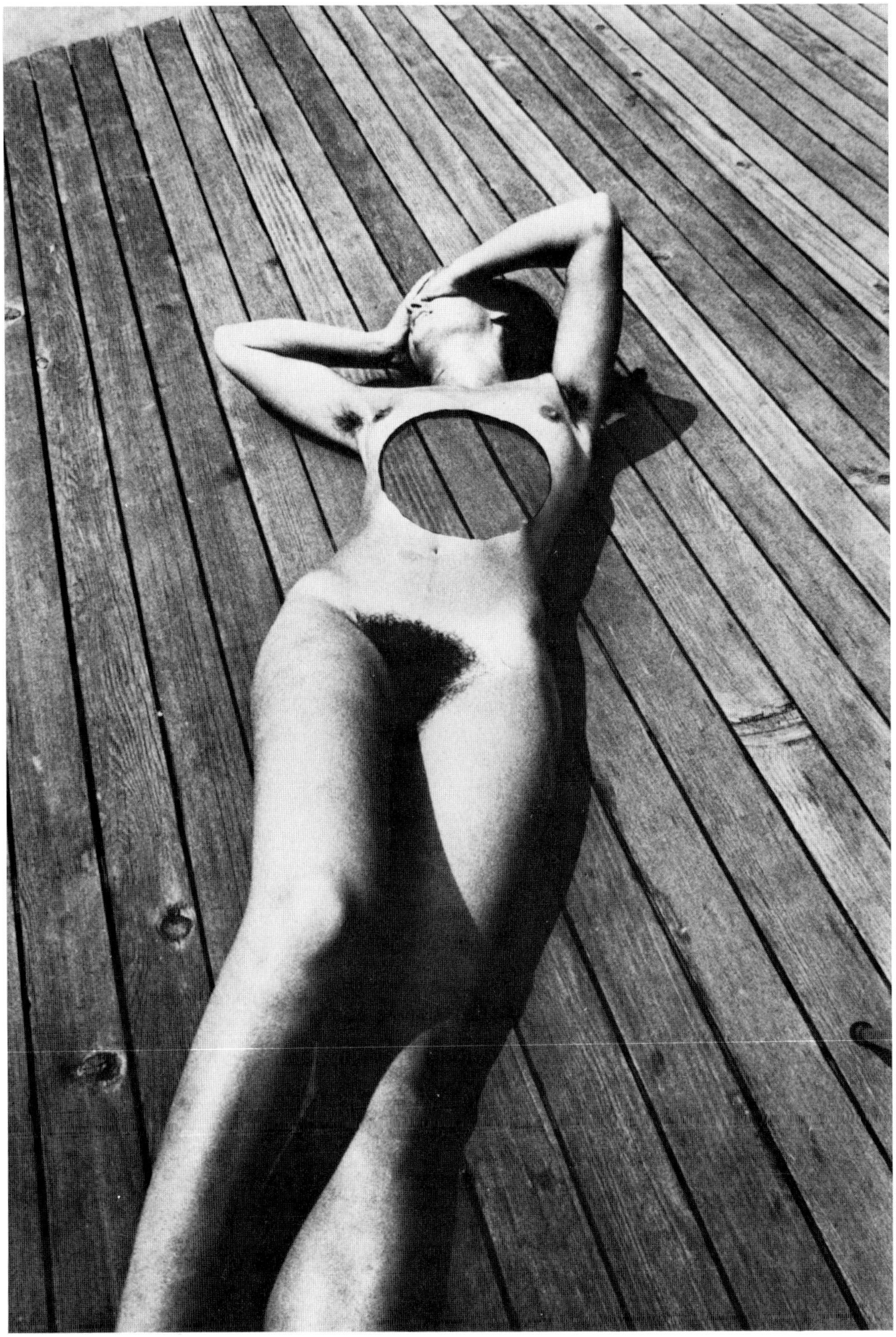

Dinah Portner used two separate negatives to make this image, titled The Shell. *Cut cardboard masks were used to print the boardwalk and figure separately. The oval area in the chest was made with a separate mask. This photograph was first published in* Combinations, *a journal of photography Vol. No. 1, Spring 1977.*

An Alternative Blending Technique. You can blend foreground and background images together by using the filter holder found below the lens of most enlargers. Again, you have to test each image individually and make a sketch to determine positioning and sizing.

Place a small piece of black cardboard on the filter holder to act as a mask. Position this mask so it blocks part of the paper. Because the filter holder is several inches below the lens, the piece of cardboard will appear on the print as a soft, out-of-focus edge. By switching the position of this cardboard mask for each image, the soft edges will overlap and blend. You might want to use small pieces of masking tape as a guide for proper placement of the cardboard in the filter holder.

If you're fortunate enough to have a darkroom with several enlargers, you can set each enlarger up with a different negative and mask. The paper can then be moved from one easel to another. But, with only one enlarger, you have to use things like masking tape and sketching to change negatives and masks accurately.

Specialty Masks

Blending techniques are more than adequate for most multiple printing needs; but occasionally more elaborate masking techniques are necessary to combine several images. This is especially true when combining images with hard edges, dropping-in type, or when you need more exacting control in order to produce a large number of identical prints.

The basic procedure for combining images is always the same. It's necessary to individually test each image, and to make a sketch for positioning and size reference. But specially made physical masks ensure accuracy and exactness, since you don't have to rely on manual masking and blending techniques. Depending on the complexity of the image, masks can be made out of matteboard or film.

The easiest, least expensive method is to make the masks out of matteboard. This works well with images that have hard-edge areas to be printed together, but that don't need to be perfectly registered. The edges of matteboard vary and the results aren't as exacting as with film masks that are registered together. However, the accessibility of the materials, and the ease with which matteboard masks can be made, make them a logical choice when planning a multiple print requiring more than simple blending techniques.

An image of a square printed within a square, as shown in the accompanying illustration, can be made with a matteboard mask. To do this, first determine the size relationships and the exact placement of each image by making a sketch from the enlarger-projected negatives. Then use that sketch as a guide for making the mask.

Cut a piece of matteboard the size of the print you plan to make. Using your sketch as a guide, cut the center square out of the piece of matteboard. The cutting must be done very carefully, as any mistake or unevenness will show up in your print. If necessary, use a piece of fine sandpaper to smooth the edges of the boards, but be careful not to sand too much because the pieces must fit together tightly. The smaller, cutout piece needs to fit snugly into the open portion of the larger piece so an edge line won't be noticeable when the masks are used to make a print.

Once the mask is cut, tape one end of the larger mask to the edge of your print easel, or the baseboard of your enlarger. This ensures that the images will be printed in register, while allowing you to lift the larger mask out of the way when not needed.

Put the negative for the outside portion of the image in the enlarger first. This should be the negative you'll be enlarging the most. With the sketch or the mask as a guide, position everything to make an exposure. Set the timer and aperture (and filtration if working with color) according to your prior tests. With safelight illumination and the larger mask taped in place on one end, take a piece of unexposed paper and position it under the mask.

Since the outside dimensions of the larger mask are the same size as the paper, it should be easy to position the paper. Once the paper is in position, lower the larger mask so it lays on top of the printing paper. Then put the smaller mask in place. When it's securely in place, hold the smaller mask in position with one hand and lift the larger mask up out of the way. Then make your exposure for the larger image.

After the first exposure is completed, lower the larger mask again. It's taped on one side so it should go right into place with the smaller mask fitting securely in position. If you have trouble lining up the two masks, something has moved out of position and the two images will be out of register.

Once both masks are in position on top of the print, cover the whole thing with an oversized piece of cardboard. This helps prevent fogging when you change the negatives. Then replace the already exposed negative with the one to be printed in the open center space. Working with a safelight, change your enlarger height, focus on a surface the same height as your print easel, and set the timer and aperture (and filtration if working with color).

When everything is set, remove the oversized cardboard. With both cardboard masks still in place, turn on the enlarger light and position the image using the masks as a guide. When the image is properly positioned, turn off the enlarger and remove the center mask, leaving the larger outside mask in place. Make your exposure. The print is now ready to be processed.

This procedure is a simple, practical method you can use to print a square image within a square or rectangle. Variations of this procedure can be worked out to suit other needs once you understand the basic approach. Try using different shapes, or several separate ones on the same sheet

The main drawback to this procedure is that cardboard masks don't always register perfectly. Slight variations and imperfections are the nature of the materials. For more exact masking, you have to make film masks with registration holes fitted to registration pins. This ensures clean, sharp masks with perfect registration. For detailed information on the films to use, and registration procedures, refer to chapters 8 and 9.

8

High-Contrast Techniques

The ability to alter contrast gives photographers another method to heighten the impact of their images. High-contrast films can achieve special effects beyond the capabilities of normal films and papers. Normal black-and-white films are continuous tone and panchromatic; meaning they reproduce a wide range of tones, and are sensitive to all colors of light.

Litho films, the most commonly used high-contrast films, are not sensitive to all colors of light. They are orthochromatic, meaning they do not record red light. Litho films have no gray tones. They reproduce all values as pure black or white, simplifying photographs by increasing their graphic qualities, but also reducing their realism.

Litho film was designed for use in lithography and graphic arts, but photographers have adapted it to achieve special effects like posterization. It is also used in many non-silver photographic processes, such as Van Dyke and cyanotype printing, photo silkscreen printing, and gum bichromate printing.

There are a variety of different brands of litho films, including Kodak Kodalith Ortho Film 6556, Type 3; Ilfolith by Ilford; and Cronar by Dupont. They are available in most sheet film sizes, from 4×5 inches (10.16 to 12.7 cm) to 4×100 foot (1.2×30.5 m) rolls. Most camera stores carry 4×5 inch sheet film in 50-sheet boxes. For 35 mm cameras, you can also buy rolls of High-Contrast Copy Film by Kodak which is similar to litho film. Because litho films are designed for copy work rather than regular shooting, they have an extremely slow film speed of approximately ASA 6.

Processing Litho Films

Litho films are normally developed in special litho developers which can be purchased in either powder or liquid concentrates. These developers consist of two parts, A and B, that you mix separately into two stock solutions. When you're ready to begin working, you mix equal parts of the A and B stock solutions together to make the developer active. Use only the amount needed, because the working solution's life

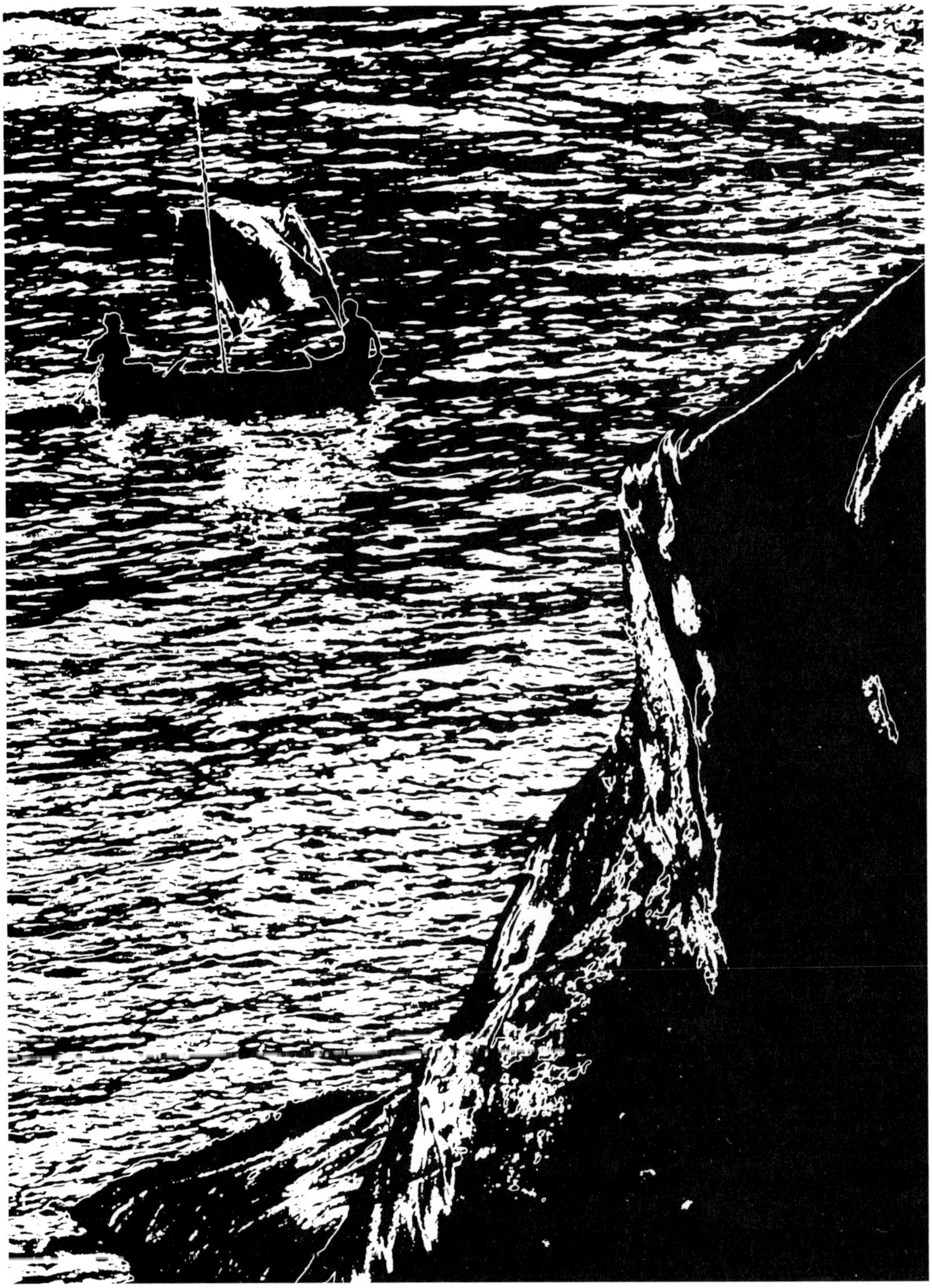

This high-contrast photograph by Robert Routh is from a litho negative altered by the Sabattier effect.

is only about one hour after the stock solutions are mixed.

Litho films are easy to process. Because they are orthochromatic, they can be handled under a red safelight (number 1A). Tray processing is the simplest and easiest method. Develop litho film for three minutes at room temperature with continuous, yet gentle, agitation. Immerse the film gently into the developer, and tap it against the side of the developing tray to dislodge any air bubbles, and help avoid pinholes. During the first 30 seconds of development, agitate the film vigorously, then continue with constant but gentle agitation. The film will look fully developed after two minutes, but develop it for three minutes, to get a pure black.

Properly exposed and developed, litho film will not have any middle values, just black and clear film. Underexposed or underdeveloped film does not have solid blacks. The black should be opaque

Litho films, such as these by Barbara Burchfield, are used for their graphic quality and manipulative nature. A normally exposed and processed litho negative, produces images without any middle tones, like the one immediately below. By reducing the exposure time from eight to two seconds the silver-gray tone of the print on the bottom resulted. Variations in the exposure of litho negatives can produce a variety of tones.

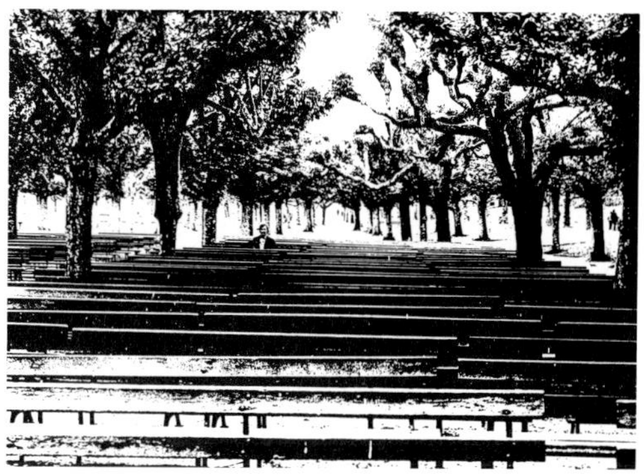

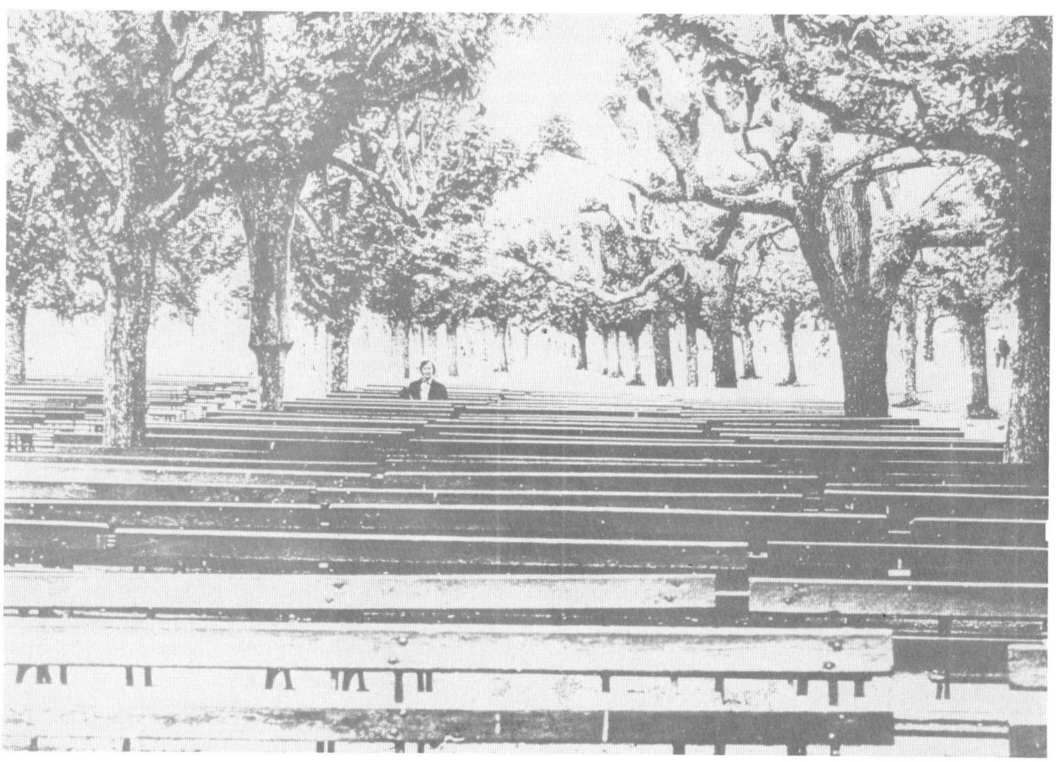

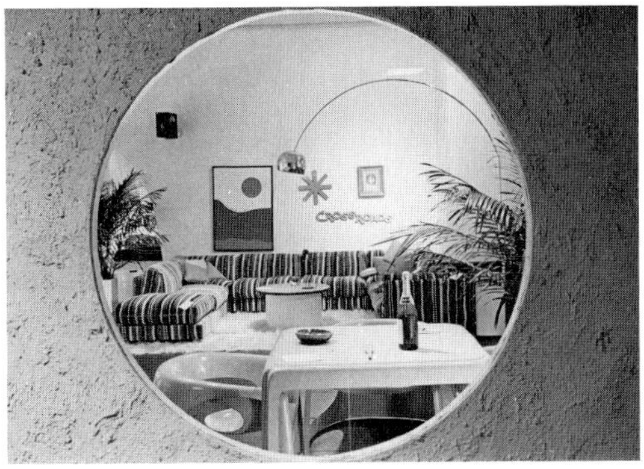

This print of a furniture display room was made from a 35 mm negative.

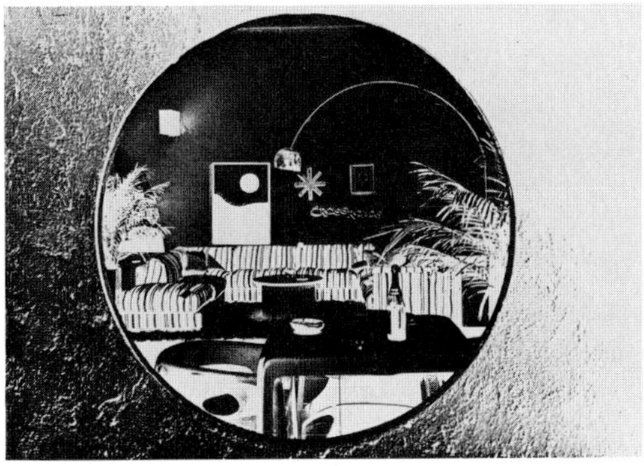

The original 35 mm negative was printed onto litho film, producing a film positive. This negative print was made from that litho-film positive.

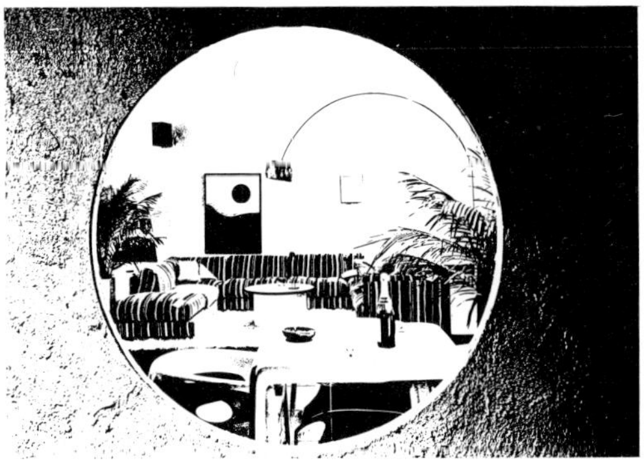

The litho-film positive was contact printed onto another piece of litho film to make a litho negative. The logo and star-like shape were opaqued out on the litho negative, and that litho negative used to make this print.

enough to prevent you from seeing any light through it, even when held next to a light bulb. Overexposed and overdeveloped films have less sharpness and a slight overall fog.

Following development, rinse the film in a water stop bath for 30 seconds. Don't use acid in the stop bath, because it has a tendency to cause pinholes. Fix the film in your normal fixer for five minutes. One side will have a milky appearance that goes away after several minutes, depending on the freshness of your fixer. This means that the film has cleared. The majority of the unused silver has been bleached out and the lights can be turned on. But this does not mean that the film is thoroughly fixed. Once the film clears, it must continue fixing for the amount of time it originally took to clear, even though the lights are on.

Wash the film for ten minutes in running water. (A hypo eliminator can be used to speed up washing.) Then immerse it in a wetting agent, such as Photo-flo, squeegee, and dry.

High-Contrast Images from Color Materials

High-contrast images can be made on litho film from your original black-and-white negatives or color slides. However, color negatives, which have an overall orange cast to them, don't reproduce well on orthochromatic litho film. The same is true of color slides that contain important details in shades of red. To make high-contrast images from color materials, it's best to use Kodak's Kodalith Pan Film 2568. This film is available in 50-sheet boxes and larger sizes; but most camera stores don't stock it, and it must be special ordered. Kodalith Pan has an ASA similar to Kodalith Ortho film and produces the same high-contrast effect when processed in an A and B litho developer. However, you have to work without safelights because it's a panchromatic film.

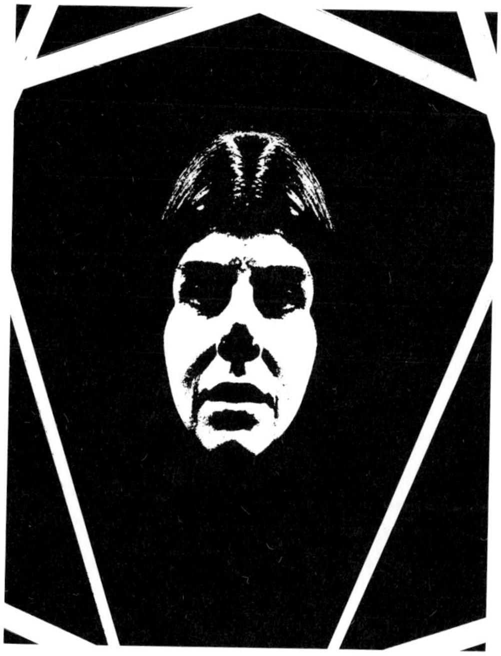

Two identical litho negatives were flopped opposite each other and sandwiched together to make this photograph.

Steve Polite combined a continuous-tone image with a litho image to make this photograph.

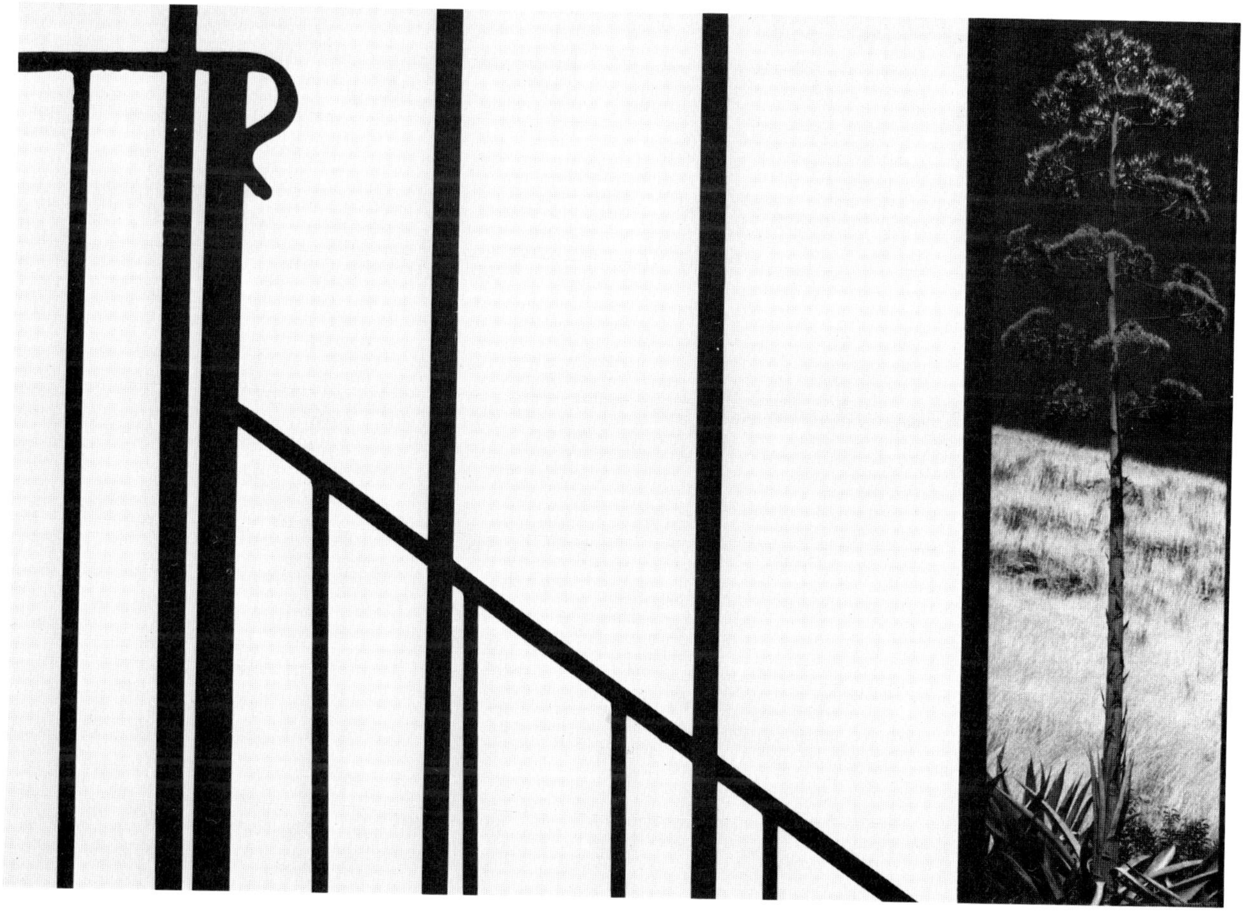

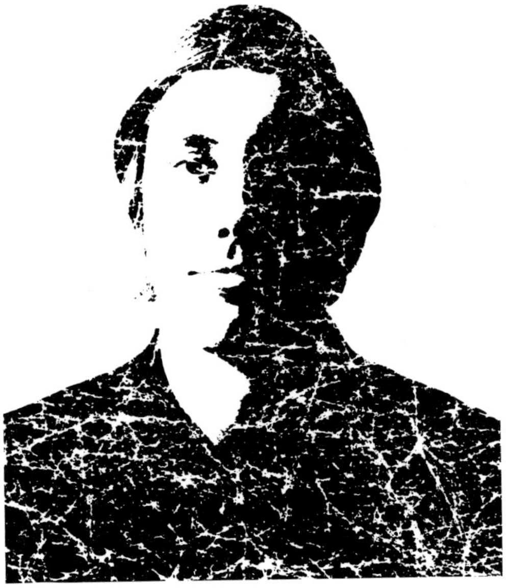

A texture screen was sandwiched with a litho negative for this photograph. Since litho film is pure black and white, it's easy to sandwich another image and have it print only in the clear areas.

Exposing Litho Films

To expose litho film, first put your negative into the enlarger and project it onto an enlarging easel. Adjust the height of the enlarger so the projected image is a size that fits your enlarger. If your enlarger takes 4×5 inch negatives, make the image as large as possible. The bigger the negative, the easier it is to work with and to manipulate later.

If your enlarger only takes 35 mm negatives, contact print your image onto the litho film. Two negative strips, each 3 frames long, can be contact printed onto a piece of 4×5 inch film. This gives you six litho film positives with one exposure. Individual frames can then be cut out to fit your negative carrier and enlarged.

Even though litho film has an antihalation backing, it's best to cover the easel with a piece of black paper when making exposures. This eliminates any possibility of light being reflected back onto the film from a light-colored easel, which could cause a loss of definition.

Taping a piece of black paper the same size as the litho film to the baseboard is another method that eliminates the use of the easel. This is a good method for contact-printing film. Position the black paper directly in the path of light from the enlarger. When you're ready to make an exposure, place the film emulsion up on top of the black paper and cover it with a piece of clean glass to keep the film flat as you make your exposure. (The emulsion side of the film is lighter and not as shiny as the base side of the film.)

Determining Exposure. To determine the proper exposure, you have to make a series of test exposures. The easiest way is to make a test strip in the same manner used in black-and-white printing. Use a consistent developing time and procedure. Even though this film is easy to use and very forgiving, consistency is important if you plan to get the most out of the materials. When evaluating your tests hold the film up to a light source to see if the blacks are solid.

If you're working with negative film, the litho image will be a film positive which can be used to make negative prints. To make positive prints, you have to contact-print the litho film positive with another piece of litho film. This produces a litho negative to be used in making positive prints.

It is sometimes necessary to make a number of film generations when working with litho films, so it's a good idea to establish standard procedures to save you time and material. If your processing procedure is consistent and the processing time is always the same, you can determine an average exposure time and aperture for that enlarger height. This can become a standard exposure for you to work from. The only time you'll have to deviate from it is when printing negatives that vary greatly in their density.

The same is true for contact printing litho positives and negatives. Since litho negatives and positives have no middle values, the exposure should never vary unless you change the enlarger height.

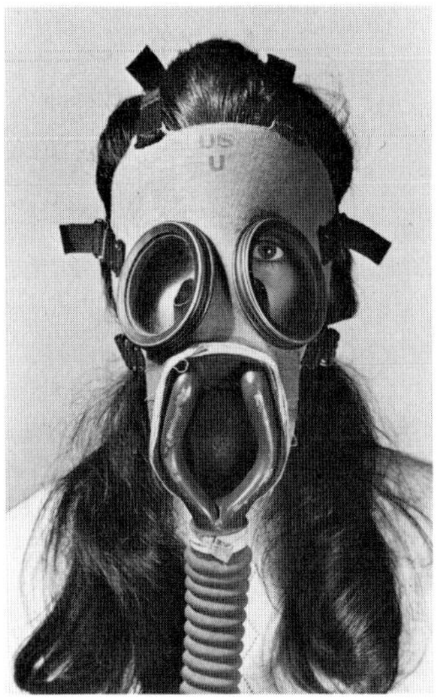

This straight print lacked the graphic impact necessary to illustrate an article on air pollution.

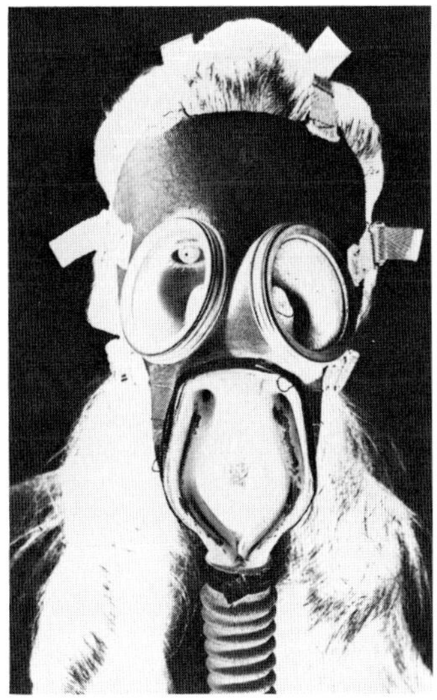

The original negative was printed on litho film to produce a litho positive, and the positive used to make this negative print.

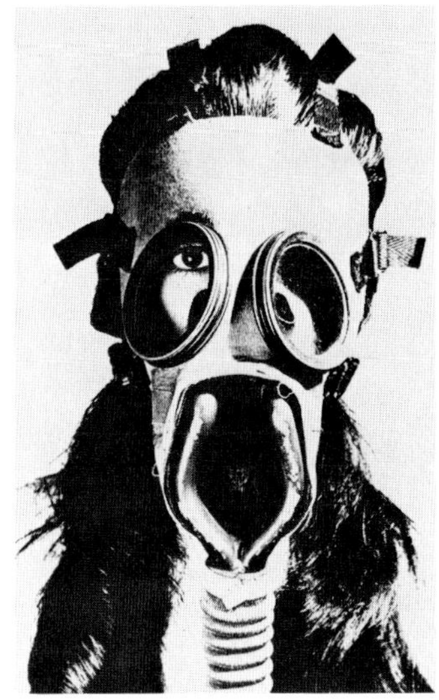

The litho positive was contact printed onto litho film to get a litho negative. This print was made from that litho negative.

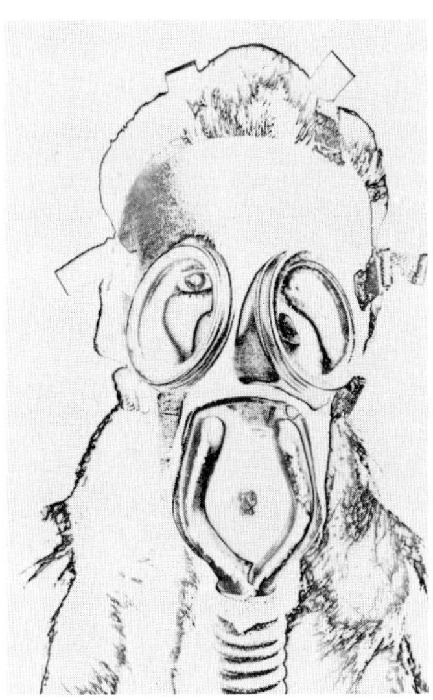

The litho negative was Sabattierized to produce this image variation.

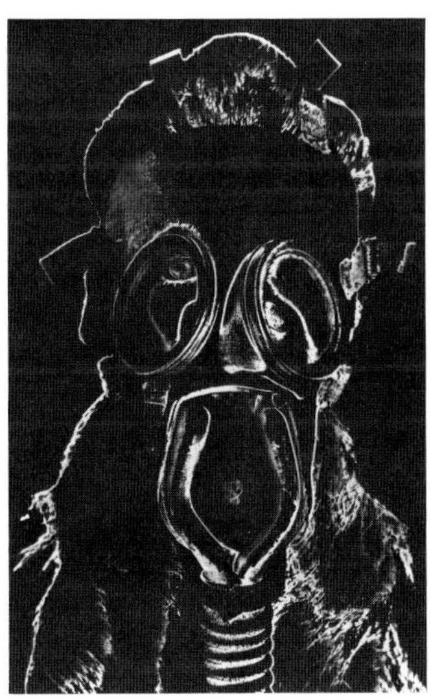

The Sabattierized litho negative was contact printed onto another piece of litho film. The resultant litho positive was used to make this print.

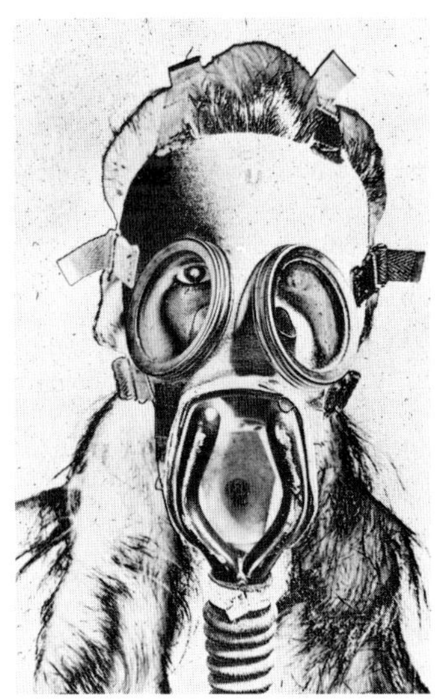

The litho negative and film positive were sandwiched together, slightly off-register, to get this semi-bas-relief print. The litho negative was not developed for maximum density, and this caused the gray tones in the middle.

Varying Developers to Control Detail

The normal developers for litho films are formulated to reduce all tones to pure black and white; therefore some images can lose important details. But there are several ways to save detail and tones while still achieving the graphic characteristics of a litho image.

Fine-Line Developer. When copying artwork, or working with photographs with a lot of fine-line detail, try using Kodak's Fine Line Kodalith developer. This lets you maintain more detail and get better definition than with the normal litho developer. This product is also a two-part developer, and the A and B stock solutions last for extremely long periods of time. However, once they are mixed they deteriorate within an hour. Use the same processing procedure with this developer as with regular litho developer. Since Fine Line Kodalith developer is used more in the graphic arts than photograrhy, it may have to be specially ordered.

Continuous-Tone Developer. Even with fine-line developer, you may run into a situation where the tonal values of the original scene are too similar, and the subject disappears into the background. If this is the case, you can build up the contrast more slowly by beginning with a continuous-tone developer.

When making the initial film positive, try developing it in Dektol diluted one part developer to three parts water. The resulting film positive will still be continuous tone, but with more contrast, and slightly denser than your original negative. Check carefully to make sure the important detail is maintained. If it looks as if the detail is going to be lost, remake the litho film positive and use less exposure, or dilute the developer. If necessary, the developer can be diluted as much as one to ten. The dilution of the developer can be slowly decreased as subsequent generations are made, enabling you to slowly build up contrast while maintaining detail.

When the film positive seems right, contact print it onto another piece of litho film, and develop it in the same developer or one with slightly less dilution. This results in a continuous-tone negative with slightly more contrast than the film positive. Continue this procedure of going back and forth from positive to negative until the overall contrast seems sufficient to hold the important details when a final litho is made and developed in either fine-line or regular litho developer.

This way the final litho negative should contain the necessary detail, while still abstracting the photograph to a pure black-and-white image.

Opaquing Litho Films

A print is seldom made that doesn't require spotting. The same is true of litho negatives and positives. Pinholes and dust spots seem to appear no matter what you do to avoid them. You can use a water-base opaque paint to spot out the pinholes, and make other corrections, when working with litho film. As the name implies, the pigment is opaque and blocks light completely. The water base makes it easy to use, and if you make a mistake it washes right off.

Opaque paint comes in both red and black. Many people prefer red because it is easier to see against the black of the film.

A litho negative and the Sabattier effect were used by Robert Routh to create the interesting image on the facing page.

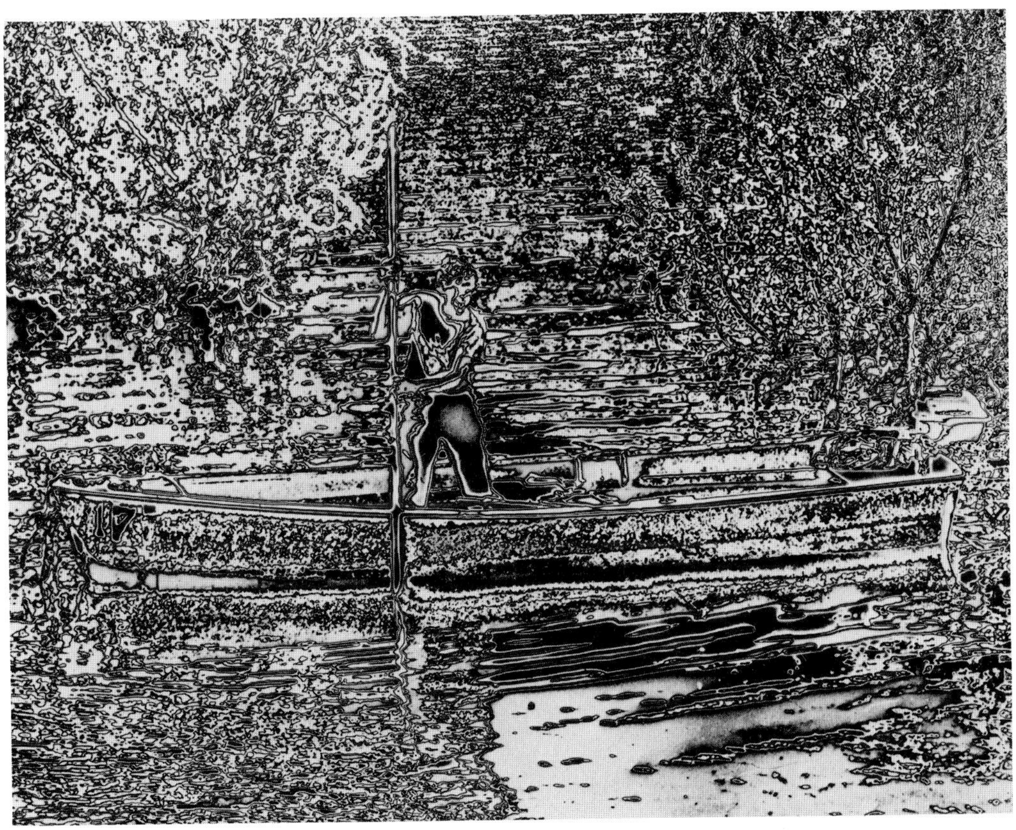

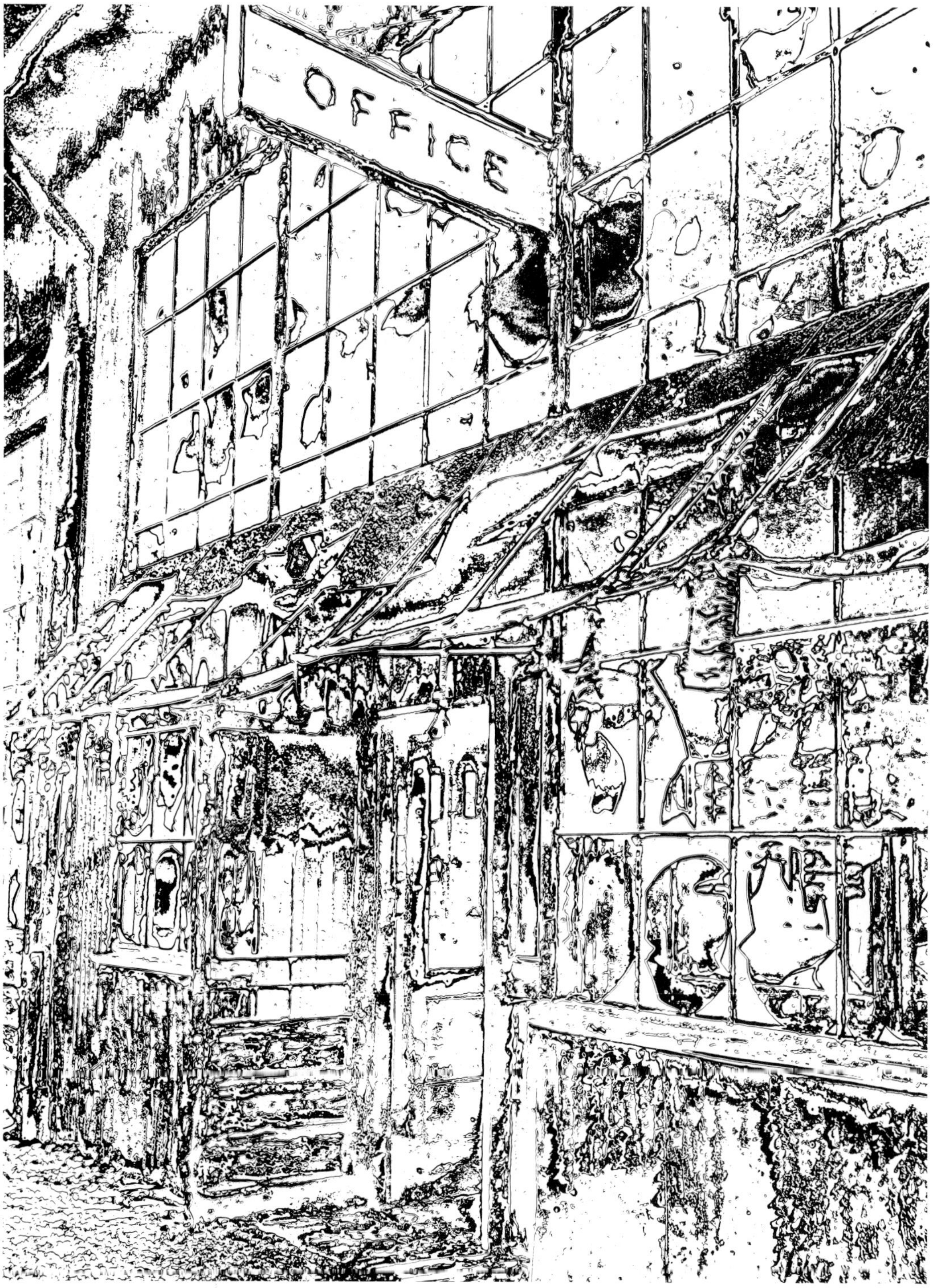

Robert Routh used litho film and the Sabattier effect to produce this beautiful abstraction.

However, if you plan to use the lithos with color-printing materials, it is best to use the black opaque as red opaque lets its own color through to expose the paper.

With black-and-white and color negatives, opaque is also used to touch up small clear spots caused by particles of dust in the camera or film holder. These spots are usually too small to touch up with the normal pencil procedure; but when enlarged they cause big black spots on the print. With opaque, you can spot them out so they won't show on the print. Opaquing can be done on either side of the film.

Eliminating Distractions with Opaque. Opaque can also be used to eliminate distracting objects in a photograph. And you can use it on both the positive and the negative. Since the film is clear and black, it's easy to block out what you don't want and then make a new negative with the correction. Also, details which were lost can be brought out again by opaqueing. For example, an eye can be drawn in or taken out completely.

Applications of Litho Films

In addition to making high-contrast photographic images and being the main workhorse of the graphic-arts industry, litho films can be used to make titles for slide

Bill Collins sandwiched a litho negative with two original negatives to produce this multiple-image photograph.

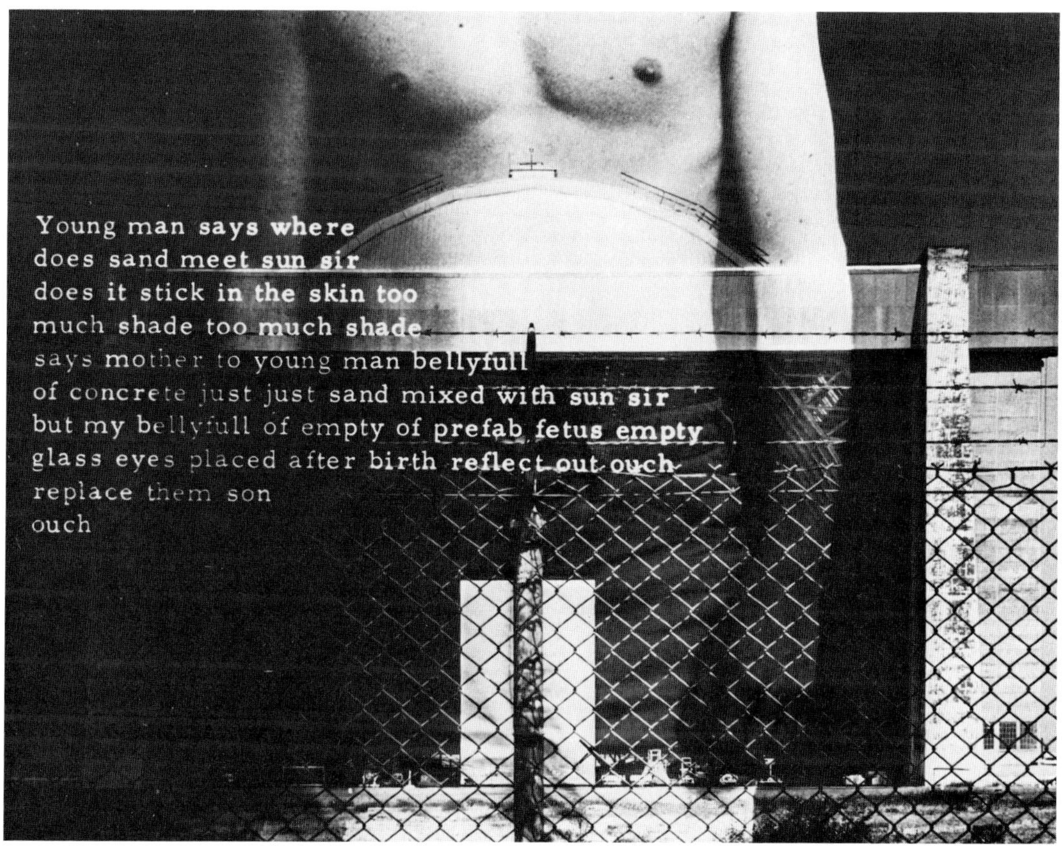

shows, to print words or text in normal photographs, and to make posterizations.

You can etch, color, use the Sabattier effect on the films, or combine the films together for bas-relief effects. To color them, try Edwal toners or food coloring. You can use the same basic procedure used to produce the Sabattier effect on prints with litho films. To heighten the effect, they can be bleached with Farmer's Reducer. Once you've used the Sabattier effect on a piece of litho film you can make an unlimited number of identical prints.

Bas-relief is another effect that is interesting to experiment with. Take a litho negative and sandwich it with a litho positive made from the same negative by contact printing. When the two are sandwiched slightly out of register a line image forms, resulting in a black outline when printed. Also consider how the image would look if you exchanged the high-contrast litho positive for one developed in diluted Dektol with continuous tones. The sandwich would then be made up of a high-contrast, continuous-tone, positive image and a litho negative of the same image. When the two are put together slightly out of register the resulting print appears to have a bas-relief effect. Parts of the image will be pure white, there will be some gray tones, black lines will outline everything, and a dimensional feeling results.

Also, when making prints from litho negatives, try using one or two stops less exposure than normal. A beautiful silver-gray tone may result. When working with litho films, it's so easy to think only in terms of black and white that few people realize the wonderful range of grays that can be achieved by giving less exposure than normal. These lighter print values add depth to an image when multiply exposed onto the same print. They can also be used in combination with normally printed images to get duo-tone effects.

A litho-film image can also be an end in itself. It can be framed between two pieces of glass, and become a free-standing or hanging photo object. Or you can mount it with a backing material such as colored paper or cloth, and frame to it create a silhouette. The applications of this film are numerous. Litho film is a creative material you should become comfortably acquainted with.

9

Posterization

Posterization is a creative process that lies between the graphic arts and photography. With posterization, an image is broken down into gradations of tone that can be printed separately. The value or color can be varied to suit the photographer. The number of variations is limitless. The result can be a graphic image that still symbolizes reality, or it can be total abstraction.

You can make a posterization in either black and white or color. Tonal separations can be made photographically from black-and-white negatives, color negatives, or color slides. To make a color posterization, it doesn't matter if the original is color or black and white. The colors are added at your discretion.

The separations are made from individual sheets of 4×5 inch litho film. These are punched at the edges so that they can be printed in register. Each sheet, or separation, represents a tonal area of the original image. These separation negatives and positives, as components of the photograph, can be varied to alter the value relationships of the final image. If your enlarger isn't large enough to accept 4×5 inch negatives, you have to modify these procedures to fit your circumstances.

Like any process, the success of posterization is dependent upon the image you work with. Not all photographs lend themselves to this technique. Images with simple patterns and strong designs normally produce the best results. The greater the *variety* of continuous tone areas within the original image, the more complex and varied the finished posterization. Photographs with large areas of similar values result in posterizations containing large masses of single colors or tones.

Posterization breaks an image down into tonal values. Four different tonal-value negatives were used to make this posterization.

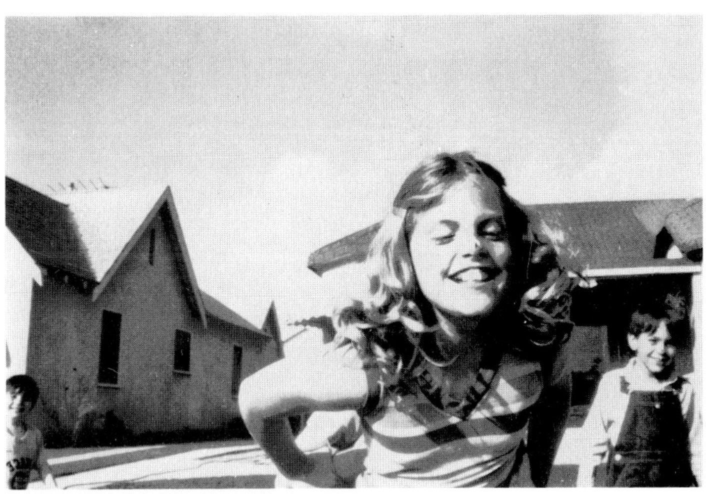

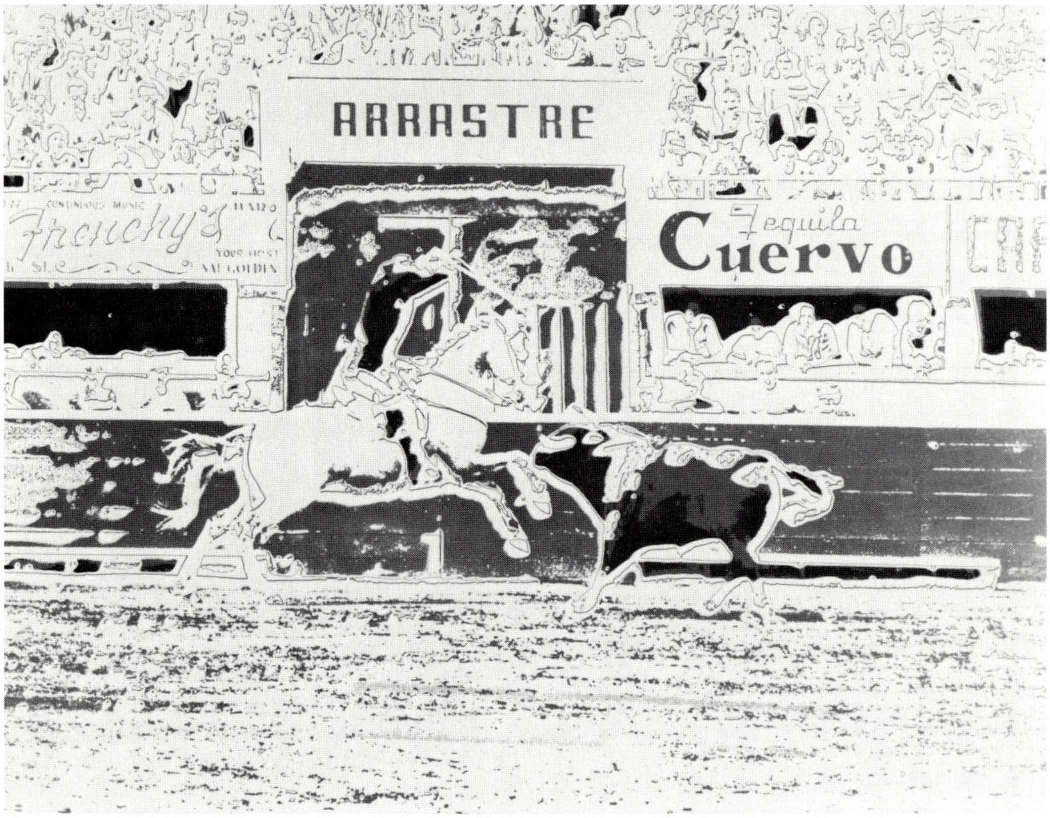

A combination of posterization and multiple-line abstraction was used by Don Mengason to create this image.

Making a master positive from your original image is the first step in making a posterization. However, before beginning you have to devise a registration system for the master positive and resulting posterization separations.

Making Your Own Registration System

Commercial registration systems for posterization, dye-transfer, and lithographic printing are expensive and only necessary if your work varies in size and must be extremely exact. Robert Routh, a well-known photographic artist, writer, and instructor at California State University at Long Beach, devised a homemade registration system for posterization that not only does an excellent job, but costs less than $15 to assemble.

With the registration system you need a *non-adjustable*, two-hole, ¼-inch (0.63 cm) diameter office punch. Before purchasing any punch, make sure the diameter of the holes punched are the same as the diameter of the pins. Otherwise, the punched film won't fit tightly around the registration pins. Registration pins can be purchased at a graphics-arts supply store. In the United States, buy Bregman registration pins (R-3) which are ¼-inch (0.63 cm) in diameter and .04-inch to .06-inch (app. 1.27 cm) in height. The pins should have a flexible stainless-steel base about 1½-inches (3.81 cm) long and about ½-inch (1.27 cm) wide. You will also need two pieces of plate

Registration System

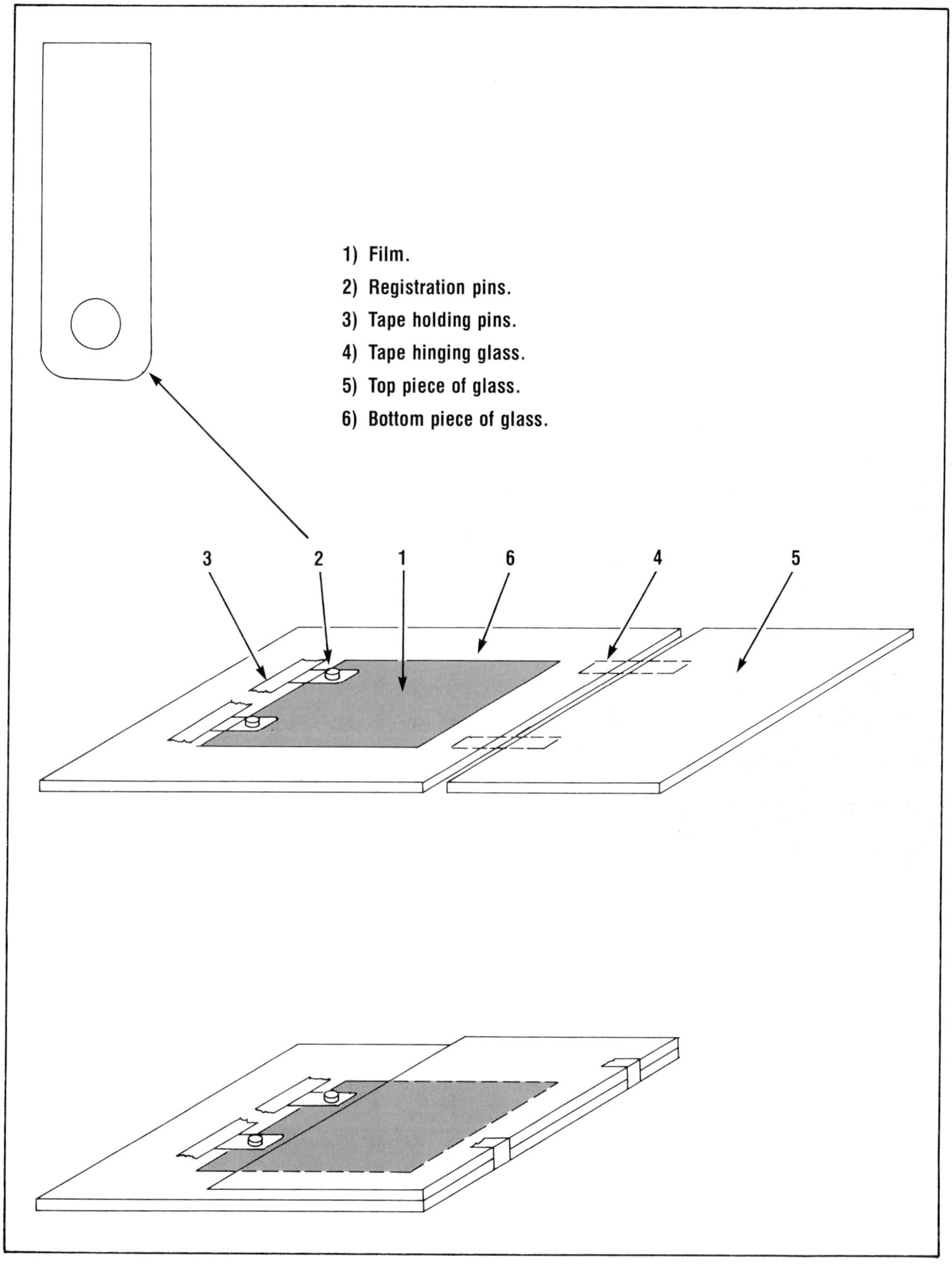

To make posterization separations you will need a registration system. This registration system, devised by Robert Routh, can be made at home. For an inexpensive system, it does an excellent job.

Registration Projection Easel

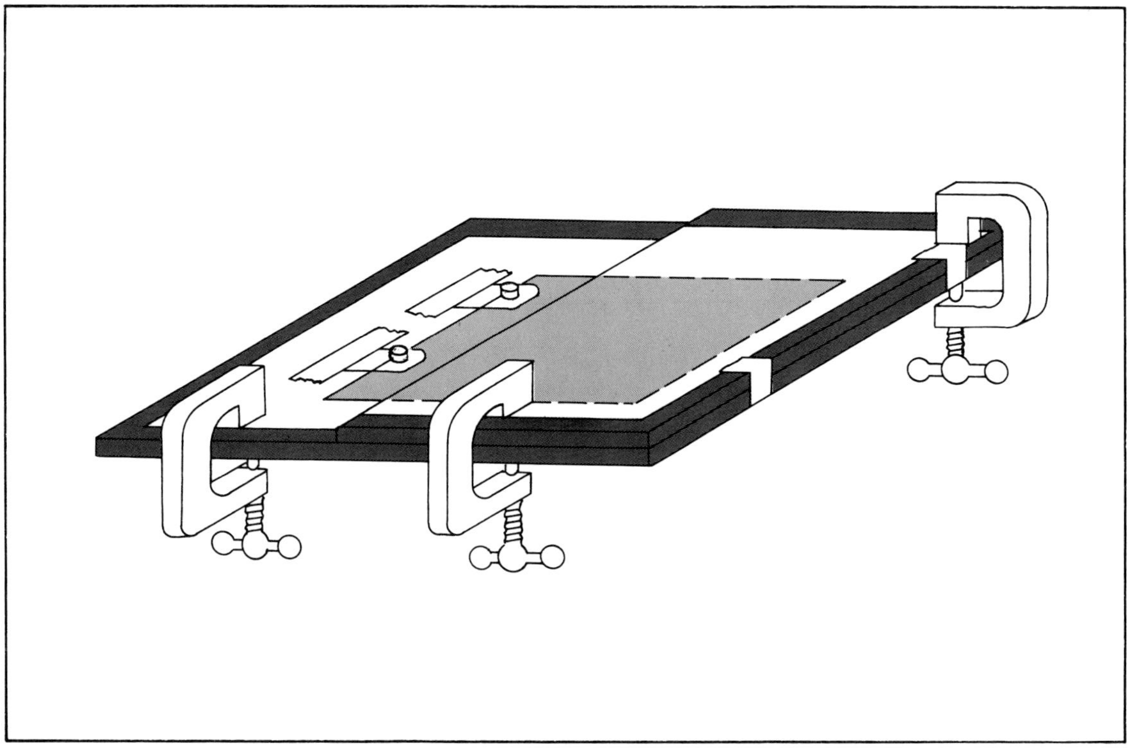

The registration easel can be modified with black tape and three C-clamps for use as a negative carrier in making enlargements. The black tape around the edges keeps light from spilling out. The three C-clamps provide points of contact with the enlarger, permitting the system to be removed and replaced in the enlarger with exact registration. The positioning of the easel and C-clamps will vary with enlargers, but the basic principle is the same.

glass about 1/8-inch (0.32 cm) thick, some black tape, three C-clamps and three 1/8-inch (0.32 cm), or so, bushings. One piece of glass should be 7×9-inches (17.8×22.8 cm) while the other should be 7×5 inches (17.8×12.7 cm).

The registration system you construct will serve as both a contact-printing easel for making separations, and as a negative carrier for making enlargements. Tape the pins to the larger piece of glass. To space them correctly, take a piece of litho film and punch the shorter end with your two-hole punch. Push the registration pins into the holes, and position the film in the center of the glass. Tape the pins to the glass securely. They will need to stay in place when sheets of film are changed.

Use tape to hinge the smaller piece of glass to the larger one at the opposite end from the registration pins. Position the pins and the top piece of glass so the edge of the top piece aligns with the edge of the registration pins. Next, punch holes in a sheet of black paper the same size as your film, and place it on the registration pins instead of the film originally used for spacing. This serves as a base that won't reflect back light when making your separation exposures.

The registration easel is now ready for use in contact printing, but further modifications will be necessary before it is used for enlargements.

The Master Positive

Now you're ready to make your first master positive. The master positive, made from your original negative, is used to make all of the separations. If your original is a slide, make a master negative rather than a positive. Once the master positive is made, the original film is no longer needed; everything can be made from the master positive. The master positive, and the separations, should all be punched in register to make it possible to go back and make additional separations later.

The master positive should have a higher contrast than your original negative or transparency. If the master positive is too weak and lacks contrast, the separations won't be strong enough. Then it becomes necessary to expose several generations back and forth from each separation to build up the density. Generally, the positive separation for the extreme highlights has to be contact printed for several generations to build up its density, but the other separations shouldn't need this.

Exposing the Master Positive. To make the master positive, project your original negative on a piece of white paper that's been punched and placed on the pins of the registration easel. Use the white paper to focus only, then remove it and replace it with a piece of black paper. Next, under safelight illumination only, put a piece of punched litho film emulsion up on the black paper and secure it with the registration pins. Lower the top piece of glass to make the film lie flat.

Now you're ready to make your first exposure test. Begin by exposing four separate sheets of film for 3 seconds each at *f*/11. Develop them in Dektol (diluted 1:3) at room temperature. Develop one for 30 seconds, one for 60 seconds, one for 90 seconds, and another for 2 minutes. Use a water stop bath for 30 seconds and fix and wash normally. (You can use a blow hair dryer to decrease drying time.) One of these tests should result in a continuous-tone positive that is strong in contrast while containing good shadow detail. If the detail isn't adequate, or the positives are too dense, then adjustments are necessary and you have to try again.

Making the Separations

Once you've made a good master positive, you're ready to make the posterization separations—pairs of high-contrast negatives and positives. Each pair represents a different tonal value of the original negative. You'll make the negative separations first, directly from the master positive. Then the positive separations are made from each negative. This results in negative-positive pairs of separations for each tonal value. The negative separations are all you need to make black-and-white posterizations. But if you plan to make single or multiple line images, or color posterizations, you'll have to make positive separations as well.

Exposing the Negative Separations. Prior to making the separations, punch registration holes in a number of sheets of litho film so they're ready for use. Put an empty negative carrier into the enlarger and raise it to a height that allows the light beam to easily cover a 4×5 inch area. Focus the enlarger until the edge of the negative carrier is sharp. (This concentrates the light source.) Next, position the registration easel in the light beam, tape it to the baseboard of your enlarger, and insert the piece of black paper.

Then, with only a safelight on, take a sheet of punched, unexposed litho film and place it emulsion up over the pins. Put the master positive, emulsion down, on top of the litho film. Cover this combination with the top piece of glass and you're ready to

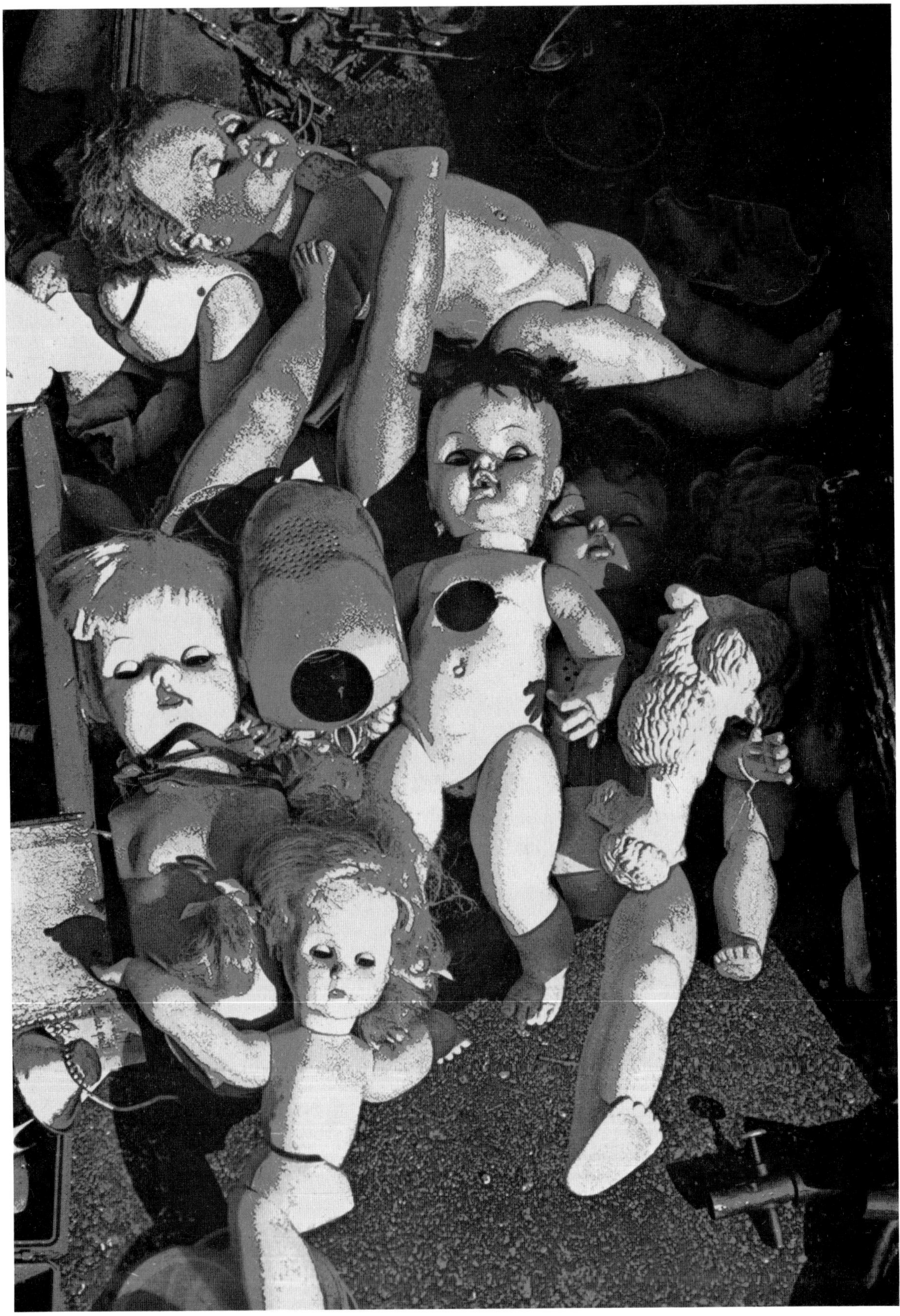

This posterization was made with five negative separation masks.

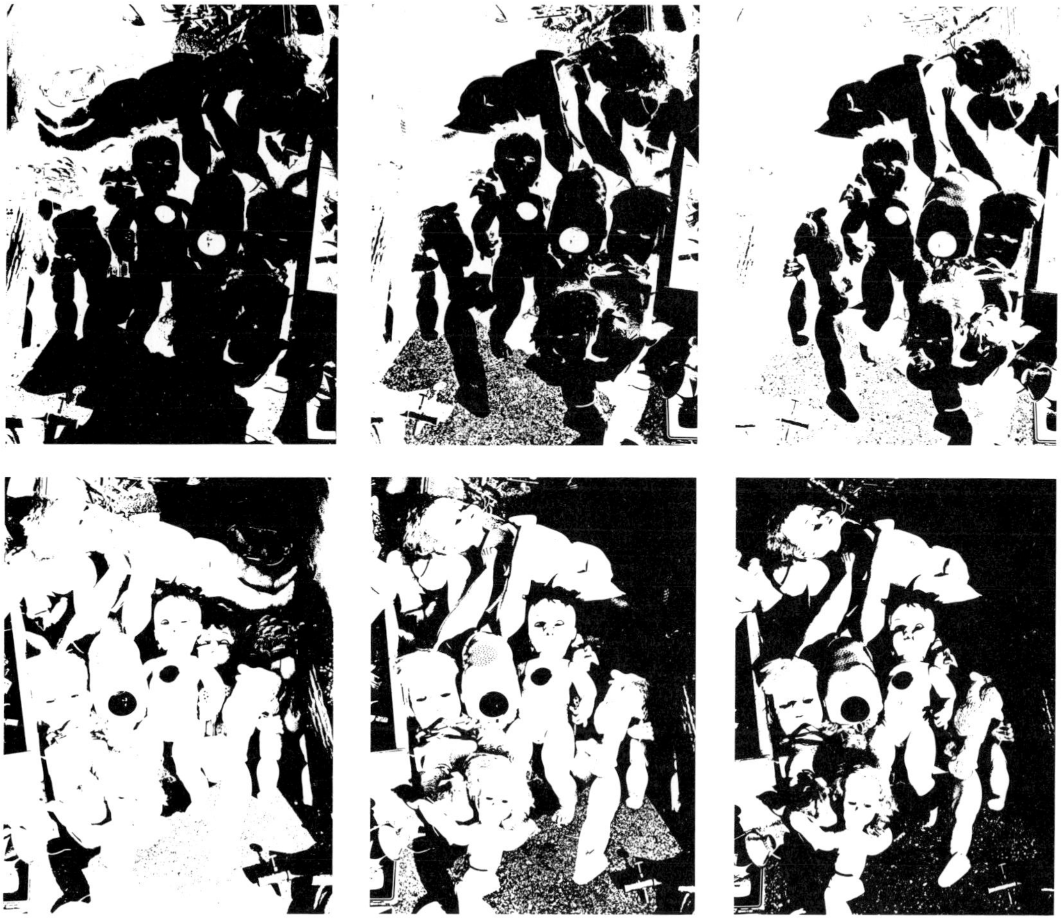

The five negative-separation masks in the first and third rows were used to make the image on the facing page. Negative separations are all you need to produce black and white posterizations. The five positive separations in the second and fourth rows were made by contact printing the negative separations. Both negative and positive separations are necessary to produce multiple-line images and color posterizations.

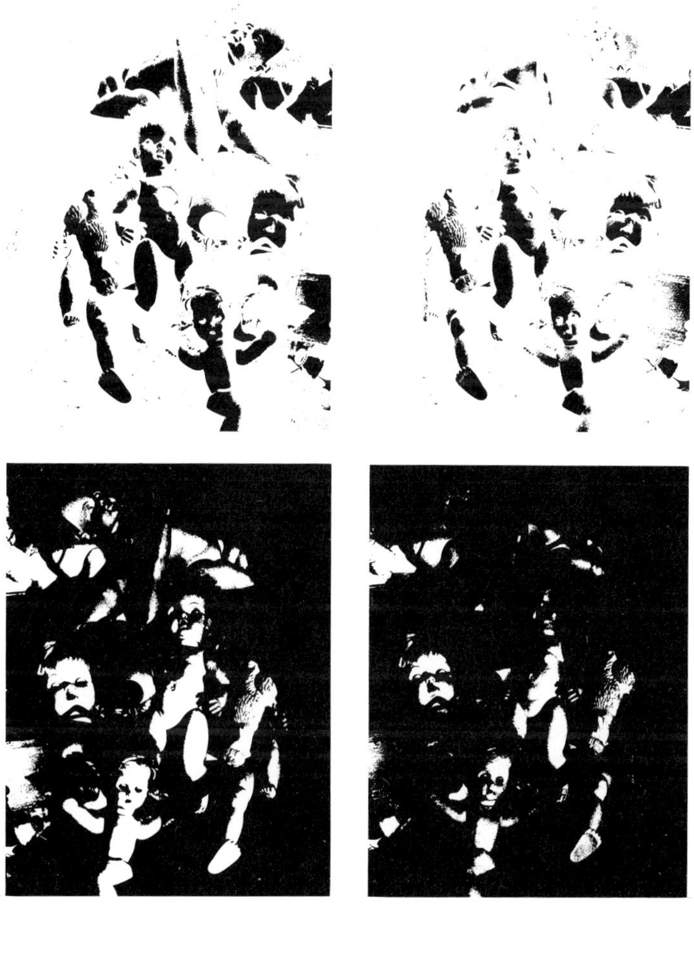

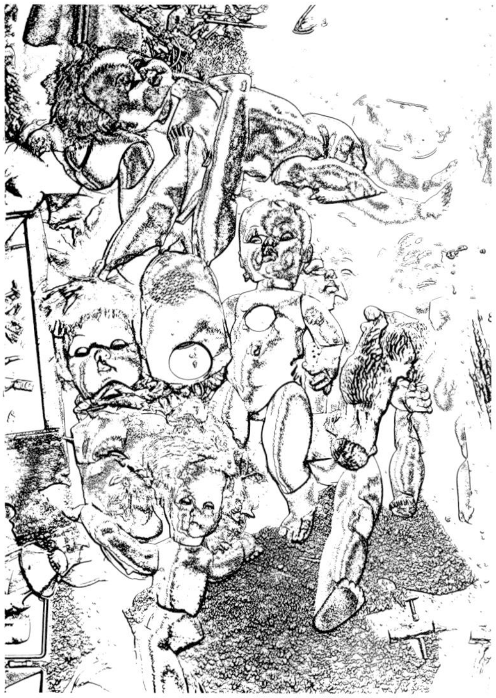

This tone-line abstraction, or multiple-line image, was made by exposing a sheet of litho film to all five negative- and positive-posterization separations of the previous page.

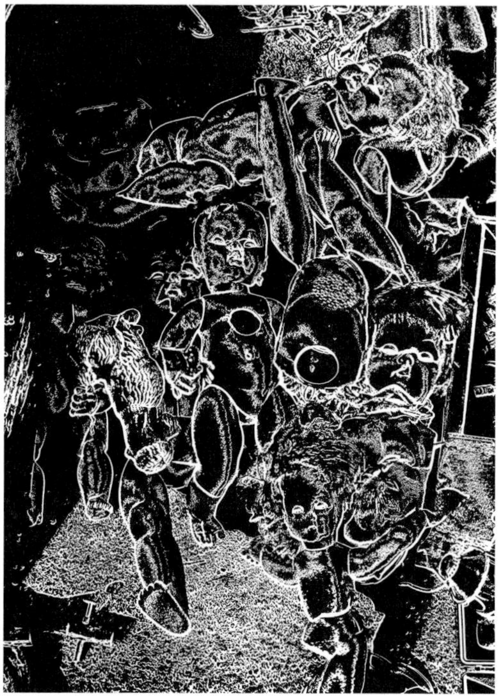

A negative multiple-line image was made by contact printing the original multiple-line negative onto a piece of litho film, which in turn produced a film positive.

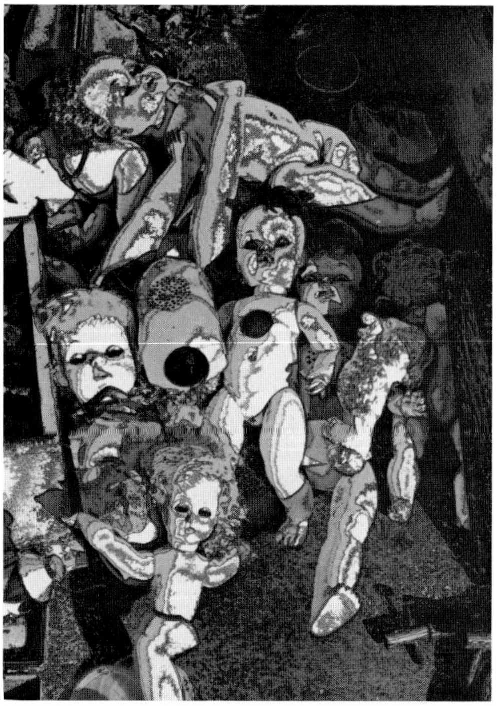

The multiple-line image was combined with a five-separation posterization to create this variation of the image.

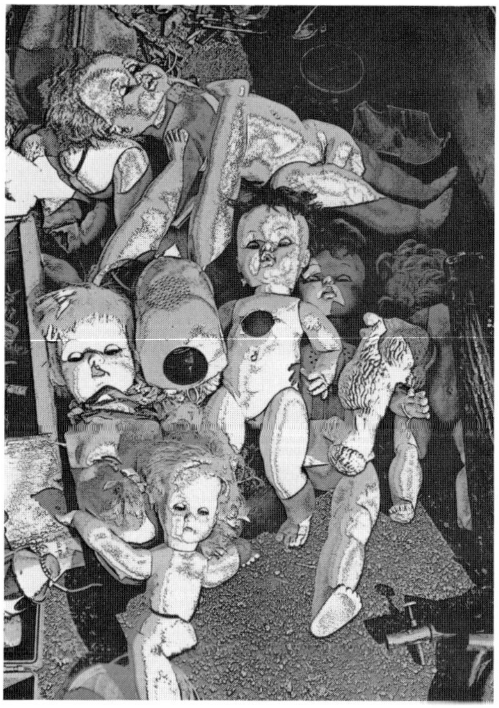

A single-line image was used with the five-separation posterization for this variation.

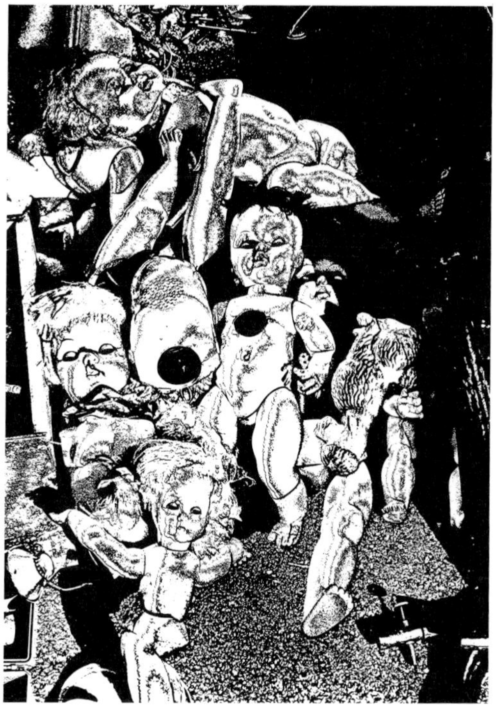

A multiple-line image was printed with a number four negative-separation mask to produce this photograph.

make your first exposure. Try an exposure of ten seconds at *f*/8, and develop the film in litho developer for three minutes. After fixing, examine the image. If the negative is not dense enough to block light completely in the black areas, you may need to make another more contrasty master positive. If the negative has a good solid black, you're ready to begin. Normally, at least five separations are needed for you to have some options to work with later. So, if the negative separation you just made appears satisfactory, make several exposures, bracketing in one-stop increments on either side of your initial exposure. This results in a series of masks that range from the extreme highlights of your image to the shadow areas.

Sometimes the highlight-separation masks lack enough density. For the proper density, the black areas of separation masks must be pure and opaque enough to block light completely. Normally, this isn't the fault of the master positive, but happens because the highlight mask is at the extreme end of the film's range of sensitivity. If your highlight mask lacks enough density, you will have to contact print the negative highlight separation onto another piece of litho film. This produces a positive film image which should be developed normally in litho developer. This positive will have more contrast than the negative, because contrast increases with each generation. The new positive must then be contact printed again to produce a usable negative highlight-separation mask.

Exposing the Positive Separations. After making a set of negative separations, a set of positive separations should be produced from each of them. These are also made by contact printing with the registration easel. The same exposure will probably work for all of them, since each one should have the same density of black. The density of the positive separation masks should match that of the negative separation masks, so no light is transmitted when they are held up to light in perfect register. The exposed areas of one should completely block the clear areas of the other. Once the positive separations are made, you should have five pairs of matching negative-positive separation masks.

Black-and-White Posterizations

Once the separations are completed, you have the tools necessary to make a wide range of variations from just one original image. You might start with black-and-white posterizations, which are made from the negative separations. Before attempting enlargements, make a series of small posterization variations by contact printing to determine which combination of masks and exposures is most satisfying and to economize on time and materials.

As the first step, take one of the negative separations and put it in place on the registration easel. (First remove the black paper so the negative can be projected.) Place the registration easel with the negative in the enlarger, so the image can be projected onto a printing easel. Adjust the height of the enlarger until the projected image is the same size as the final print. Then remove the registration easel from the enlarger head and replace it with an empty 4×5 inch negative carrier. Focus the light beam of the enlarger with the edges of the negative carrier. This will be the height used for the contact-posterization tests. This way, the exposures for the final enlargements will be the same as those used to make the contact tests (because the light will be traveling the same distance).

Testing Procedure. Next, cut some normal contrast (grade 2 or 3) black-and-white enlarging paper into 4×5 inch sheets. Punch them on the 4-inch end with your two-hole punch. Put the black paper back in the registration easel, position it under the light beam of the enlarger, and tape it in place.

Arrange the negative separations in sequence from the most- to the least-dense negative. Number your negatives to avoid confusion. Once everything is organized, take a piece of punched 4×5 inch printing paper and place it emulsion side up on the black paper in the registration easel. Put the shadow separation (#1) emulsion down on top of the printing paper. Cover this combination with glass, and try an initial exposure of 12 seconds at *f*/32 or *f*/22 if you plan to make an 8×10 inch enlargement. (Exposure adjustments will be necessary for enlargements up to, or greater than, 8×10 inches.) This first exposure determines the areas of the print that will be black. Later, if you decide you want another part of the picture black, you'll have to vary the sequence of the separations. After the initial exposure has been made, remove the shadow separation, *leaving the printing paper in place*, and replace it with the next separation in the sequence. Make a three-second exposure at the same aperture.

For the remaining separations, follow the procedure used with the second separation and give each one a three-second exposure. With each additional exposure, light is added to a different part of the print. At the same time, parts of the print exposed by previous separations get added exposure. Consequently, each separation creates a different tonal value. No two areas of the print receive the same amount of exposure.

This sequence can be altered, or separations omitted, to create variations of the image. If there is a particular area you'd like to remain white, leave that separation in place throughout all the exposures. Try a number of variations, but be sure to record all the data, so you can repeat the image when you decide to make an enlargement.

Enlarging With the Registration Easel

To make an enlargement, you have to modify the registration easel. To modify the easel, you need black tape, three C-clamps, and three of the ⅛-inch bushings mentioned earlier. You're modifying the easel so it can be removed from the enlarger to change separation negatives and then be put back in the same place to maintain registration.

The positioning of the easel and C-clamps will vary with enlargers, but the basic principle applies to all enlargers. The C-clamps are positioned on the glass easel so that there are two clamps on one side and one clamp on an adjacent side. This creates three stopping points on two sides that come in contact with the edge of the enlarger. Since there are three points of contact, the positioning should be the same each time you put the easel into the enlarger. The ⅛-inch bushings are used between the C-clamps and the glass to produce a spacer with a vertical edge which makes contact with the edge of the enlarger.

If you plan to do a lot of posterizations, you may want to make two easels, one for contact printing and one for enlarging. You could then permanently glue the bushings, or similar objects, in place on the bottom of the easel so it's always set up and ready to use. The important thing to remember is the three-point contact necessary to maintain registration. (You'll probably also find it necessary to reposition the registration pins on the easel so the film will be located in the center of the enlarger.) Once these modifications have been completed, use the black tape to mask off the rest of the glass so stray light won't leak out around the negatives. The edges of the glass also have to be taped, because the light will travel out the edges. This is especially important when working with color materials.

When the modifications on the easel are done, make your enlargements in the same order you made the contact test prints. As long as the enlarger height is the same, the same exposures should apply. The only difference this time is you'll be leaving the printing paper in a printing easel, and changing the separations on your registration easel in the enlarger. The data recorded when you made the test prints should result in enlargements that have the same tones as the tests provided the enlarger height was the same.

Color Posterization

Color posterization, with printing paper designed for negative printing, is approached in a manner similar to black-and-white posterization. But, unlike the procedure for black-and-white posterizations, both the negative and the positive separations must be used to avoid overlapping the colors. Overlapping is an advantage with black-and-white posterization, but with color posterization you should avoid overlapping to keep the integrity of the colors.

By sandwiching the negative and positive separations properly, it is possible to expose a different color each time with no overlap. To maintain a pure white, refrain from exposing one or more of the separations. In order to save time and materials, make contact tests before enlarging. The same procedure used for black-and-white contact tests and enlargements applies with color, except the separation sequencing is different (refer to the accompanying diagram). The enlarger light is filtered to produce the colors.

Controlling Color. The simplest way to control the color is by using the primary filters, red (25A), green (61), and blue (47B) as explained earlier in the chapter on photograms. An exposure through any one of these three filters produces its complementary color. (The complement of red is cyan, the complement of green is magenta, and the complement of blue is yellow.) A separate but equal exposure through any two primary colors produces the third primary color. Thus, an exposure of five seconds through a red filter and a five-second exposure through a green filter will produce the color blue. Equal exposures made separately from each of the three primary colors produces gray or black, depending on the amount of the exposure. Any hue in the rainbow can be achieved by varying the exposure combinations of these colors.

Color-negative papers are balanced for use with color negatives, which have an orange color cast (mask). Therefore, it is best to balance the colors by putting a piece of unexposed but developed color-negative film above the negative carrier. This helps alleviate exposure problems when using the blue filter.

Determine your exposure times by making a series of test strips for each of the primary and secondary colors. Make a series of 15 one-second exposures for each color. Shorter exposures produce paler pastel colors, while longer exposures produce richer, more saturated colors. Refer to the chapter on photograms for further information on making color test strips. These test strips provide a basis for producing the desired color, value, and exposure.

Separation Sequence For Color Posterizations

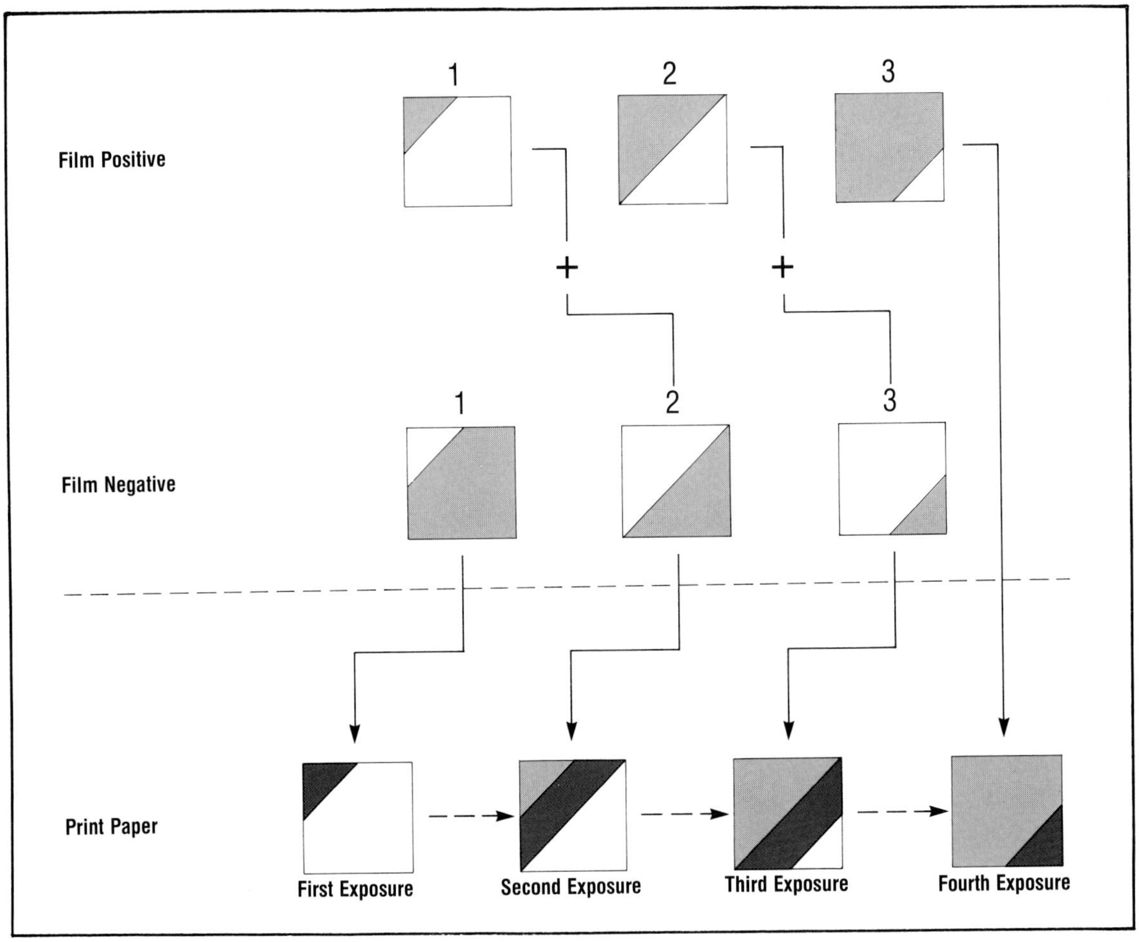

For color posterizations both the positive and negative separations must be sandwiched to expose a different color each time with no overlapping. To maintain a pure white, don't expose one or more of the separations. The above diagram shows an image divided into three separations, but the number of separations is up to you.

Tone-Line Abstractions

A tone-line abstraction is a line image derived from the various tonal values of a photograph. The result looks a lot like a pen and ink outline of the original photographic image. The lines represent the various contours and value separations within that image. The separation negatives used to make posterizations are also used to make tone-line abstractions.

Both single-line abstractions and multiple-line abstractions are possible. The single-line abstraction is a simple outline of the obvious contours and shapes within the photograph; a multiple-line image is more like a contour or relief map of the image. You can print these line abstractions individually in either positive or negative form, or in combination with a black-and-white or color posterization.

Making a Tone-Line Abstraction. To make a tone-line abstraction, you'll use both the positive and negative separations. A single-line abstraction is made from one separation. Take a single separation and sandwich the negative and positive together in registration. Then hold them up to a light. If the litho separations were properly exposed and developed, you won't see any light directly through the sandwich. But when you hold them at an angle, a line image will be visible. If you see light bleeding through the black areas of the film your litho separations aren't dense enough, and some fogging may result when you make tone-line abstractions and posterizations. To correct this you have to go back and rework some of your separations.

To begin, set your enlarger up at its standard height for contact printing lithos. The tone-line abstraction can be made directly on printing paper or litho film. It's best to make it on film first, so you can get a negative and a positive tone-line abstraction on film for use in making enlargements any size you want. The same exposure information you arrived at when contact printing your second generation of litho separations applies here. Use the registration easel for making tone-line abstractions. Put a punched piece of black paper on the bottom, over the registration pins. Then put a punched piece of unexposed litho film in, emulsion side up. Secure the positive and negative litho separations over the unexposed film, with their emulsions apart. Hold them in firm contact with the top sheet of glass.

You are now ready to make your exposure. Light won't pass through the sandwiched positive and negative separations because the separations in register block the light. But, if the light comes at a 45-degree angle, it will go between the separations, expose the film below, and create a line image.

If the light comes from only one side, just part of the image will be exposed. This problem was solved in the past by using a record turntable in the darkroom with a small light set up next to it at a 45-degree angle. The unexposed film and litho positive and negative were sandwiched and placed on the turntable. When the turntable revolved, the film was exposed from all sides at a 45-degree angle.

Fortunately, Robert Routh has devised a simpler method. His method uses an enlarger as the exposure device. Take your registration easel—with the black paper on the bottom, the unexposed litho film emulsion up, and the positive and negative separations on top of that—and place this combination under your enlarger at a 45-degree angle to the light. Make an exposure using the time you arrived at to contact print litho films. After making the first exposure, turn the registration easel 90 degrees to the right while maintaining the 45-degree angle. Make another exposure for the same amount of time. Continue turning the easel 90 degrees until you make separate but equal exposures from all four sides. This results in a fully exposed single-line abstraction.

Multiple-Line Abstractions. To make a multiple-line abstraction, follow the same procedure as for single-line abstractions, but once you've completed exposing one separation, remove it and put a new one in its place. Then expose the same piece of film in the identical manner, but with a different positive and negative separation. This procedure can be repeated as many times as you like. If you have five separations, each one can be used, and the multiple-line image will be very detailed. To get a wider, bolder line, increase the angle of the registration easel during exposure, or place a piece of matte acetate, frosted side up, between the positive and negative separations.

Switching the placement of the positive and negative separations is another variation. Reverse them so the one previously on top is now on the bottom, making sure their emulsions are apart. This results in a variation of the line image. When they are one way, you get a single line; but by switching them, a double line results. If you make both a single and a double line from the same separation, they can be printed in register on the same print. The single line ends up between the two lines. The single line can be printed one color and the double line, which will be on either side of it, can be another color.

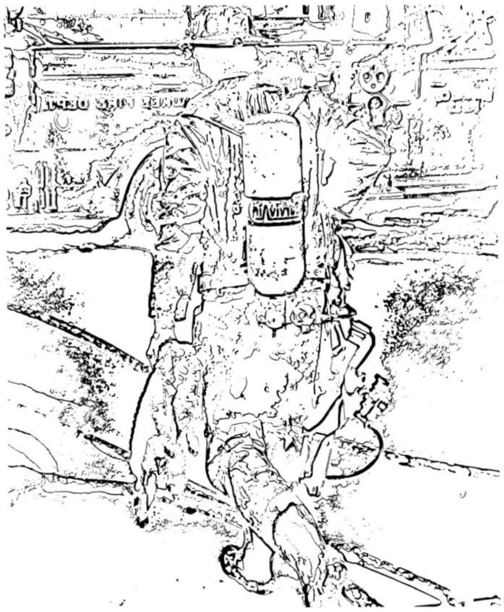

This multiple-line image was made from five separation negatives and positives.

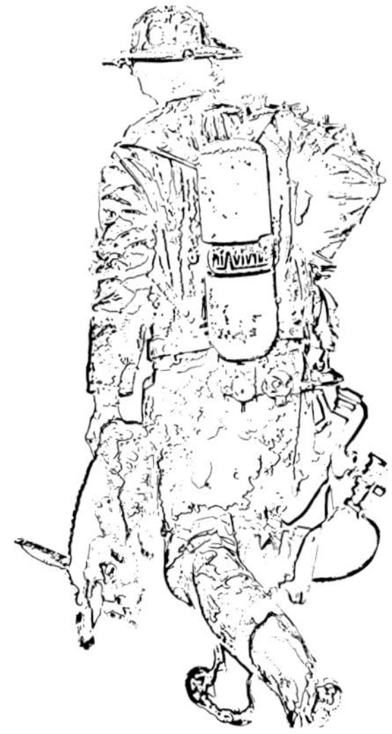

A simplified version was made by painting out the background on the negative with opaque.

Posterization Combinations

You can also combine tone-line abstractions with posterizations. Sine your abstractions were made in register from the same separations, you can easily add them to a color or a black-and-white posterization. You will need both a positive and a negative tone-line abstraction. The positive is kept in place on the registration easel during all of the exposures for the posterization to prevent exposure in the area where the line image is to be printed until you are ready. Then replace the positive tone-line abstraction with the negative one and make an exposure just for the line image.

Continuous-Tone/ Posterization Combinations

In addition to combining tone-line abstractions with posterizations, you might want to try combining a continuous-tone image with a posterized version. This can be done with either black-and-white or color materials, and lets you create images somewhere between fantasy and reality. Use your master positive to get a negative continuous-tone image to combine with the posterization. Or, you can make a continuous-tone negative image in register, and use that to combine a positive image with the posterization. A continuous-tone color image can be combined with your posterization if you plan in advance to make the separations, and attach registration tabs to the original film. Make your master positive by contact printing the color original directly. Thus, all of the separations will register with the color original, and it can be printed into a posterized version.

Once you've mastered the technique, and know how to work with the registration system to make separation masks, any number of variations and options are open. You can use this registration system to make masks for multiple printing continuous-tone images together. Printing paper can be punched and registered so it can be moved between exposures, and then negatives can be changed without losing registration. The possibilities are exciting, and provide an open door to explore the medium to the full extent of your imagination.

10

Altering the Finished Print

You can go beyond the darkroom to further extend the level of your photographic creativity. After you make prints, you can add to, or alter them by toning, bleaching, hand-coloring, drawing, and painting. Some toning techniques also increase the permanence of photographs. To heighten the impact of a particular image or idea, try a montage or cut and alter the print surface. These techniques can change the impact of your images, while spotting and retouching provide finishing touches that make an image complete.

Toning Black-and-White Prints

Chemical toning is a traditional method of adding color to black-and-white prints. Commercial toners are available in a variety of colors. Sepia and brown have always been the most popular, but prints can also be toned red, blue, green, yellow, or even a combination of several colors.

Substances such as coffee, tea, and food-coloring dyes can also be used to tone prints. However these items tone the paper base while most commercial photographic toners react with the emulsion. Consequently, the effect is different.

With non-photographic toners such as food coloring, the longer the print is in the dye the deeper the color gets (until it reaches a saturation point). After the print is toned, it must be thoroughly squeegeed. If any liquid remains on the surface of the print it will cause unevenness in the tone. Don't rinse the print in water before squeegeeing, and be careful not to get any liquid on the surface once it's dry. Since food coloring affects only the paper base, the dye will bleach out to a lighter value when in contact with another liquid.

If you plan to tone a print, make sure it's properly processed. Improper processing, especially in the fixer and final wash, can cause uneven toning and staining. Your prints should be fixed for the recommended amount of time, with frequent agitation. The best method of fixing prints is to use a double fixing bath. The first bath can be a slightly used fixer, but the second bath should be fresh. Fix the prints for three min-

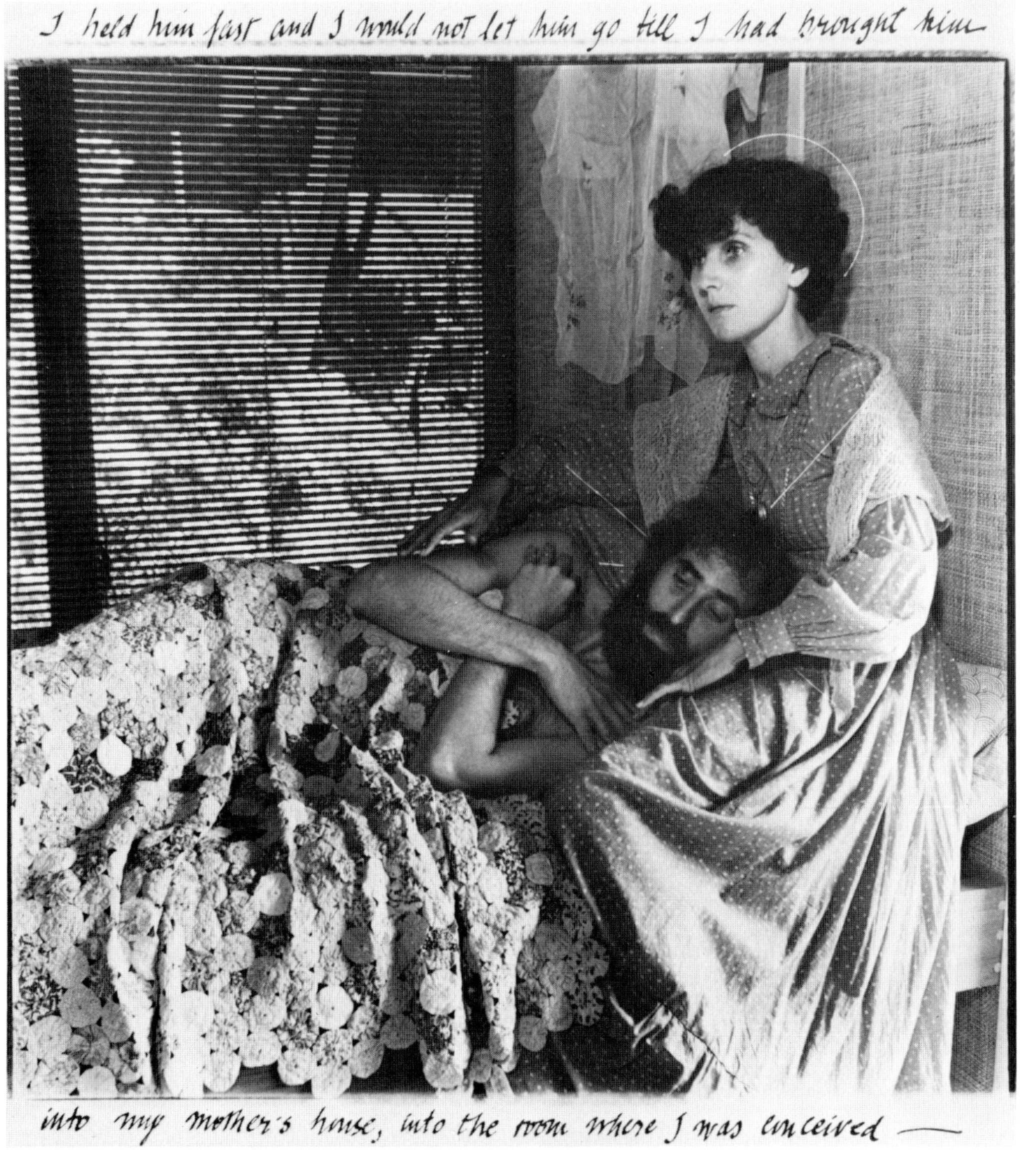

The finished print is considered a sacred object by many photographers, while for others it is only a beginning. Holly Wright has written directly onto the surface of this image.

utes in the first bath and then for three more minutes in the second. This provides a thorough fixing and reduces the possibility of staining when the prints are toned. When the first bath is exhausted switch the second bath with the first, and replace the second with a fresh batch of fixer.

After fixing prints, bathe them in a hypo eliminator. Then thoroughly wash them. Fiber-based papers need at least a half-hour of washing, while resin-coated papers should be thoroughly washed in two to five minutes.

Edwal Toners. Some of the more unusual toning products available are manufactured by the Edwal Scientific Products Corp. Edwal toners, which can be used to tone both black-and-white films and papers, are single-solution toners available in red, blue, green, yellow, and brown. These toners are designed to be used individually, but you can get intermediate colors by toning a print first in one color and then in another.

Edwal toners come with thorough instructions which should be followed carefully. Inside the cap of each four-ounce bottle is a small container holding reddish crystals. These crystals must be completely dissolved in the liquid part of the toner to make it active. Prior to mixing the crystals with the liquid the toners will last indefinitely. Once mixed, they last only six to eight weeks. (The one exception is the blue toner which lasts up to a year.)

When using Edwal toners, save a batch of prints and tone them all in one session. The toners will stain trays, hands, and anything else they come in contact with, so caution is advised.

Once the toner is activated, dilute it with water to make 64 ounces (approximately 2 litres) of working solution. This is enough to tone about thirty 8×10 prints. Toning can be done at room temperature. Normal toning takes from four to ten minutes; however, the hotter the toner the faster it works. The permanence of the dyes is about the same as those of modern color films.

To tone a print, immerse it in the desired toner and gently agitate it. When the toning depth is suitable, remove the print from the toner and wash it in running water for 10 to 20 minutes. Even though the toner is chemically fixed to the silver image, some of it affects the paper base. With extended washing times, toner washes out of the paper base and the highlight areas come out whiter.

If possible squeegee and then air dry the toned prints on fiberglass window screens. Avoid blotters and print dryers with aprons or rollers, because toned prints will stain anything they come into contact with while drying. If you find blue or green spots appearing on your toned prints, they are probably due to iron particles in your water. If you used porcelain trays, the spots could be a result of chips in the trays.

You can get unusual effects by extending the toning time and using the toner full strength. Try to work with a print that is darker than normal. Due to the extended toning time of 15 to 20 minutes, and the increased activity of the full strength toner, the silver salts will be bleached away and the image converted to chalk-like tones. The toner reacts according to the density of the image; therefore the resulting effect looks somewhat similar to a monochromatic color print with the Sabattier effect. However, if some dark areas are left in the print, additional color effects can be obtained by transferring the print from one color toner bath to another. This results in an unusual colored outline effect.

Conventional Toners. A wide variety of other toners are available, but most of

Land-Site #5, *by Laurie Brown, is composed of nine separate black-and-white prints mounted together to form one piece. The ground areas are selectively toned brown, while the sky is left normal.*

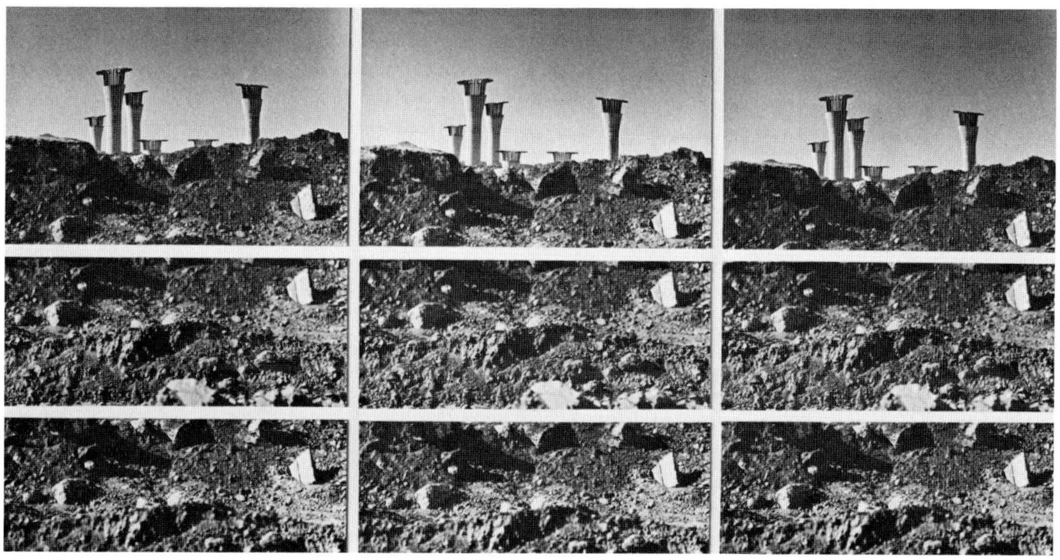

them produce various shades of brown. Kodak's Sepia, Selenium, and Poly-Toner are popular toners that yield different shades of brown when used with various warm- and cold-tone papers. Depending on the print paper used, a blue toner made by Kodak produces reddish-orange tones when used on sepia- or brown-toned prints.

All these toners are easy to use and come with adequate instructions, but it's advisable to do some experimenting with them. Remember the prints must be fully processed for the toner to react properly. The results will vary depending on the printing paper you are using. Don't expect to get the same coloring if you switch papers or go from resin-coated to fiber-based paper. Also, the color cast may change slightly once the print dries, and heat driers can cause the color to shift.

Masking for Multiple Colors. Most of the time we are satisfied with a one-color toned print. But you can totally alter the effect of an image by toning part of it one color and the rest another. Or try toning part of it, leaving the rest black-and-white. To do this, use either photo maskoid or rubber cement. Thoroughly coat the part of the print that you don't want to tone. The maskoid or rubber-cement coating provides a liquid-proof covering and prevents the toner from affecting the covered areas of the print. After you have toned the print, rinse it in water and then rub the protective coating off the untoned portion of the print. Then squeegee the print. You can also coat the toned portion of the print with maskoid or rubber cement while still wet, immerse it in another color toner, and end up with a multi-color print.

Toning Black-and-White Prints for Permanence

All photographs, both color and black-and-white, deteriorate with time. How fast this happens depends on whether they were properly processed, how they are stored, how they are displayed, and the amount of contact with light. Aside from fading problems due to exposure to light, most print deterioration is a result of contact with air-borne sulfur gases and other harmful compounds. Also, wrapping papers, cardboard, and matte boards can be very damaging to photographic materials over a period of time, unless they have a neutral pH and are buffered.

Fortunately, black-and-white images can be protected by special toners that combine with the metallic silver in the photograph and form a compound with above-average stability. A special formula of selenium or gold toner is commonly used for this purpose. These toners, depending on their dilution, won't impart color to a print. Their purpose is to make the prints more permanent, not to tint them.

For maximum permanence, gold toning is considered the most effective. But it's much more expensive than selenium toning, which many photographers also prefer for aesthetic reasons. Selenium toning intensifies the blacks in a print, adding a brilliance to the image. However, by varying the dilution of selenium toner, you can produce some color shift; less toning makes no visible change in the print.

Protective Selenium Toning Bath. To make a protective selenium toning bath, begin with a one-gallon (3.78 l) working solution of Kodak Hypo Clearing Agent (or other washing aids, such as HEICO Permawash, Orbit, or GAF Quix). Then add 1½ to 7 ounces (45 to 207 ml) of Kodak Rapid Selenium Toner to the clearing agent, depending on whether or not you want the intensification effect in the blacks. The more toner you add, the stronger the intensification and color shift. Next add 2½ ounces (74 ml) of Kodalk Balanced Alkali to the solution, and mix thoroughly.

Before using the toning bath, be sure to properly fix your prints with a double fixing bath. Rinse the prints in water for ten minutes, then transfer the prints directly into the selenium toner solution at room temperature, and continuously agitate them for three to five minutes. After toning, wash the prints for the normal amount of time. Each gallon of solution provides protective toning for fifty 8×10 prints.

Bleaching Black-and-White Prints

Eliminating part of an image can be almost as magical as making an image appear when you develop it. "Now you see it, now you don't" is what bleaching is all about. Bleaching can correct tonal values, or completely eliminate tones, and make an image more graphic. Most photographers use bleaching as a corrective tool to lighten part of a print or to bleach out skin blemishes and other disturbing elements. But it can also be a powerful and intriguing visual tool for totally altering the impact of an image.

There are a number of bleaching methods. Some photographers even use common household bleaches such as Clorox to bleach a print. But Farmer's Reducer is the most controllable and commonly used bleach for reducing black-and-white photographic prints and films.

The active ingredient in Farmer's Reducer is potassium ferricyanide. It changes the black (metallic silver) areas of a print into a silver salt that dissolves in hypo. The second ingredient in the bleach is hypo. The recommended procedure is to use sodium-thiosulfate crystals, rather than normal hypo, but a regular fixer with a hardening agent will work. Unless hypo is used with the potassium ferricyanide, the altered silver compounds will eventually stain the print. But the hypo dissolves the silver compounds completely and washes easily out of the print.

Small packets of Farmer's Reducer can be purchased in photo stores. But once the ingredients are mixed, they only last about 15 minutes. This makes it a very expensive proposition unless you buy the chemicals in bulk and mix them yourself. Most photog-

These two photographs illustrate how bleaching can alter a print. In the one on the right, select areas of the print were lightened by bleaching, altering the effect of the image. The unaffected areas were protected from the bleach by a covering of rubber cement. Further bleaching could have reduced these areas to pure white.

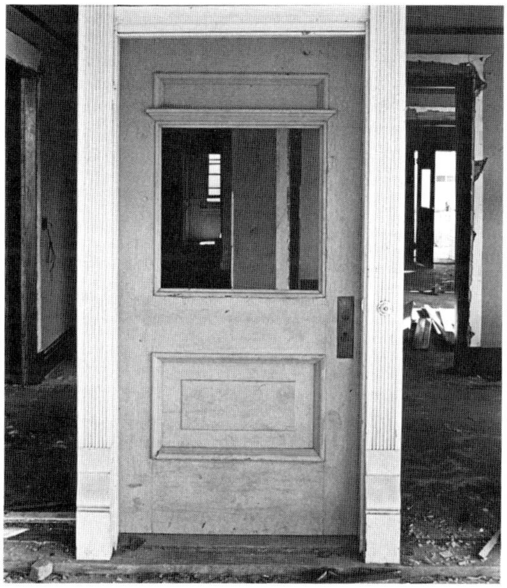

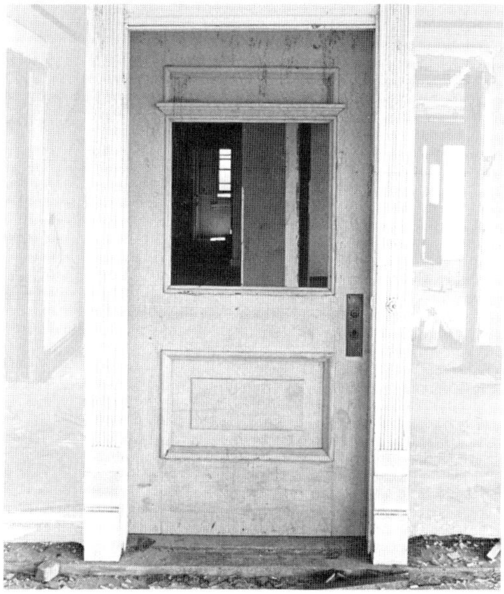

raphers do exactly this. They buy pure potassium ferricyanide in larger quantities that cost relatively little and last a lifetime. Plain hypo or sodium thiosulfate can also be purchased quite inexpensively.

There are several approaches to making an active reducing bath. The easiest method—used by professionals who like to get the job done without a lot of fuss—involves pouring approximately a tablespoon of potassium ferricyanide into a 5×7 inch processing tray. Then add a similar amount of sodium thiosulfate. Fill the tray with about a half-inch (12 cm) of water, and thoroughly dissolve the chemicals. This makes an active solution ready for immediate use. If the bleach is too weak, add a little more potassium ferricyanide; dilute it with more water to make a weaker solution. After about 15 minutes the bleach will be exhausted and should be discarded.

A more methodical method is shown in the accompanying chart.

Handle these chemicals with caution! Potassium ferricyanide is poisonous. Avoid contact with eyes, mouth, or any cuts you might have on your hands. If your skin is especially sensitive, wear rubber gloves when working with Farmer's Reducer.

Bleaching can be done locally to accent small areas of a print, or it can be done overall to lighten or increase contrast.

Overall Print Reduction. Overall print reduction is useful when you want a print to be slightly lighter, or need to boost its contrast. Prints with the Sabattier effect that are dark and lacking drama can be enhanced by overall bleaching. Mackie lines that may be too dark to command attention, will stand out after bleaching.

To put more life into a flat, low-key print, intentionally overexpose it 20 to 50 percent. This results in a print that is darker than normal. After fixing, a fiber-based print only needs to be washed for about 15 minutes to be ready for bleaching. If the print is already washed and dried, resoak it in water for 15 minutes before bleaching, so the effect of the bleach will be uniform.

Following washing, submerge the print completely in the working bleach solution with continuous agitation. After ten seconds, quickly remove the print from the tray, and place it under a stream of running

FORMULA FOR FARMER'S REDUCER

	Amount	
Chemical	**U.S. Customary**	**Metric**
Stock Solution A:*†		
Potassium Ferricyanide	1.3 oz.	37.5 gr
Water to make	16.0 fl. oz.	500.5 ml
Stock Solution B:†		
Sodium Thiosulfate (hypo)	17.0 oz.	480.0 gr
Water to make	64.0 fl. oz.	2.0 l
Working Solution:		
Stock Solution A	1.0 fl. oz.	30.0 ml
Stock Solution B	4.0 fl. oz.	120.0 ml
Water to make	32.0 fl. oz.	1.0 l

*Less active bleaching results from using half of the recommended amount for Solution A.

†Stock solution B will keep indefinitely, but Stock Solution A is only good for about six months in a well-sealed, brown-glass bottle. The working solution must be used about 15 minutes after mixing.

water. If you wait for the print to look right while in the bleach, it will be too late. Since the print continues to bleach for a while after being removed from the bleach, you have to learn to anticipate the change that will take place. When the print is in the water, the bleaching action is slowed and you can examine your results. After rinsing the print for several minutes, decide whether or not it needs more bleaching. If so, put it back in the bleach and repeat the process, being careful not to overdo it. The highlights should not be reduced to bare paper; some tone should be retained.

After the print is bleached to your satisfaction, resoak it in hypo (fixer) for five minutes. The water rinse slows down the action of the bleach, but does not stop it completely. Hypo dissolves the remaining silver salts and prevents any further bleaching or subsequent staining of the print. After refixing, wash and dry the prints as usual.

Local Bleaching. To eliminate small unwanted details in a photograph—such as air bubbles caused by faulty film processing, or wrinkles or facial blemishes—try local reduction. This can also bring out shadow detail and accent highlights. But it should be considered with caution. It is very easy to ruin a print if you aren't careful. Practice is necessary.

To reduce a print locally, first soak it in water. Then place it, emulsion side up, on a smooth, flat surface. Lean the print at an angle with the part you want to bleach at the bottom, so running bleach will be less likely to damage other parts of the print.

Carefully squeegee off all surface liquid. With a small piece of cotton, a cotton swab, or a brush apply the working solution to the area you want to reduce. Use a light circular motion, and don't allow the bleach to stand too long on the print's surface. Work slowly and apply the bleach lightly. Then rinse the area with running water, squeegee, evaluate the print, and apply more reducer if necessary.

If it takes too long to get the desired amount of reduction in a really dark area of the print, try dipping a wet brush into straight potassium-ferricyanide crystals. Rub the brush on some surface to make sure all the crystals are dissolved and then apply them directly to the print. This straight solution acts much faster, but avoid excessive use because the print will be more prone to staining than with the normal solution. To minimize the possibility of staining, keep a sponge soaked in hypo handy to stop the bleaching quickly. After you've finished, refix the print, then thoroughly wash and dry.

Bleaching Color Prints

Photographers seldom consider the creative option of bleaching color prints. Bleaching is normally only used for retouching. Most photographers avoid it altogether and have a professional retoucher solve problems that involve bleaching. But don't overlook the potential for creatively altering color prints with bleaches.

The most commonly used bleach is a nonselective, or total, bleach that removes all three dye layers. This bleach is normally used to remove black spots on prints by bleaching them to white. Then retouching dyes are spotted on to match the surrounding colors of the print.

There are also selective bleaches designed to remove the color from a specific dye layer. A selective bleach lets you bleach cyan, magenta, and yellow individually. With this process you can selectively bleach out unwanted color casts in a print, or totally alter the visual relationships by removing colors.

Bleaches can be used on most types of color prints. However, some print materials react better than others. Cibachrome prints are easy to bleach, while bleaching is not recommended with most Kodak color print materials. The chemicals necessary to make the bleaches are generally not available in camera stores, but they can be specially ordered through chemical-supply outlets. The following companies carry the necessary chemicals, and let you order through the mail:

Lauder Chemical Co., 350 Peninsula Ave., San Mateo, CA 94401

Student Science Services, 622 W. Colorado St., Glendale, CA 91204

Porter's Camera Store, P. O. Box 628, Cedar Falls, IA 50613

Cibachrome Bleach Formulas. The solutions described in the accompanying charts are for bleaching Cibachrome prints, and have been reproduced (with permission) from Cibachrome literature.

Caution should be used in handling all of the chemicals mentioned for Cibachrome bleaching. Some are highly poisonous and highly corrosive. Avoid all contact with skin and eyes. Wear protective goggles and rubber gloves when working with them.

For further information about the hazards of artistic and photographic materials, a good book is *Artist Beware*, by Michael McCann, PH.D., published by Watson-Guptill Publications, 1515 Broadway, New York, N.Y., 10036.

Dye Bleaching Cibachrome Prints

Cibachrome selective dye bleaches reduce a particular color, while the total bleach removes all the dyes. The total bleach is especially useful for Cibachrome, because it removes black spots caused by dust on the transparencies.

Selective Bleaching of Cibachrome Prints. For bleaching specific *yellow* areas of a print, apply the dye with either a nylon brush or a piece of cotton. Allow the bleach to remain on the print for 1½ to 8 minutes. For overall yellow reduc-

CIBACHROME YELLOW-DYE BLEACH*

Chemical	Amount
N, N-dimethyl-formamide	2 volumes
Water	1 volume

*Mix to make a stock solution, which will keep for several months

CIBACHROME MAGENTA-DYE BLEACH*

	Amount	
Chemical	U.S. Customary	Metric
Solution A:		
Chloramine T	0.5 oz.	15.0 g
Water	32.0 fl. oz.	1.0 l
Solution B:		
Acetic acid (10% solution)	any	any
Solution C:		
Sodium bisulfite	0.3 oz.	10.0 g
Water	32.0 fl. oz.	1.0 l

*Each solution should be mixed and stored separately in plastic-capped glass bottles for a longer life. The individual solutions will keep for several months. Once used, they should be discarded.

CIBACHROME CYAN-DYE BLEACH*

Chemical	Amount	
	U.S. Customary	Metric
Sodium dithionite	0.1 oz.	3.0 g
Sodium bicarbonate	0.1 oz.	3.0 g
Water	32.0 fl. oz.	1.0 l

*Prepare only for immediate use. Once mixed the solution lasts approximately eight hours.

TOTAL BLEACH FOR ALL CIBACHROME DYES*

Chemical	Amount	
	U.S. Customary	Metric
Solution A:		
Potassium permanganate	0.25 oz.	8.0 g
Distilled water	16.0 fl. oz.	500.0 ml
Solution B:		
Water	32.0 fl. oz.	1.0 l
Sulfuric acid (2-normal)**	2.0 fl. oz.	56.0 ml
or		
Water	11.0 fl. oz.	340.0 ml
Sulfuric acid (concentrated)**	.75 fl. oz.	20.0 ml
Solution C:		
Sodium sulfite	0.3 oz.	10.0 g
or		
Potassium metabisulfite	0.3 oz.	10.0 g
Water	16.0 fl. oz.	500.0 ml

*For use, mix equal parts of solutions A and B. Solution C is used separately to remove yellow/brown stains. The stock solutions keep for several months, while the mixed solution only keeps for approximately 8 hours.
****Never add water to the acid**, for it can spatter the acid. Always add the acid to the water. **Be very cautious with sulfuric acid**. It is highly corrosive. Avoid all contact with skin, and store in a polyethylene bottle. If you are unable to get the weaker 2N solution, mix it from the more concentrated solution.

tion immerse the print completely in the bleach. After bleaching, wash the print for ten minutes in running water, then dry. To determine the proper amount of bleaching time, experiment on scrap prints. Avoid prolonged bleaching because it may affect the magenta dye layer.

The working solution for *magenta* dye bleaching is made by adding a few drops of solution B to solution A. The amount of solution A depends on how much you feel you need to do the job. Unless you plan to immerse the whole print in the bleach, mix a small amount. For normal retouching applications two to three ounces (69 to 80 ml) should be enough. Add drops of solution B until the solution turns milky. The amount of solution B varies with the volume of solution

A. Apply the working solution to the print surface until the desired bleaching occurs.

Rinse the print in water for 30 seconds. Next, immerse the print into solution C for two minutes. Finally, wash the print for ten minutes and dry.

A yellowish stain may result in the white areas of the print. To remove the stain, immerse the print in the following solution until it disappears:

Hydrogen peroxide, 3%	10 volumes
Ammonia, 10%	1 volume

Then wash the print for ten minutes and dry. This solution keeps just one day so discard it after use.

For bleaching small areas of *cyan* dye, use the undiluted bleach solution. It normally takes two to three minutes to completely bleach out all of the dye. Reduce the entire print by immersing it in the bleach. To slow the bleaching action, lower the concentration by diluting the bleach 1:1 with water. After bleaching, wash the print for ten minutes, then dry.

Total Dye Bleaching. Make the working solution by mixing equal parts of solutions A and B. Apply it to small areas of the print with a nylon brush or cotton swab. Use only a small amount of bleach and be careful to apply it only where needed. After a minute and a half, blot the spot with cotton or blotting paper, and examine it to see if more bleaching is necessary. Apply more bleach if needed.

The bleached areas will have a yellow-brown stain. Remove this stain by applying solution C, or P-3 fixer, to the spot for several minutes. It's better to blot and reapply the clearing bath (solution C) than to let it sit on the print for long periods of time, because it has a tendency to damage the print surface. When the bleaching and stain removal is complete, wash the print for ten minutes and then dry as usual.

Masking for Bleach Control

The easiest way to reduce large areas of a print is to totally immerse the print in the bleach. To keep the whole print from being bleached it is necessary to *mask* the parts of the print that you want to remain normal. A liquid frisket, such as Photomaskoid or rubber cement, works best. You can get both at art supply stores. Liquid friskets are easy to apply and give you a liquid-proof coating to paint over the print areas that need protection from the bleach. When applying a mask, be careful to thoroughly coat the areas you are protecting. Any break in the coating will allow bleach to get through.

Leave this mask or protective coating on during the bleaching procedure. Strip it off later with a piece of Scotch tape, or rub it off. With this technique you can prevent the bleach from affecting other areas of the print.

Creative Applications of Bleach

Bleaching can be a very useful retouching procedure. With Cibachrome—bleaching is an important tool for ridding prints of black spots from dust on slides. But most photographers consider the use of bleach more trouble than it's worth, especially since color prints are easy to remake with current processes.

The creative application of bleach has been used extensively with black-and-white prints, but few photographers have taken advantage of it with color prints. Yet the potential for visually altering the photograph is even greater with bleaching color, since bleach can be used to bring out color relationships that are impossible to achieve any other way.

You can apply the bleach in a specific, controlled manner, or loosely for a painted effect. Masking with liquid friskets offers you the option of totally bleaching some areas while leaving others completely untouched. The use of selective, or total, bleaches also offers a number of options for altering color relationships. The possibilities are unlimited. Altering prints by bleaching is a lot like hand-coloring, only instead of adding color to the print you are subtracting it.

Coloring Prints by Hand

There are many materials used to hand-color both black-and-white and color photographs. These are used more often on black-and-white prints than on color, although the latter are frequently colored for retouching purposes. However, photographers seldom apply additional colors to color photographs for aesthetic reasons, even though there is definite creative potential.

The materials used to color prints by hand can be divided into three categories: oil-based, lacquer-based, and water-based. They can be used individually or combined. Oil- and lacquer-based colorants will adhere to water-based colorants. But water-based colorants won't adhere to oil or lacquer.

Each material gives a different effect. Experiment and choose the one that works best with your image. Frequently, photographers tone a black-and-white print before coloring it. Most hand-colored portrait pho-

Dinah Portner masked this print with maskoid and then selectively hand colored the image to alter the spacial relationships. The illusion of floating was increased by rephotographing the image with a cut-out portion placed on top of the print. By having the cut-out elevated above the surface of the print, a shadow was cast creating more of an illusion.

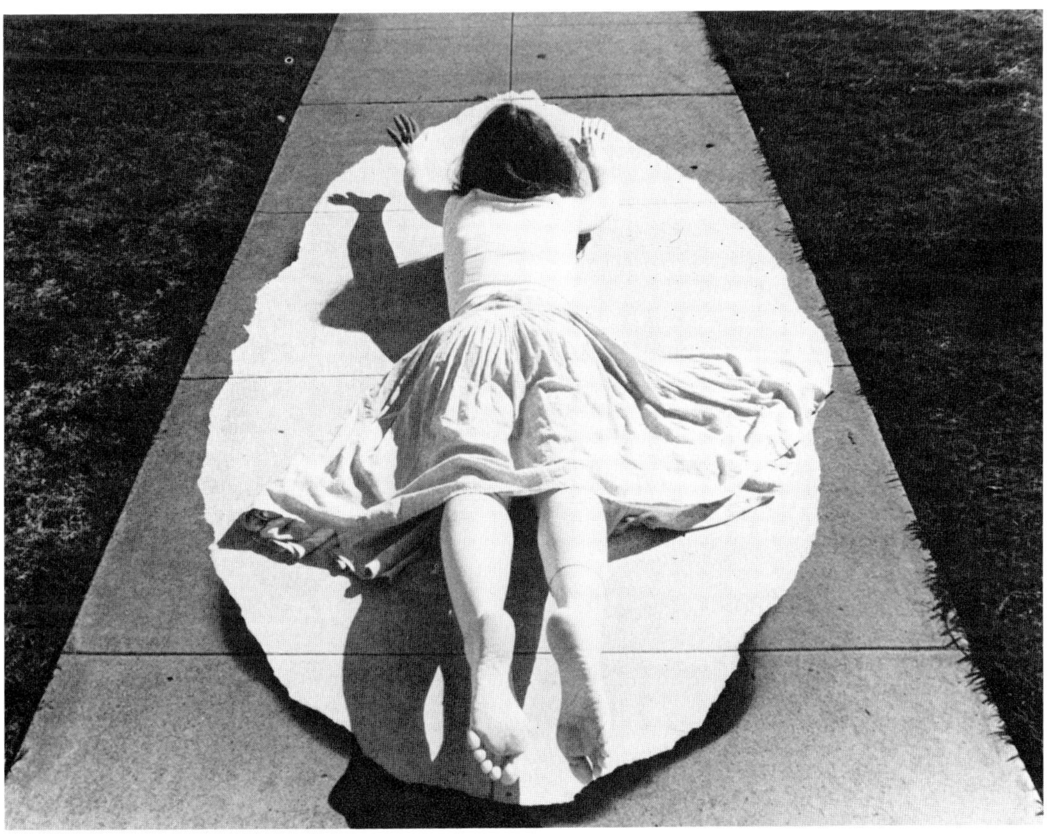

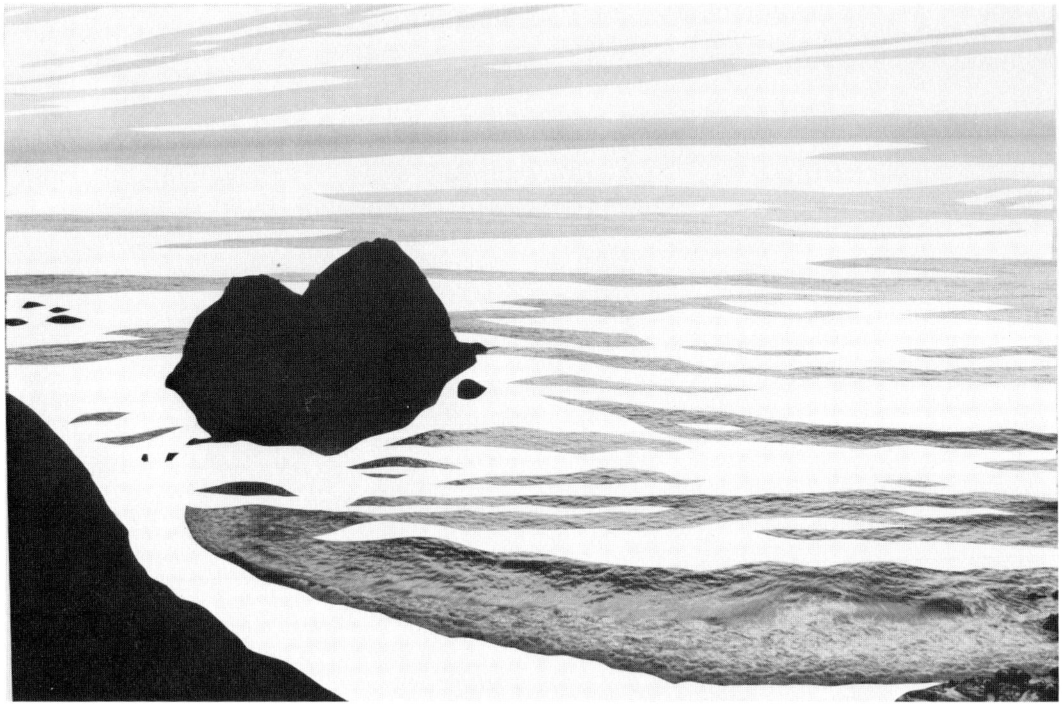

The RC emulsion was selectively cut and peeled off the paper backing to alter the graphic impact of this photograph by Keith Nakata. The original was in color.

tographs have been sepia- or brown- toned before coloring. This makes it easier to get a believable skin color. However, in her *Painted Women* series, Karen Truax toned her prints blue before coloring to create a detached feeling, symbolizing a woman of the night.

Oil-Based Colorants. Oil-based dyes and paints are the easiest to control and thus good materials to begin working with. Any oil paint can be used, but some are designed specially for photographic purposes. The ones generally used for photographs are transparent, compared to the opaque pigments used for painting. The transparent oils allow the photographic image to show through while opaque oils cover the photographic detail.

Transparent oils, such as Marshall's, work best if the print surface is primed with a fine film of turpentine rubbed on with cotton. The colors are also applied with cotton. For detailed work take a small amount of long-fiber cotton and wrap it around the end of a toothpick. This will work better than a normal cotton swab because the long-fiber cotton doesn't have regular cotton's stray ends. You can apply the dyes straight from the tube for rich, vibrant colors, or blend them with other colors. You can tone them down by buffing with the cotton. Mistakes can be erased with turpentine and cotton. One disadvantage of oils is that they take a long time to dry, but they are the most permanent method of coloring photographs.

Transparent oil-based dyes are known for their soft, subtle colors. If you want bolder, more saturated colors, try opaque oils. Consider using transparent oils for an overall effect and opaque oils for accents. But remember, opaque oils cover photographic detail, so don't use them unless this is acceptable.

Lacquer-Based Colorants. You will get the advantage of lacquer-based paints only if you use spraying devices—such as spray cans or air brushes. They can be used to add textural feeling to the print. Color can be sprayed on an overall area, or the print can be partially masked with cardboard, maskoid, rubber cement, or ruby lith (available at art supply or graphic-arts supply stores).

Water-Based Colorants. Acrylic paints and water-based dyes designed for photographs, such as Marshall's Photo Retouch Colors and Edwal Toners, are frequently used to color photographs. Acrylic paints dry slowly and stay on the surface of the print. They have a definite painted-on look, compared to the dyes that penetrate the print surface and cannot be removed. Acrylic dyes can be applied directly for intense color, or diluted with water for subtle effects. The best way to apply them is to use a paint brush. The Edwal toners, which can be painted on, are the same ones discussed in the section on toning black-and-white prints.

Pencils and Chalks. In addition to using paints and dyes, you can also use colored pencils and chalks. These provide different effects and give a definite textural feeling to the print. With colored pencils you must prime the print surface with a fine film of turpentine. When using colored chalk, be sure to use a protective fixative spray when you are finished; otherwise, the chalk will rub off. Lacquer sprays designed to coat photographs work well for this. For other effects, consider using colored felt pens, India ink, or crayons. Just about anything can be used to color, or alter the feeling and surface character of, a photograph. The material you use should be determined by the effect you want. Again, the possibilities are almost endless.

Surface Alterations

Cutting, sewing, and montage making are a few of the options available to alter the surface of a photographic print. They can loosen up your image, and possibly lead you to discover new ideas and approaches to the medium.

Resin-coated papers are good for surface alterations. By taking an X-Acto knife to delicately cut the surface of a print, it is possible to peel the emulsion away, without going through the back of the paper. This gives you the opportunity to alter the spatial relationships of the photograph and to vary the surface texture. The white paper base, with its fiber texture, is a nice contrast to the smooth plastic surface of a resin-coated print. Also quite nice is the effect created by cuts in the print surface alone.

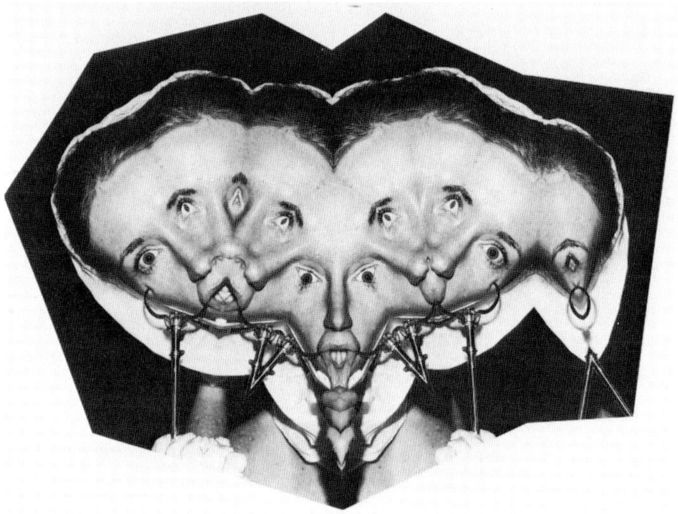

Lanie Strahler montages a number of prints to arrive at her final images. Unlike most photographers who do montaging, Lanie doesn't rephotograph the piece. Her montage is done with such finese that the final piece is the montage itself. For this photograph, titled Self Portrait as Anomaly, *12 separate prints were used.*

A montage is a combination of several images together. Instead of going through elaborate multiple-printing procedures, you can simply cut up prints and glue parts of them together. Very few photographers do this, but it offers tremendous creative potential which should not be ignored merely for reasons of photographic purity.

If you decide to make a montage, use a glue specially designed for photographic purposes. (Never use rubber cement for any image you want to last, unless you like yellow prints.) Most glues are extremely bad for photographs. To avoid problems use glues or adhesives with a neutral pH. One of the best is wheat paste. It's messy, but inexpensive and easy to use. Spray-mounting adhesives designed for photographs are another option, but they can give way with time, and change with humidity. There are also double-stick and transfer-type dry-mounting materials available that are easy to use. The traditional dry-mounting technique with a heat press also works, but it's very time consuming and awkward to use for montages.

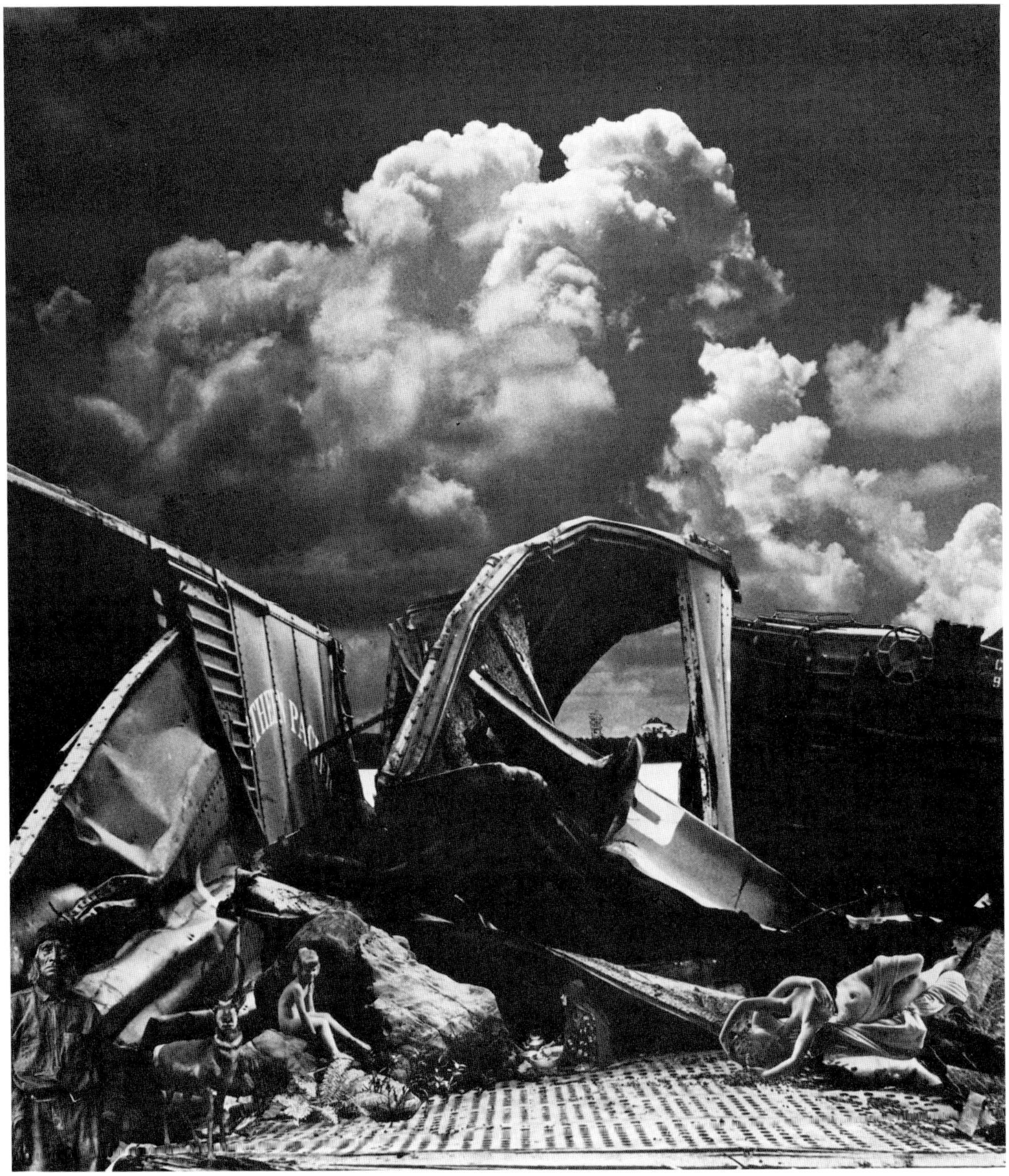

This print by Jim Farber, In the Ruins, *was made by montaging separate images and then rephotographing them. Jim carefully prints each image to size, combines them, and photographs the montage with a large-format camera to get as much detail as possible.*

Sewing is another way to alter the surface and character of a photograph. Many photographers, such as Suda House, Betty Hahn, and George Blakely, have used sewing and stuffing as a means to add dimension, color, and additional meaning to their images. It may seem strange, but a print can be sewn just like material. In fact, cloth, parts of other photographs, and pieces of film can be sewn onto a print. The degree to which you alter your prints is purely a personal choice.

Spotting and Dye Retouching

Once your creative energy is spent and the prints are complete, it is time to consider finishing touches. Seldom is a print so clean it doesn't need spotting. In addition, dye retouching on color prints provides an extra accent that gives an image real drama.

Spotting black-and-white prints is easy. Dyes come in either liquid or dry form. Preferences vary, but the dry form seems easier to control. A problem many people have with liquid dyes, such as Spot-Tone, is that they get too much on their brush, and apply more than is needed. Since the dye adheres on contact, this leads to a great deal of frustration. With dry dyes, wet the brush slightly, then rub it in the dye. You need just a small amount of dye, so keep the brush fairly dry. By occasionally wetting the brush, then blotting it on a paper towel, dye can be applied slowly and evenly to the print. Build the density of the dye slowly. It's not necessary to totally cover a spot. You only have to add enough color so the spot blends in with rest of the print and is not obvious. Avoid trying too hard, as this usually leads to an obviously overworked spot. To remove mistakes, soak the print in Photo-flo.

Dry dyes, such as Kodak Spotting Colors, are usually expensive. You can make your own from liquid dyes dried in small quantities on a piece of glass. The brush you use for spotting should be a good-

Moonrise Over Hernandez Bar and Grill, *is another montaged photograph by Jim Farber.*

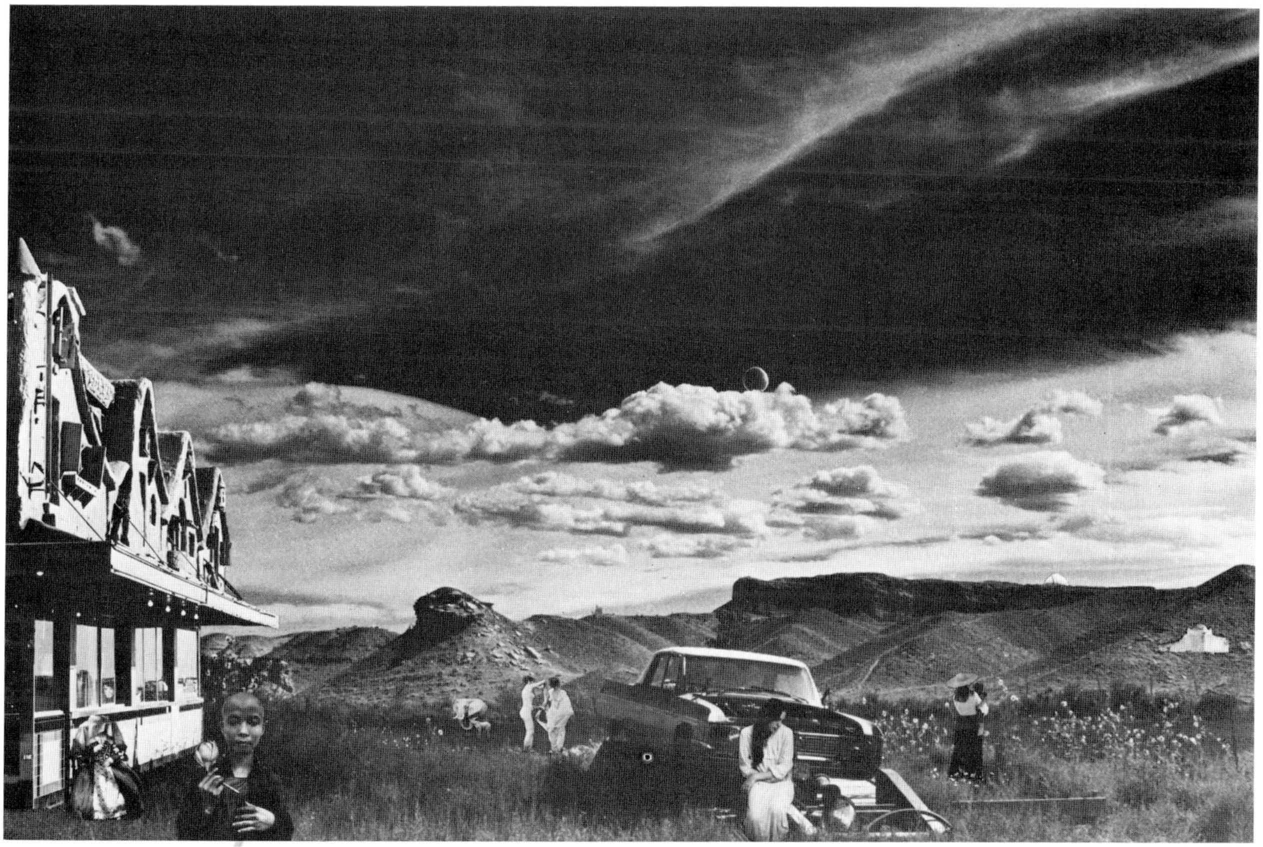

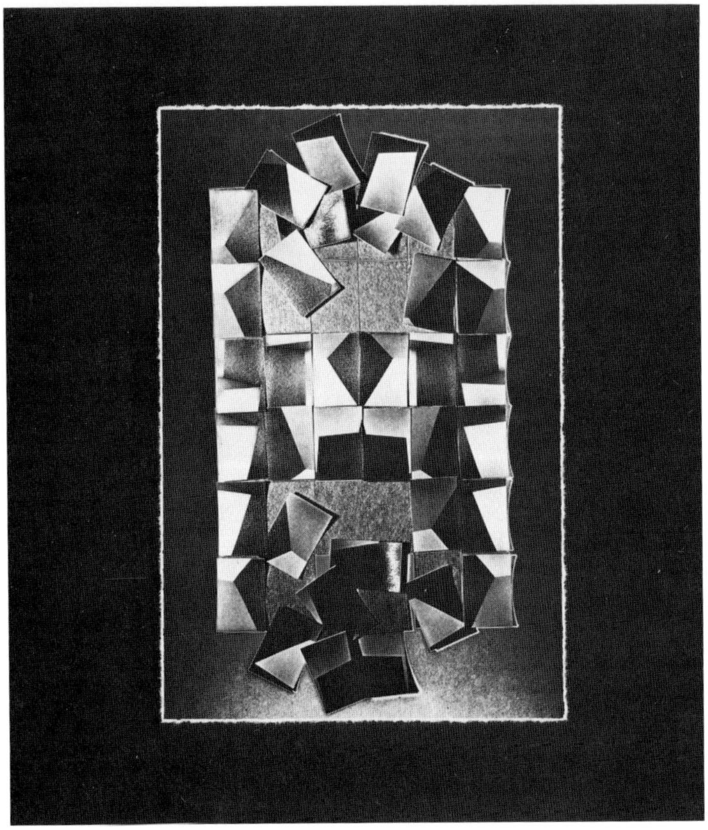

Corners, by Chuck Nicholson was created by rephotographing carefully arranged prints. The final image was Sabattierized, and then scored with a knife. This created a ragged white edge after the rest of the print paper was torn away.

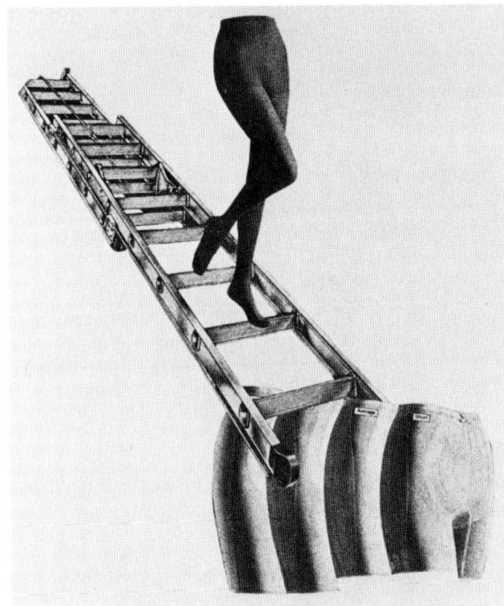

In *American Loveboat #3*, by Robert Flick, separate prints were made, montaged together, and then rephotographed on 2475 Recording film to get the grainy quality.

quality sable brush that comes to a nice, sharp point without stray hairs. Some photographers prefer a very small brush, while others prefer brushes with more bulk. It is really a matter of what you get used to. A good size to start with is number 0 or number 2.

Color prints are spotted the same way as black-and-white prints. The only difference is that colored dyes are used. The easiest to find among the many products available are Marshall's Photo Retouch Colors. These liquid dyes come in a variety of colors. The easiest way to use them is to take a drop of each color and put it on a piece of glass to dry. The you can use the dry-dye/dry-brush technique.

Black, a neutral color, can usually be used for spotting color prints. However, some colors—such as yellow, light blue, and flesh tones—have to be spotted with their own color. The important thing to remember is that you don't have to completely cover the spot, you simply have to blend it into the surrounding image area.

Black spots are the most difficult to correct in both black-and-white and color prints. These are the result of clear spots or holes in the film. Before the days of resin-coated papers, photographers etched out black spots with a sharp razor. But this is impossible with resin-coated papers since the razor will cut through the plastic surface. There are two alternatives—bleaching, or spotting with an opaque white paint. Bleaching is awkward and time consuming, so most photographers use white paint. A white dye comes with the Kodak Spotting Colors, but it is expensive and doesn't last long. Try buying a white water-base poster paint. This works just as well and will last for years.

Another important finishing technique professionals have taken advantage of for years is dye retouching color prints. This is a simple process used to accent, intensify, or alter color casts to save a print, rather than remaking it. Dye retouching can be done in large areas of a print as well as in small, detailed portions. With Cibachrome, the dyes are added while the prints are wet. With most other processes, the dyes are added when the prints are dry.

With Kodak, and other similar color-print materials, use the Kodak Retouching Colors kit. These dyes, which come in small bottles, have a wax-like consistency similar to shoe polish. They can be used in two ways. One method is to use them like a spotting dye: that is, wet a brush and rub it into the dye. Once the dye is applied wet, it sets and becomes permanent on the print, and cannot be altered or removed. The other method of using these dyes depends on the dye not setting upon contact.

Flexichroming, or dye retouching, is the dry method of using the Kodak Retouching Color kit. To apply the dye, use a dry piece of cotton or a cotton swab. This way you can blend the dye into the image and cause subtle alterations and corrections of color. To get the dye onto the cotton, breathe onto the cake of dye before rubbing the cotton in it. The dye will adhere to the cotton, and it can then be applied to the print. Be careful not to get any moisture on the dye, or it will adhere to the print immediately and permanently.

Rub the dye onto the surface of the print. Smooth it with the cotton so it blends into the image. At this stage, the dye can be rubbed off with cotton, or with the reducer supplied with the kit. When you're finished adding color, set the dye with steam. The easiest way to do this is to hold the image over a steaming tea kettle for about ten

Another approach to montaging is employed by George Blakely in this image, Big Delineations #1. *He takes small machine-processed color prints and sequences them, causing the photographs to overlap when mounted together. The prints are attached at the top and loose at the bottom so that they can be lifted for closer examination.*

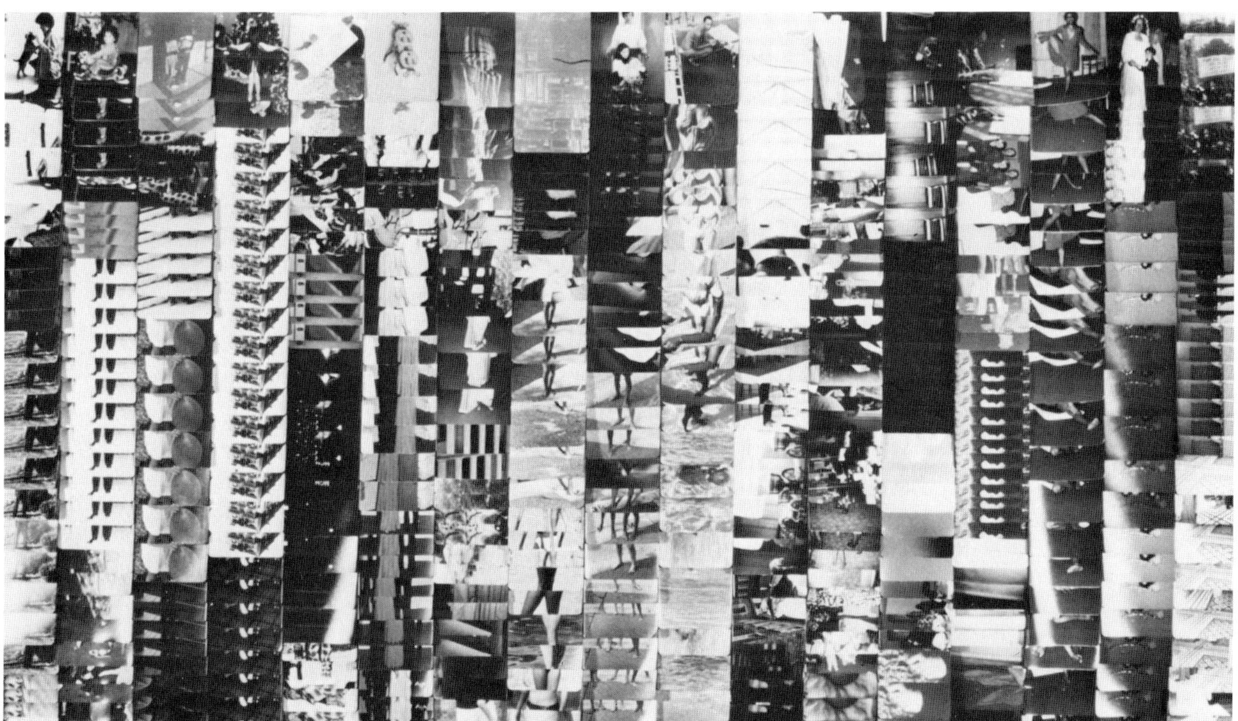

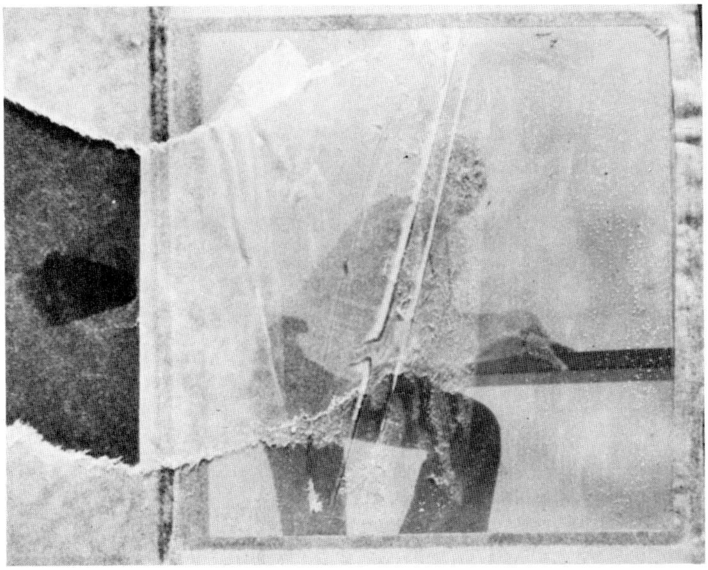

The popularity of photography has produced a tremendous amount of pictures, many of which have little sustaining value. Rather than add to that bulk, George Blakely recycles images. This photograph is from a series of images which Blakely made from discarded polaroid negatives. He rephotographs them onto color film and makes color enlargements.

seconds until the dye is absorbed into the surface of the print. Let the print dry without anything touching it, because steaming makes the print surface tacky and very delicate.

Once the print is dry, the dye should be totally absorbed. If you still see some dye standing on the surface of the print, try re-steaming it. If it's still there after a second steaming, you applied the dye too thickly. If you need more intensity apply several coats, but steam-set the dye between each coat.

You can use this second approach to add a little color to a person's cheeks, to intensify a blue sky, or to accent a particular color.

Flexichroming can also be used to alter subtle color biases in the lighter areas of a print. For instance, prints of snow may have a slight color bias. You can correct this by Flexichroming the print with the complementary color.

With Cibachrome prints the approach is slightly different. They have to be retouched with dye while the print is wet. Use Cibachrome Transparent Dyes, as these have the same basic dye structure as Cibachrome paper, and the same permanence.

Start by wetting the print in plain water. Then lay it on a smooth, flat surface, and squeegee off the surface liquid. The dyes should be applied with pieces of cotton or cotton swabs. Apply the dyes with caution. They set upon contact with the print, making this process much more critical than flexichroming.

These dyes affect only the middle and light values of a print. When you apply dye to a light area of a print, don't worry if some of it gets on an adjacent dark area, because it won't show when the print dries. If too much dye is applied to the print and unevenness results, try soaking the print in water for an hour. Most of the dye should wash out. Once the dye is properly applied, dry the print. The dye will soak into the emulsion and be invisible when dry. This technique takes some practice to execute properly; but it can save you money, as well as time, by letting you add color to washed-out highlights, rather than making the print over.

A Final Note. Spotting and dye retouching are important finishing procedures necessary to properly dress up your photographs. But these techniques, like all the others covered in this book, only provide a means to a particular effect. The strength of your photographs can't exist on effect alone. It's what you do with these techniques and how you apply them to express your ideas, feelings, and reactions, that will make your photographs important, not only to you but to others. No matter what your special interests are, consider this thought by Ansel Adams: "We must remember that a photograph can hold just as much as we put into it, and no one has ever approached the full possibilities of the medium."*

*Quoted in Nathan Lyons, *Photographers on Photography* (Englewood Cliffs, N.J.: Prentice-Hall, Inc., 1960), p. 29.

Index